67

MAURICE HA

SELECTED ESSAYS

MAURICE HARMON

SELECTED ESSAYS

Edited with an Introduction
by BARBARA BROWN

Foreword by
TERENCE BROWN

IRISH ACADEMIC PRESS
DUBLIN • PORTLAND, OR

First published in 2006 by
IRISH ACADEMIC PRESS
44, Northumberland Road, Dublin 4, Ireland

and in the United States of America by
IRISH ACADEMIC PRESS
c/o ISBS, Suite 300, 920 NE 58th Avenue
Portland, Oregon 97213-3644

WEBSITE:www.iap.ie

British Library Cataloguing in Publication Data
An entry can be found on request

ISBN 0-7165-3400-2 (cloth)
ISBN 0-7165-3401-0 (paper)

Library of Congress Cataloging-in-Publication Data
An entry can be found on request

Typeset in 11/11.5pt Ehrhardt by FiSH Books, Enfield, Middx.
Printed by MPG Books Ltd, Bodmin, Cornwall

CONTENTS

CONTENTS

FOREWORD

When Maurice Harmon was born in Dublin in 1930 the Irish Free State was a mere eight years old. At that date its continued existence was by no means certain; and in his life- time Harmon would see the Irish state reconstituted twice: in 1937 and 1949, as the twenty-six counties of independent Ireland became in modern European terms the comparatively mature polity it now is. Many Irishmen and women today, who take the existence of the modern republic for granted, would probably find it difficult to appreciate that until quite recent times (entry in 1973 to the European Economic Community, now the European Union, was perhaps the watershed date) there were those at home and abroad who doubted whether Ireland in its twenty-six county manifestation could survive as an independent entity.

It is in this context that the academic career of the author of the essays and papers collected in this volume has a special interest. For these works by one of Ireland's most responsible and productive literary scholars largely focus on the literature of independent Ireland in the period of state formation and consolidation, with key contributions dealing with such writers as Austin Clarke, Patrick Kavanagh, Mary Lavin, Francis Stuart, Benedict Kiely and Thomas Kinsella. Seán O'Faoláin figures in numbers of them, which is surely salient, for not only has that writer been one of Harmon's major interests (early in his career he produced a ground-breaking critical study of O'Faoláin, more recently a distinguished biography), but because it was O'Faoláin who perhaps most self-consciously of the writers considered in this volume, saw himself working in the context of the newly independent state. His contributions as a public intellectual are saluted here in a central essay. Appropriately therefore the contribution that O'Faoláin made as writer to modern Ireland, honoured here and elsewhere in Harmon's writings, encourages the reader of this volume to discern a prevailing theme in the collection. That is how the production of literature in English by Irish men and women in independent Ireland helped to give to the insecure state in a turbulent century a sense of identity necessary to its survival. Accordingly it can seem apposite that this book begins with a study of the representation of the peasantry in pre-1916 Anglo-Irish literature, as if to instruct us that Irish literary achievements in English in the twentieth century were works of necessity that would restore a people's sense of themselves after the calamitous experiences of nineteenth century Ireland.

So as we read this book we get a sense of a modern literature in English accretively developing in a period in which so many hoped for the revival of Irish and when some believed that only a literature in the Irish language could truly be the basis of a secure national identity. This thoughtful gathering together of Maurice Harmon's essays on Anglo–Irish literature helps us therefore to understand how after the triumphs of the Literary Revival which can be associated with the movement for independence, a literature in English emerged as accompaniment to an independent state in southern Ireland. And this book also helps us to appreciate how that literature acquired its critical readership in the academy.

In the central essay on O'Faoláin, 'Seán O'Faoláin: Man of Ideas', Harmon reminds his readership of the isolated conditions in which that writer was forced to operate as a public intellectual in the 1940s and 1950s. He remarks: 'it is difficult to understand and appreciate what O'Faoláin was doing and why it was necessary, because the country and the culture have changed so much....The absence of an intellectual tradition meant that O'Faoláin hardly even had an adversary with whose ideas he could wrestle'. This prompts the reader to reflect that in an analogous sense Harmon was almost as solitary a figure when in the early 1960s he turned his scholarly attention to the academic field he has since made his own: the study of Anglo–Irish literature, with a primary focus on the literature of independent Ireland. For as Barbara Brown highlights in her helpful introduction to this volume, when Harmon began his career the writings of Yeats and Joyce had the world's attention. Few academic critics either in Ireland or abroad bothered with more recent and presumably lesser lights, who were eclipsed by the greater luminaries. Harmon accordingly was one of those who helped define a subject and who as editor of the crucial *Irish University Review* laboured tirelessly to create the context in which younger scholars can take for granted the existence of a literature which now finds itself studied as an element in the burgeoning academic discipline of Irish Studies. It is accordingly a pleasure to welcome a book which not only offers essays and papers possessed of real critical and scholarly worth in themselves but which allows us to reflect on the role that work of the painstaking, generous–minded, kind Harmon undertook in unpropitious circumstances, played in the cultural life of modern Ireland.

Terence Brown
Trinity College, Dublin
March 2006

INTRODUCTION

Barbara Brown

IN 1990 Maurice Harmon retired from University College Dublin as Emeritus Professor of Anglo-Irish Literature and Drama. His colleagues celebrated his career as scholar, editor, and poet with the *Festschrift Serving the Word*, essays and poetic tributes reflecting his range of cultural and literary interests. He continued to be productive in retirement, as evidenced by public lectures and readings, chapters in collections, articles and reviews, and books.[1] He translated and edited with an Introduction the medieval Irish compendium of stories and poems *The Colloquy of the Old Men* (*Acallam na Senórach*), 2001, revised in a forthcoming second edition as *The Dialogue of the Ancients*. Editing *Poetry Ireland Review*, 2001–02, provided material for this collection's 'Afterword: Dear Editor'. Salmon Publishing launched his latest book of poems, *The Doll with Two Backs and other poems*, in December 2004. One of his former colleagues is reported as saying, 'Isn't that fellow ever going to burn out?'

He was born in Dublin on 21 June 1930 and has lived there for much of his adult life, but his true home, he maintains, the source of his moral and imaginative life, is the Ardgillan estate in north County Dublin, where he roamed as a boy. Even when he went to the Redemptorist boarding school in Limerick, he wrote commemorative lyrics about its woods and shore under the influence of Shelley and Wordsworth. His English teacher, Father Minihan, read extracts from *The Bell*, the monthly magazine edited in Dublin by Seán O'Faoláin, and told pupils about his correspondence with the Limerick novelist Kate O'Brien, whose novel he thought should not have been banned (*The Land of Spices*, 1941). For Harmon, this was an awakening and a foreshadowing.

Later he would recreate the Wordsworthian life he had known at Ardgillan in *The Last Regatta*:

> We lived so far from town I did
> not go to school for years,
> truant of woods and shore.
>
> ... What I knew best
> was climbing slowly through dreamy firs
> until I hung above a swaying world,
> could see the castle turning on its hill,
> could feel the ocean roll towards Rockabill.[2]

The effects of boarding school are recreated with less enthusiasm in the long narrative poem 'The Boarder':

> No matter where he walked
> No matter what he thought
> No matter how he prayed
> his mind could not respond
> to the change that had come inside him.
>
> ...
>
> he had fitted in
> left the woods
> left the shore
>
> grey cement, dull stone
> dull stone, grey cement
> beds, corridors, desks
>
> his mind shrank
> his tongue
> sank in its bed.[3]

At University College Dublin, which he entered in 1948, Harmon came under the influence of Roger McHugh, who was mapping out the territory of Anglo-Irish Literature. His fellow students included Thomas Kinsella and John Montague. He took every available class on Anglo-Irish Literature and attended a special series of lectures on Early Irish Poetry given by Gerard Murphy. When John V. Kelleher came from America to give several talks on Modern Irish Literature, Harmon was an avid pupil. At this time he was writing an MA thesis on Liam O'Flaherty and thinking about further study. Jeremiah J. Hogan, Professor of English, wanted him to enter for a travelling studentship that would have taken him to Oxford or Cambridge, but he had his eyes set on America and further work with Mr Kelleher, Professor of Modern Irish History and Literature at Harvard University. He completed a master's degree in Comparative Literature from Harvard and in 1961 received his PhD in English Language and Literature from the National University of Ireland.

In 1965, after teaching at Lewis and Clark College in Portland, Oregon, and the University of Notre Dame, he returned to UCD, where he accepted an appointment in the Department of English. He was an influential teacher. His essays, lectures, and talks have as a primary aim the possibility of enabling others to understand and to appreciate. Sometimes in a general consideration of approaches to Anglo-Irish Literature, he may speak of the axes on which the literature turns – East–West, Present–Past, Inward–Outward – and may use them to interpret and illuminate particular writers or texts. At the same time he believes that one must focus on the entire work, not on selections, and that interpretation must be based on the whole text. It is also one of his guiding principles that one should be humble facing a text, patiently attending to its inner workings until its techniques and significance are disclosed.

While still in his forties, he was elected to the Royal Irish Academy (MRIA). As founder and editor from 1970 to 1986 of the *Irish University Review. A Journal of Irish Studies*, Director of the inter-disciplinary programme in the MPhil in Irish Studies, and organiser of international conferences, Harmon extended the range and scope of his intellectual interests. He held professorships at a number of institutions, among them the University of Notre Dame, The Ohio State University, the University of Washington, Marshall University, and Boston College. In 1990 he retired to have more time for research and writing. By then he was regarded as one of the leading figures in Anglo-Irish literary studies.

International lecturer, scholar-critic, biographer, translator, editor, and poet – what the summary of Harmon's scholarly activities and publications attests is his lifetime of study and research in Anglo-Irish Literature, with particular emphasis on Irish poetry after Yeats and modern Irish fiction. The pieces in *Selected Essays* manifest that commitment. To them he has brought impeccable scholarship, linguistic skill, and lively wit. The collection as a whole addresses important issues. Fifty years ago, when he began to apply himself seriously to the study and the teaching of Anglo-Irish Literature, there were many questions to be answered, including the actual nature of the subject. What was Anglo-Irish Literature? When did it start? What were its main characteristics and sources? What were its defining texts? How did it relate to English Literature?

It is clear that he did not see Anglo-Irish Literature as a discipline in which there were two or three major figures who could be studied out of context. Although he gave lectures and seminars on W. B. Yeats and James Joyce, he saw that other writers were being neglected and that the whole issue of an indigenous literature in the English language written by Irish men and women was receiving insufficient attention. While the attention devoted to major writers increased, there were few articles and books written on other Irish writers. Indeed, in the critical climate of the time, it was difficult to place a serious article on a minor writer in any of the scholarly journals.

In the mid-1960s, when Harmon returned from America to help with the development of an undergraduate and graduate programme in Anglo-Irish Literature at UCD, it was significant of his approach that he included the work of contemporary writers in his lectures and conducted seminars in contemporary fiction and poetry. Now when he attended conferences, such as those run by the American Committee (later Conference) for Irish Studies, he was as likely to present a paper called 'New Voices in the Fifties' as one on Joyce or Yeats or Synge. His pioneering study *Seán O'Faoláin: A Critical Introduction*, 1967, discussed O'Faoláin's work in its social, political, and cultural contexts, and concentrated on the text. Noting what Howard Mumford Jones had done in *Guide to American Literature and its Backgrounds since 1890* (1953), he set about listing the main periods into which Anglo–Irish Literature might be divided and creating a bibliography of the main texts in various categories, including background reading. The outcome was *Modern Irish Literature: A Reader's Guide*, 1967, a study which led eventually to *A History of Anglo–Irish Literature from its Origins to the Present Day* (1982), which he wrote with Roger McHugh, the first Professor of Anglo–Irish Literature at UCD.

Working with graduate students led him to see that the reference works that were available for those in English or American studies were not available for his students. A subsequent publication was the *Select Bibliography for the Study of Anglo–Irish Literature and its Backgrounds*, 1977, in which he provided annotated information on those reference works which were useful for students of Anglo–Irish Literature and, significantly, included sections on mythology, history and early Irish literature, folk culture and anthropology, Gaelic literature and archaeology. The interdisciplinary approach was in his view essential and by 1982 incorporated in UCD's MPhil programme in Irish Studies. Meanwhile, from 1970 to 1986, the *Irish University Review* under his guidance became one of the foremost periodicals in its field and provided an outlet for emerging scholars and writers as well as established figures not only in Ireland, but internationally. It is in keeping with Harmon's approach that its special Spring issues focused on so–called minor writers, such as Austin Clarke, Seán O'Faoláin, Mary Lavin, Richard Murphy, and many others, and demonstrated his professional and personal association with them.

In the Introduction to the *Select Bibliography* he defined some of the principles that guided his own work. Central to the emergence of a distinctive Anglo–Irish literature, in his opinion, was that it drew upon two cultures, the Irish and the English. The degree and nature of the interaction between them may vary from time to time and may vary from one writer to the next, but the dual heritage is, he argued, an inescapable element. Irish literary studies exhibit this duality and increasingly involve the studies of its contexts.

> In such matters our inquiry is dictated by the writers. If they find it necessary and valuable to draw upon mythology, folklore, history, Gaelic literature, and so on, we have no alternative but to follow in their footsteps. That principle is fundamental to the

development of a critical response that is adequate to the literature. Increasingly among Irish writers there is the impulse to explore and to understand the roots from which they have come and there is the habitual need to compensate for deficiencies within the heritage by drawing widely from outside cultures. Both of these lead to the production of a literature that draws deeply and widely from the whole spectrum of the Irish past and that ranges well beyond the shores of the island and beyond the confines of the two major traditions of the Irish and the English.

The influence of this interdisciplinary approach is visible in *The Poetry of Thomas Kinsella* (1974), underpinned by a search for references and sources. Similarly, *Austin Clarke: A Critical Introduction*, 1989, shows for the first time how Clarke's poetry can be understood, if one goes to the trouble of tracking down the allusions. Both demonstrate the kind of work that is required, if one follows what Harmon advocated in the Introduction to the *Select Bibliography*. At the same time he also emphasised the international dimensions of the literature, the necessity for assessing the connections Irish writers have with cultures outside Ireland.

It is difficult to make a representative selection of Harmon's essays. The idea in this selection is to bring together different kinds of essays ranging from the scholarly contribution to a reputable journal, to papers delivered at international conferences, talks to summer schools, a radio talk, a centenary commemoration, an overall assessment of the work of a particular novelist, practical advice to young poets, editorials in a poetry magazine, a conversation with a short-story writer. Some essays are in the form of critical interpretations, some in the form of cultural, contextual considerations; others are shaped as literary history. They range chronologically in Part I, Beginnings in Prose and Poetry, with essays featuring writers in the nineteenth century and the beginnings of an emergence of a national literature in the prose works of William Carleton, 'Cobwebs before the Wind: Aspects of the Peasantry in Anglo-Irish Literature, 1800–1916'; the poetry and essays of Samuel Ferguson, 'The Enigma of Samuel Ferguson', and dramatists in the early years of the Irish Literary Revival. Investigations of poet Austin Clarke and essayist and fiction writer Seán O'Faoláin in the changed circumstance of the post-revolutionary period follow in 'The Rejection of Yeats'. Although there is no essay on W. B. Yeats included here, his historical and literary presence permeates the collection and is a continuing influence in the development of the Irish poets who come after him. By the mid-1920s the work of Yeats, Synge, Joyce, and O'Casey had established a separate Irish tradition in English literature with distinctive characteristics and standards. But for the writers who succeeded them the question was to find an individual voice and areas not dominated by their achievements. 'Writers on Radio: A Seventy-Fifth Anniversary Talk' outlines the contributions from 1931 of writers in every genre as available in the Archives of Radio Telefís Éireann (RTE 1) in Dublin.

Part II, Developments in Prose, continues the critical examinations of prose fiction in the novels and short stories of Seán O'Faoláin Mary Lavin, Francis Stuart, and Benedict Kiely. In Part III, Developments in Poetry, the achievements of Austin Clarke and Patrick Kavanagh are detailed, followed by descriptions of the work of poets in the next generation, such as Thomas Kinsella, John Montague, and Seamus Heaney. Together, the essays explore their indebtedness to the indigenous nature of Irish writing but also their emergence with confidence as writers with an international stature. The final essay, 'Irish Poets: Fresh Perspectives, Different Voices', provides a general assessment of contemporary Irish poetry, and a recapitulation.

Harmon is conscious of the ways in which this indigenous literature emerged in the nineteenth century and of the problems faced by writers such as William Carleton and Francis Ferguson as they sought to produce work that was different from what was being done at that time in England and to define an Irish tradition. He shows that the appearance and influence of such major figures as Yeats, Joyce, and Synge, who clearly belonged to a different tradition, made it impossible for literary historians to fit them easily within the development of English literature. His studies of Clarke and O'Faoláin as well as his observations in the *History of Anglo-Irish Literature* reveal how much thought he has given to these issues. The post-revolutionary generation of writers was one of his main interests, as may be seen in the essays depicting its central figures and in his under-standing of the pressures and responses they confronted – the restrictions imposed on Clarke by a repressive Catholic Church, O'Faoláin's struggle against a puritanical society, Patrick Kavanagh's blunt refusal to imitate those who 'sailed in puddles of the past/chasing the ghost of Brendan's mast', and the pervasive feeling throughout the post-revolutionary period of a dangerously introverted society.

The gradual emergence of a new generation of writers among Harmon's contemporaries was a source of great interest, and indeed of satisfaction, to him. He knew from personal experience what Ireland had been like in the early 1950s at a time when only two Irish poets were visible – Austin Clarke, who had become silent, and Patrick Kavanagh, whose output was small – and when the short-story writers were producing less and less. The growing strength of poets such as Thomas Kinsella, John Montague, and Richard Murphy, together with the work of Aidan Higgins, John McGahern, and Edna O'Brien, who in turn were followed by an increasing number of gifted writers, such as Seamus Heaney, heartened him. His enjoyment of literature is palpable and this, too, is reflected in his style, as it has been in his work as a teacher.

When asked to consider the most outstanding characteristic of Irish writing in the later period, he has identified the feeling of self-confidence that liberates writers from Heaney to Eavan Boland to Paul Muldoon. That development incorporated the freedom from English dominance and influence, the confidence to use native Celtic and Irish sources, and the outward movement towards internationalism. A literature that had seemed to be in decline reversed direction and went from strength to strength; the issue is heard in the final essay in this collection. If there is a single celebratory tone in the essays on writers in this second literary revival, that same note of self-confidence is heard also in the dignity of an aesthetic criticism in essays about these writers, as though the need to clarify social pressures and to explain their effects has been lifted with the arrival of a less repressive, more open Ireland. There are, of course, other indispensable pressures, as Kinsella's *Nightwalker*, Heaney's *Station Island*, and Boland's *Outside History* show; but in general the untrammelled, sometimes ludic, and generally confident operation of the imagination of these writers and of many of their contemporaries – John Banville, Derek Mahon, Brian Friel, Marina Carr, Paul Muldoon, and many others – absorbs and transmutes material for the joy of its expression alone. Criticism itself has been released in a variety of different approaches.

Harmon's approach has always been driven by a respect for language. As a poet himself, he has a particular interest in the ways in which writers handle language; it is indeed his primary focus. Just how acute is his perception of literature from the point of view of the poet may be gauged by his 'Advice to a Poet', which has become a much-used source on the Poetry Ireland website and is presented here in the Afterword. At the same time his influential anthology *Irish Poetry after Yeats: Seven Poets*, 1979, the product of years of seminar work on modern Irish poetry, not only demonstrated to the wider world that the tradition continued after Yeats but in the much-quoted Introduction also defined the main issues and responses of poets who emerged from his influence and who changed Irish literary tradition. The essays included on Clarke, Kavanagh, Kinsella, Montague, and Heaney develop some of the ideas set out in that path-breaking Introduction. It is a text-centred approach, seeing the work from the inside as well as within its historic and cultural perspectives.

In the last fifty years the map of Irish literary scholarship has changed. When Harmon went to America in the mid-1950s to study with John V. Kelleher, he saw how isolated the literary scholars and historians were, individual figures in different parts of the country. Publications were few. Gradually the situation improved with the creating of the American Committee for Irish Studies, followed by the Canadian Associations of Irish

Studies, and, in 1970, by the International Association for the Study of Anglo-Irish Literature, a title later changed to the Study of Irish Literatures (IASIL). In 1951 Liam Miller established The Dolmen Press in Dublin, where the new writers were published. Just as the poets, novelists, and dramatists in Ireland began to flourish, so a succession of new voices emerged in criticism, both in Ireland and abroad. In particular Harmon has been aware of the generations of literary scholars in America in which the succeeding generation consciously engaged with those who had gone before them. At one time that was not possible in Irish Studies; now it is.

Harmon's assessment of three centuries of a wide field of literary activity is generous, challenging, and characteristically modest. It provides an original account of a varied range of Irish writers that reflects the collection's ecumenical breadth. For the scholar, the student, and the general reader alike, it complements rather than competes with other work in the field. In the final lines of 'Stone Games' – in which he describes skimming stones with his brother off the Ardgillan seashore – Harmon defines his credo:

> We took failure in its stride
> and ever since I've sought
> satisfaction in work being done, done right,
> and not in praise or honour to be won.[4]

Notes

1   Other publications are the authorised biography *Seán O'Faoláin: A Life* (London: Constable, 1994); *No Author Better Served: The Correspondence between Samuel Beckett and Alan Schneider* (Cambridge, MA: Harvard University Press, 1998), the only edition of a Beckett correspondence to be published to date; and the collection *The Dolmen Press: A Celebration* (Dublin: The Lilliput Press, 2001), for which he wrote the Introduction and essay 'The Dolmen Miscellany'. Poetry collections include *The Book of Precedence* (Cork: Three Spires Press, 1994); *A Stillness at Kiawah* (Cork: Three Spires Press, 1996); *The Last Regatta* (Cliffs of Moher, Co. Clare: Salmon Publishing, 2000); *Tales of Death* (Belfast: Lapwing, 2001); and *The Doll with Two Backs and other poems* (Cliffs of Moher, Co. Clare: Salmon Publishing, 2004).
2   'Slow Learner', *The Last Regatta* (Cliffs of Moher, Co. Clare: Salmon Publishing, 2000), p. 55. Subsequent citations are from this text. 'Rockabill' is a lighthouse near Skerries, County Dublin.
3   'The Boarder', pp. 45–6.
4   'Stone Games', p. 56.

Part I

BEGINNINGS IN PROSE AND POETRY

COBWEBS BEFORE THE WIND:
ASPECTS OF THE PEASANTRY
IN ANGLO-IRISH LITERATURE, 1800–1916[1]

Studies of Anglo-Irish literature by Maurice Harmon include Modern Irish Literature 1800–1967: A Reader's Guide, *1967,* Select Bibliography for the Study of Anglo-Irish Literature and its Backgrounds *and* A Literary Map of Ireland, *both 1977. He edited and wrote the Introduction for the four volumes of William Carleton's* Traits & Stories of the Irish Peasantry, 1830–33, *1973, published in the Mercier Irish Classics Series. The lecture 'William Carleton: Language and Vitality' was given at the annual William Carleton Summer School, Clogher, County Tyrone, in 2000, and he spoke again at the school in August 2003 and 2005.*

E VEN though Ireland has been until quite recently predominantly an agricultural country, very few of her important writers have come from the peasant background or have made peasant life their major concern. The awareness of the peasant world emerges in James Joyce's *A Portrait of the Artist*. As a product of the urban culture of Dublin, Joyce was conscious of the chasms of experience, culture, and language that separated him from the rural background. It may also be taken as a curious fact of Irish literary history that George Moore, the other founder of the modern prose tradition, should have entitled his book of stories about rural Ireland *The Untilled Field*, 1903, as though nothing of value had yet been written. Granting that the Irish Literary Revival was generally weak in dealing with rural life, it is significant that for Moore, a sophisticated and experienced man of letters, the task of depicting the peasantry still needed to be done. Together with William Carleton, the dramatists T. C. Murray, Padraic Colum, and J. M. Synge, he provides the main material for the consideration of the realistic literary treatment of the Irish peasant in the period from 1800 to 1916.

On the one side in nineteenth-century Ireland were those Ascendancy writers, from Maria Edgeworth to Somerville and Ross, whose approach to the peasants was circumscribed by cultural, racial, and religious barriers. On the other were those writers of ability, from William Carleton to T. C. Murray, who took it upon themselves to present the peasant in realistic terms. In this general division, J. M. Synge stands apart in that he broke through the barriers of the Ascendancy world and penetrated deeply into the native, Catholic, and rural world. Anglo-Irish literature, which may be said to have begun with Maria Edgeworth and William Carleton, to grow toward Yeats, Joyce, and the flowering of the Revival, then to taper off into the literature of the post-revolutionary period, does not in fact show a progressive deepening in the portrayal of the Irish peasant. William Carleton (1794–1869) is unrivalled at the beginning of a line that fades with his death in 1869, revives with George Moore's single collection of short stories, shines strongly in J. M. Synge, and thereafter – in the period outside our present focus – emerges strongly in the work of Liam O'Flaherty and Patrick Kavanagh.

Carleton's own, much-repeated claim that he wrote with knowledge about the peasants is validated through his best work: *Traits and Stories of the Irish Peasantry, 1830–33*; three good novels, *Valentine M'Clutchy*, 1845, *The Black Prophet*, 1847, and *The Emigrants of Ahadarra*, 1848; and his *Autobiography*, 1896. No other writer of the nineteenth century can be placed in the same class, not Michael Banim, whose *Crohoore of the Bill Hook*, 1825, and *The Croppy*, 1828, flash with intermittent realism, nor Crofton Croker with his endless folk material, not Gerald Griffin, whose best work, *The Collegians*, 1847, is not about peasant life and whose best short story, 'Suil Dhuv', 1827, is too fragmented and lurid in the tradition of Banim, and not the romantic Dion Boucicault.

By birth and experience, Carleton was firmly rooted in peasant life. He was born on a small farm in County Tyrone; as a storyteller, his father belonged to the oral tradition and had a prodigious memory so that behind Carleton we have the sense of the bottomless mind of the storyteller. Furthermore, his father moved easily from Irish to English, although his mother felt more at home in Irish, as do Carleton's characters at moments of particular emotional intensity. Carleton was fortunate, too, in that the Clogher Valley, where he grew up, was rich in native culture: 'My native place is a spot rife with old legends, tales, traditions, customs and superstitions…charms, old ranns, or poems, old prophecies, religious superstitions, tales of pilgrims, miracles and pilgrimages, anecdotes of blessed priests and friars, revelations from ghosts and fairies.'[2]

As well as being an assertion of pride in Carleton's knowledge of his people, this is a claim made in the context of the whole antiquarian activity of the mid-nineteenth century. Carleton makes explicit reference to the work of George Petrie, Samuel Ferguson, and John O'Donovan. In other words, he knew that he wrote of a disappearing entity; he was within a movement that leads directly to the activities of Douglas Hyde, Lady Gregory, and W. B. Yeats, who, in turn, would recognise the value of the peasant background and would seek to record some of its culture.

Frank O'Connor has pointed out that Moore's *The Untilled Field* established some of the recurrent themes of modern Irish literature – rural insufficiency, anti-clericalism, and emigration.[3] But these were also part of Carleton's response, whose treatment of peasant society, while lacking Moore's greater literary awareness and sense of form, was nevertheless more profound and intimate. To place the two achievements side by side is to realise with considerable force how much had been lost between 1830 and 1903. Moore's advantages stem from his contacts with European and English literature, Carleton's from his immersion in his own material. And it is a revealing comment on what happened in between that Moore could regard his subject as virgin country.

Carleton's claim for the authenticity of his work is more than a question of home and environment. He is not the only Irish writer to assert the truthfulness of his own work. But he is the only Irish writer of his century to present his material in the kind of confident and complete manner that indicates the literary imagination in a fully creative relationship with its material. Again the contrast with Moore is instructive. Moore's stories are filtered through a defining and controlling intellect so that a basic idea holds the material together. Carleton writes in several voices and, while not all of these are successful and while the rational control is often weak, the emotional range and imaginative force are considerably greater than in Moore. Carleton's work is praiseworthy for its verisimilitude, for its realistic portrayal of the lives of the people and for the insight which he gives to their secret and often chaotic lives; for his personal experience of the church, the hedge school, and the life of the poor scholar; and for his knowledge of the pilgrimages, the stations, the weddings, Ribbonism, rackrenting, eviction, and peasant violence – on these levels his fiction is a record of the actual and the concrete. But his greatest claim to fame from the literary point of view, as distinct from the interest he has for the historian, lies in those stories and those places in his best novels where he speaks out in mature control of his material.

Carleton's use and misuse of language is central to any attempt to understand and evaluate what he has written. The narrative voice in *Traits and Stories of the Irish Peasantry* varies so much that it is impossible to identify one particular voice as distinctly his. Explanation and digression frequently interrupt the narrative voice and tone. While he sometimes writes in a realistic manner, he chooses the mask of comedy so readily that it might be seen as a way of disguising his uncertainties about language itself. His natural talent, so extravagant and capacious, at once his gift and his misfortune, draws us to his work but frustrates our best efforts at evaluation.

Does Carleton have a distinctive style? The Introduction to an edition of *Traits and Stories*, written when he was forty-four years of age, provides an example of how he uses words when not creating a fictive world.

> It is well known that the character of an Irishman has been hitherto uniformly associated with the idea of something unusually ridiculous, and that scarcely anything in the shape of language was supposed to proceed from his lips but as an absurd

congeries of brogue and blunder. The habit of looking upon him
in a ludicrous light has been so strongly impressed upon the
English mind, that no opportunity has ever been omitted of
throwing him into an attitude of gross and overcharged
caricature, from which you might as correctly estimate his
strength and moral proportions as you would the size of a man
from his evening shadow.[4]

This is not an effective style; it is wordy and assumes the weighty use of
words makes the argument more persuasive. The Introduction gives us a fix
on how Carleton speaks when he wants to impress a literate audience. He is
here the middle-aged successful author who has earned the right to speak
on this subject because he has contact with his people. Carleton went to the
English tradition to learn how to become a writer; that influence has left
marks on his style, in particular the syntax of the eighteenth-century
essayists, the distancing effects of the urbane narrator, Gothic fiction, the
literature of the Sublime, and the English romantics. On the other hand lie
the conventions of the oral tale in which there is the strong, dramatising
presence of a narrator and his interaction with an audience and in which
wonder and chance, the unexpected and the unprepared for often appear;
in an oral tale almost anything can happen even without explanation or
preparation. That degree of freedom works against the conventions of the
written story where events must be explained, where there is a logical
progression of incident, where character issues in action, where
coincidence and chance tend to be suspect.

Carleton's story 'Denis O'Shaughnessy Going to Maynooth', a portrait
of the artist as a young pedant, is distinguished by the zest with which
Carleton writes it. And, like Joyce's later semi-autobiographical novel, it is
written with an ironic and amused detachment even as it deals
compassionately with a subject that is personal and painful. The story of
the fair-haired boy, Denis, who is set aside by his family for the priesthood,
is a familiar one in Irish-Catholic experience. Carleton knows what he's
talking about, understands the attitudes of the people, and above all has an
ear for their ways of speaking. His portrait of Denis is full of vitality and
humour; it not only describes the young pedant but also brings him alive
through his characteristic speech. By use of the mock-serious tone
Carleton achieves a degree of distancing through which he can freely reveal
his own family background and his experiences as a young clerical scholar.
The control comes from the mocking tone that enables Carleton to
commemorate and judge at the same time, and to use the Philomath
English of the hedge school for the same dual purpose.

Carleton lightly and skilfully explains the attitudes towards the Catholic
Church and towards education that determine and clarify Denis's situation.

A boy set aside for the priesthood, he says, 'is cherished, humoured in all his caprices, indulged in his boyish predilections, and raised above the heads of his brothers, independently of all personal or relative merit in himself. The consequence is, that he gradually becomes self-willed, proud, and arrogant, often to an offensive degree...'. Denis is vain, pompous, fearful, flirtatious, shrewd, adaptable, and inconsiderate. The story illustrates these observations and qualities in a series of broadly comic scenes: the 'pranks of pedantry', the verbal duels with his father, the displays of learning for the neighbours, the dalliance with the girls, the vanity of dress and deportment. Carleton's portrayal of Denis depends on a successful rendering of how he speaks, as when he insists on being better treated and to enjoy what he calls 'proofs of respectability' from his family: 'I am in that situation of life in which, from my education and other accomplishments, I must be estimated as duly qualified to eat beef and mutton instead of bacon, an' to have my tay breakfast instead of stirabout...Buy me a knife and fork...The beef and mutton must follow.'

The mocking manner is found elsewhere in Carleton's work, particularly in 'Phelim O'Toole's Courtship', where it includes comic descriptions and exaggerated accounts of customs and superstitions. There is the credible detail with which he tells of various superstitions; the vitality of his descriptions is remarkable. When people have concluded the rites of the station they move to the tents for refreshments and sport, or as Carleton puts it, 'The dancing, shouting, singing, courting, drinking and fighting...'. Such passages may be found in many other stories, in 'Wildgoose Lodge', 'The Party Fight', 'The Lough Derg Pilgrim'. There is an easy authority in Carleton's language when he writes within his powers. It is in these extensions to the story that Carleton brings social perspective to the comic portraits: in the give and take between Denis and Father Finnerty; in the family's generous celebration when he is pledged a place in Maynooth, and in the subtle bargaining with the Bishop, in whose palace he sees further evidence of material wealth. A whole social canvas is built subtly and humorously around the central figure.

The issue of the educated narrator is in the forefront of his story 'The Hedge School'. In Carleton's mind this brings us to the heart of his own culture, to the system of education on which he blames most of society's ills. How does he approach it? What kind of speaker does he choose? The opening line gives the answer: 'There never was a more unfounded calumny, than that which could impute to the Irish peasantry an indifference to education.' Not a fluent style, but circumlocution, display of learning, and a disabling distancing from the material. Carleton recovers quickly when he goes on to describe the hedge school. The style becomes immediately realistic, visual, and detailed. Carleton's use of particulars, when he deals with what he knows, is always reliable and convincing.

> About two hundred yards from this, the boreen, which led from the village to the main road, crossed the river, by one of those old narrow bridges whose arches rise like round ditches across the road – an almost impassable barrier to horse and car. On passing the bridge, in a northern direction, you found a range of low thatched houses on each side of the road: and if one o'clock, the hour of dinner, drew near, you might observe columns of blue smoke curling up from a row of chimneys, some made of wicker creels plastered over with a rich coat of mud; some, of old, narrow, bottomless tubs…

Our speaker is a gentleman on a horse. The peasantry address him as Sir. He combines Carleton's ability to deal with a real world with the elevated language of the educated, cultured persona. What we may notice is the deliberate compositional nature of the description. Carleton is thinking of conventional studies of rural life, that he wants us to see his village in terms of an English landscape painting. He directs our eye carefully along the internal lines of the picture. We see the cluster of cottages, the dunghills by the doors, the smoke, those particular chimneys and out of these comes our understanding that we too, as gentlemen and ladies on our horses, react to the unsanitary conditions, the smell, and the dirt.

But Carleton creates something quite different from the conventions of British landscape painting and British descriptive writing where rural landscape tends to be idealised and Arcadian. Thomas Gainsborough composed picturesque scenes that gave a romantic appreciation of the countryside. Travel literature, of which there was a great deal, did much the same. Carleton imitates the conventions but subverts them. His village is gross, it offends the senses; it is shockingly realistic.

'The Battle of the Factions' is a story in a different vein. Here the mockery of 'Going to Maynooth' is replaced by another persona and a different voice. By presenting his material through the authoritative and exuberant figure of the teacher, Pat Frayne, Carleton achieves distance and subtly allows the confident and sympathetic relationship of narrator and story to be undermined by the actuality of his narrative. At the same time he uses Pat Frayne to provide a delightfully casual and appreciative portrait of local girls gossiping, a genial explanation of the differences between a faction fight and a party fight, and a frame story of heroic and romantic love. John O'Callaghan and Rose O'Hallaghan, Carleton's Romeo and Juliet, fail to prevent the traditional feud between their families and both die in a final tragic tableau of the dead that concludes and diminishes Pat's enthusiastic commemoration of the glory of the faction fight. The result of this rich freight of incident, detail, narrative, and tone is a powerful story of love and death, custom adhered to with stupid principle, and family and social life disrupted. All come naturally within the memory of Pat Frayne, who, like the old soldier with no more wars to fight, still hears the sounds of combat above the cries of loss that also escape from his story. At the same time his tale, being appropriate to the teller, reveals his own richly humorous, extravert, and passionate nature.

Pat Frayne's impulse is to make a myth out of the faction fight. First, in a piece of superb description, he draws a clear distinction between the sectarian party fight, fought between Orangemen and Catholics, and the faction fight, fought between rival families. 'In a party fight,' he says, 'a prophetic sense of danger hangs, as it were, over the crowd – the very air is loaded with apprehension; and the vengeance burst is preceded by a close, thick darkness, almost sulphury, that is more terrifical than the conflict itself, though clearly less dangerous and fatal.' A faction fight, he maintains, has none of this tragic and sombre element. The atmosphere is light and comic:

> Paddy's at home here, all song, dance, good-humour and affection . . . he tosses his hat in the air, in the height of mirth...He is, in fact, while under the influence of his heavily afflatus in love with every one, man, woman and child . . . To be sure, skulls and bones are broken, and lives lost; but they are lost in pleasant fighting – they are the consequences of the sport, the beauty of which consists in breaking as many heads as you can.

This conversion of hate into love and violence into an acceptable mode of self-expression is appropriate to Frayne's ritualising imagination. The meeting of members of opposing factions begins in a ritual of insult and challenge, an exchange of compliments prior to the exchange of blows in what might well appear to be a lesser form of duelling, more friendly, more informal, but just as deadly. Frayne happily commemorates scenes and deeds of appalling violence with good-humoured and appreciative equanimity, but events overtake him and the tragic centre of the narrative becomes increasingly evident. 'God help poor Ireland!' he exclaims, 'when its inhabitants are so pugnacious, that even the grave is no security against getting their crowns cracked, and their bones fractured!' And in the final scene men crawl about, bloodied and broken, women wail and curse, and even the triumphant shouts of the victors are faint when compared with their initial shouts. When, in the last stages of the battle, the young hero is killed and when Rose, who kills his murderer in a rage, then discovers she has killed her own brother goes insane with double grief, the story's celebratory tone is finally defeated. 'It was truly dreadful,' Frayne says sombrely, describing the death of John O'Callaghan.

The companion story, 'The Party Fight and Funeral', although based on an actual fight that Carleton saw in Clogher at the age of twelve, lacks the power of Frayne's full-bodied and eloquent narrative, because Carleton speaks through the figure of a gentlemanly observer whose civilised opposition to what he describes turns the story into a moral document. When his brother becomes the narrator, his language also shows him to be at a distance. The style is that of the educated, analytical observer. But there is yet a third narrator who is one of the people. At once the style, similar to that of Pat Frayne in 'The Battle of the Factions', becomes more concrete. The vitality, vividness, speed of the narrative and the speaker's voice are convincing; we feel he knows what he is talking about, that his first person story is based on experience. It is possible to consider the issue of the three voices as a technical one, but it is also possible to argue that Carleton deliberately divides his speakers, with two from the upper class and one from the people. He writes consciously, even self-consciously, for an English audience, and is aware that his material, the rough and ready world of his own people, is alien to the English, its language unfamiliar to them. Using two kinds of narrators is an attempt to deal with this problem.

The question of Carleton's use of language is central, although difficult to bring into clear focus. It may be that he never fully recovered from the defects of his education. It is to his credit that he tried to marry the literary styles of his English models with the oral expression to which he was accustomed. Pat Frayne's speech has the ring of truth, but so does the first narrator's in 'The Party Fight and Funeral'; it is authentic within its own terms of reference. And if, as I suggest, Carleton may be quietly mocking him, then that is an additional achievement. If, as I also suggest, Carleton is undermining Pat Frayne's views on sectarian conflict, then he is a more sophisticated writer than many would have us believe. Sometimes, he fails to keep a distinction between his own voice and that of his narrator, which suggests an ultimate uncertainty about language, but the intelligent inter-play of voices and values from different social and educational backgrounds is a measure of Carleton's success in illustrating and illuminating the world he knew better than anyone.

Carleton has left one other study of sectarianism at work in the story 'Wildgoose Lodge', which is an imaginative recreation of a reprisal execution that took place in Reaghstown, County Louth, in 1816 and in which eight people died. His account of the gathering of the Ribbonmen in a chapel and of the insane burning and killing of the whole family is a powerful indictment of violence. From the beginning everything in the Gothic narrative contributes to the sense of evil. Although the summons to attend the meeting seems normal, the narrator has a sense of foreboding and anxiety: 'I felt a sense of approaching evil . . .'. The day is gloomy and tempestuous; he walks to the meeting under a heavens that is lowering and angry; and when he enters the parish chapel, the scene inside is in keeping with the darkness, the storm, and the midnight hour itself. Forty people are

sitting in silence, the windows are shuttered, the candle on the altar
lengthens the shadows at the lower end of the chapel. Some of the worse
men in the parish – malignant and reckless spirits – are present. Six or
seven of them are standing on the upper steps of the altar their eyes
kindling 'with a fiercer expression of vengeance'.

The Captain at the altar takes on a satanic expression – his hands open
and close conclusively, his eyes shoot out baleful glances, his teeth grind –
and so far, as part of the story's build-up, no one knows the purpose of the
meeting or of the oath the Captain demands they take. The heightening
progression reaches a climax in the blasphemous actions that follow: those
present, with some exceptions, drink whiskey from the altar in subversion
of the rite of communion and swear the baleful oath:

> The countenances of these human tigers were livid with
> suppressed rage; their knit brows, compressed lips, and kindled
> eyes, fell under the dim light of the taper, which an expression
> calculated to sicken any heart not absolutely diabolical.

The actual setting fire to the house happens quickly. Carleton emphasises
the satanic faces of those immediately involved; they are 'demons' whose
'horrible visages' exhibit hatred, revenge, and joy. The oath is 'No mercy –
no mercy', a perversion of Christian charity, and it is this cry that now
triumphs. In one graphic incident a woman with flaming hair appears at a
window of the burning house and shrieks for mercy. Carleton grimly notes
that the only reply to this appeal

> was the whoop from the Captain and his gang of 'No mercy – no
> mercy!' and in that instant the former, and one of the latter,
> rushed to the spot, and ere the action could be perceived, the
> head was transfixed with a bayonet and a pike, both having
> entered it together. The word 'mercy' was divided in her mouth;
> a short silence ensued, the head hung down on the window, but
> was instantly tossed back into the flames!

The cry of 'no mercy' rings out again as some of those inside try to escape
but are bayoneted to death by the attackers. There are cries from those
within, the flames worsen, the windows are blown out. Those who are still
alive beg to be killed by weapons rather than suffer death by the flames but
are flung back into the horrors of the conflagration.

In Carleton's view the behaviour of the Captain and others of the Ribbon
Lodge is indicative of the demonic forces in human nature. This concept is
endemic in Carleton, just as violence and anarchy seem to be endemic in all
those nineteenth-century Irish novels that try to deal realistically with Irish

peasant society. It might be conjectured that violence and anarchy are not so much realistic accounts of social reality as modes of moral judgment, metaphors of the moral imagination conceived in the face of a huge unmanageable evil. This literary recourse to the lurid may not be so much a result of the influence of the Gothic novel or the contemporary vogue of sensationalism as a form of protest, produced in despair, against the unmanageable system of landlordism, rackrenting, eviction, injustice, famine, death, and emigration. The real subject of these novels is not their visible world of savage murders and reprisals, nor the deceit, greed, and indifference of the landlords and their agents, but the predicament of a race denied a place in society or any glimmer of hope for the future.

Carleton's near obsession with the satanic individual, seen in 'Wildgoose Lodge', 'The Midnight Mass', and 'The Lianhan Shee', becomes more pronounced in the novels. In *The Black Prophet*, 1847, O'Donnell the prophecy man is almost totally evil, a murderer pursued by nightmare, plotting evil, cruel, a man who has fallen from innocence. Solomon M'Slime and Valentine M'Clutchy in the novel *Valentine M'Clutchy*, 1845, are Carleton's most obnoxious villains, utterly devoid of moral feeling, intent on their own greedy, cunning, and hypocritical exploitation of the people. Both of these powerful, if badly organised, novels are jagged acts of wrath against the system that denies and oppresses the people. Each is a succession of metaphors of action, characterisation, and landscape for the amoral chaos to which Irish life had been reduced in the years leading to the Famine.

But the extent and hopelessness of the calamity facing his people must have made the novelist's task virtually impossible. At his best in the short form, Carleton loses control frequently in the novels, where he works with a too-complicated plot, lurches into melodrama, and speaks directly to the landlord and the reader in lengthy asides that appeal for sanity, understanding, and justice. Flawed as works of art, the novels speak from the abyss to which his people have been driven and with a tone of utter hopelessness. Characters who make the symbolic pilgrimage from the rural desolation and the brink of death to the sumptuous world of Merrion Square in Dublin on the assumption that, if they could only speak directly to the landlord in person, on the basis of common humanity, their wrongs would be righted, are analogous to Carleton's own appeals within his novels for understanding. All are equally doomed. Owen M'Carthy staggers wearily home again only to find that the light of his life has died and his family has been evicted. Old M'Mahon returns with an abject and doomed faith in the word of an Irish gentleman. There was no light and no redress, except in those unacceptable fictive solutions, those happy endings so dear to Carleton, at the end of *Valentine M'Clutchy*, at the end of 'Tubber Derg', and at the end of *The Emigrants of Ahadarra*, 1848. In such fairytale endings wrongs are righted, the good are rewarded, and a kind landlord personally restores the land to the evicted. One wonders if Carleton knew how hollow the words sound at the end of *The Emigrants of Ahadarra*:

> 'M'Mahon,' said Chevydale, 'give me your hand. I am sorry that either you or your son have suffered anything on my account. I am come now to render you an act of justice – to compensate both you and him, as far as I can, for the anxiety you have endured. Consider yourselves both, therefore, as restored to your farms at the terms you proposed originally. I shall have leases prepared – give up the notion of emigration – the country cannot spare such men as you and your admirable son.'

One ought to be able to read this as a savagely ironic comment, but Carleton lacks Swift's toughness of mind and temperament. Coming right after M'Mahon's sorrowful farewell to his buried wife, the landlord's words are stiff and lifeless. The true conclusion to these novels comes in the words of the prophet's daughter, a doomed protest made on an individual level but applicable to the whole people: 'I tried to be good, but I am only a cobweb before the wind – everything is against me, an' I think I'm like some one that never had a guardian angel to take care of them.'

Everything was against them and there were few angelic landlords. Ireland, Carleton truly said, 'might be compared to one vast lazar-house filled with famine, disease and death'. His condemnation of the absentee landlord who abandoned his tenants to the rapacious agent erupts fiercely in his novels, but is given particular ironic edge in the letter of refusal sent by the agent Henry Hickman to the Right Honourable Lord Viscount Cumber in *Valentine M'Clutchy*. Hickman, a balanced and intelligent man, writes with scorn:

> 'Should your tenantry ask me – "why are you this cruel and oppressive upon us?" what reply could I made but this – "I am cruel because his lordship is so profligate. He wants more money to support his mistress, to feed her vanities and excesses, and you must endure distress and privation, that the insatiable rapacity of a courtesan may be gratified."'

Hickman then advances a number of principles to the landlord, appealing in one that he remember that the peasants are human beings. The appeal is in vain. The novel itself is a bitter account of rapacity and greed by the landlords and their agents, a picture of almost total corruption, including the ruining of the women.

In *The Emigrants of Ahadarra*, Hycey has got two girls into trouble and has designs on the servant, Nanny. In *The Black Prophet*, Peggy Murtagh's parents refuse to forgive her because she has had an illegitimate child, despite the shame and guilt she feels. In that novel, too, the prophet ascribes his own evil disposition to the effects on his character of his first wife's adultery. But it is in *Valentine M'Clutchy* that the economic exploitation of the people is specifically related to the sexual exploitation of girls. In this novel the suspicion of sexual sin brings disgrace, parental distress, and the loss of her fiancé and friends to Mary M'Laughlin. Sexual opportunism is presented as an aspect of moral corruption: Solomon M'Slime tries to seduce Eliza, the barmaid, and gains sexual success with and effects the ruin of Susanna Wallace, his servant girl. Together with the libertine Phil M'Clutchy and with the connivance of Valentine he responds lasciviously to the young Widow Tyrrell. And it is Poll Doolin's task to bring illegitimate babies to the foundling hospital in Dublin. Carleton's treatment of the theme of sexual exploitation and the horror of sexual guilt among the people may be set against his special feeling for innocent girls and in particular for the bond between fathers and daughters, as in *The Black Prophet* between O'Donnell and Sarah; in *The Emigrants of Ahadarra* between old M'Mahon and Dore; in 'Tubber Derg' between Owen M'Carthy and his little girl; even Pat Frayne's delighted portrait of the gossiping girls may be regarded as suitably paternal.

In the face of the general oppression, so vividly presented in *Valentine M'Clutchy*, decent men are driven into the Ribbon societies. At one meeting members bring forward their individual grievances to justify their actions. 'What have they left undone?' the leader asks, speaking of the landlords, and proceeds to summarise what has been said:

> 'They have cheated you, robbed you, and oppressed you in every shape. They have scourged to death and transported your sons – and they have ruined your daughters, and brought them to sin and shame – sorrow and distraction. What have they left undone, I ax again? Haven't they treated yez like dirt under their feet? Hunted yez like bloodhounds as they are – and as if ye were mad dogs? What is there they haven't made yez suffer?'

There could hardly be any quick answer, unless we say literally everything and look about for ten Carletons.

To move from William Carleton to George Moore is to experience a strange sense of similarity, even as one begins to realise that the differences are enormous. Although Moore's themes are almost the same as Carleton's, the range and intensity of his work are much reduced. Post-Famine Ireland is a diminished reality, and the sense of vitality, of masses of people lined up for a faction fight, crowding to Midnight Mass, attending stations, going on pilgrimage, getting married, abducting teachers, drinking, courting, being evicted, emigrating, dying, is missing from Moore's world, as it is from that of his contemporaries. I know of nothing in Irish literature of the late nineteenth or early twentieth centuries to match Carleton's sheer vitality and sense of the density of human life.

Moore's restricted vision focuses generally on one or two characters and his central theme is symbolically projected through a recurrent female figure – Lucy, Margaret Dirken, or Julia Cahill. Opposed to them are not Carleton's avaricious priests but a puritanical clergy who denounce dancing, courting, and all natural expression – and encourage the made marriage. In 'Home Sickness', Bryden returns from New York to find health and peace in his own country. By their dancing he and Margaret Dirken transform the loneliness of the parish, but the oppressive quality of Irish life impinges on his happiness. The people complain of the bad times, the priest condemns the dancing, and Bryden notices how obedient the people have become. Unable to endure this new Ireland, he returns to America. In 'Julia Cahill's Curse', Father Madden, an authoritarian cleric, represses the people. Opposed to him is the beautiful and spirited Julia Cahill, who will not tolerate his interference, whose beauty draws all men, but who is therefore denounced from the altar by the priest and forced to emigrate. The legend of her curse lives on in the parish, a reason for its fatal decline, and years later men set off for America to find her and what she has come to represent.

But it is in the understated story 'The Exile' that Moore portrays this devitalised Ireland most effectively. In this sad story he deals with several interrelated themes at once: the loneliness of Irish life, the insufficiency of rural Ireland, and the necessity for emigration. The plot is simple. Two brothers, Peter and James, live on a small farm with their father. Peter, a gentle uncertain man, not really suited to farm work, tries for the priest-hood, then the police force, then the priesthood again, and finally returns home to the farm. James is a good farmer, loves Catherine and wants her to marry him. Catherine, however, loves Peter, and when he enters the priesthood she joins a convent. When Peter comes home, James emigrates and Catherine leaves the convent to marry Peter. But the plot barely indicates what the story is really saying. Exile is a general state, a condition of existence, an absence. All the figures are in isolation from each other; the impulses to do good add up to very little; there is no sense of community, of a village, or of a parish, or even of a person to whom one can readily go for advice. Ireland itself is in decay, as the descriptions of the landscape also show, and human purpose has been so eroded that men have no sense of direction and seem incapable of self-reliant or creative action. Peter follows a number of callings; even marriage holds little interest for him. James cannot get the girl, so goes into exile in a final scene in which the implica-tions of the story expand to include all the other figures at the railway station waving sad farewells to their emigrants. It is not a story that brings insight to the characters themselves, but it tells us a great deal about their wasted, humourless, and dispirited lives, about the loss of purpose, about the inadequacies of the background. Even the low-keyed style suits the faint pulse of life in the story.

It is no wonder that short-story writers in the post-revolutionary period of disillusion should look back to Moore, not just because he gave shape and design to dominant and recurrent themes, but also because he worked with what they also had to work with – the diminished reality of Irish life. Every man, says a character in one of Seán O'Faoláin's stories, as he cries out in anguished loneliness, every man lives out his own imagination of himself and every imagination needs its background. The task that begins with Moore is just that: to create an imaginative background and to find a satisfying vision of life in an Ireland that the Famine and the social and cultural changes that it brought about had changed forever.

In reality, the process by which the people finally gained possession of the land was long and bitter. By the end of the nineteenth century, as a result of various land acts ending in the Wyndham Act of 1903, the great change had been effected. The soil of Ireland, as Padraic Colum phrased it, passed from alien landlordism into the hands of the farmers themselves. The event is so momentous that it comes out strongly in the literature: a matter of pride, as Murtagh Cosgar says in Colum's 'The Land', 1915, thinking of what had been gained and the legacy that would now pass to the sons – 'their manhood spared the shame that our manhood knew. Standing in the rain with our hats off to let the landlord – ay, or a landlord's dog boy – pass the way';[5] or, as the old man in Daniel Corkery's *A Munster Twilight*, 1916, reminds his son, 'You won't have to face what I had to face, the struggling with landlords, and the law – the law, that would leave a rich man poor and a poor man broken.'

The land, that had been won through a century of struggle, becomes a dominant force in the realistic literature of the late nineteenth and early twentieth centuries, a cruel mistress to which men give their lives and their strength so that they can barely imagine the idea of a son who will not give himself to the same kind of existence. In T. C. Murray's play *Birthright*, 1911, Bat Morrisey would deny his eldest son's right to the farm and would send him into exile rather than see the land pass into the hands of a man not made in his own image and likeness: 'The sweat o' my body an' my life is in every inch o' the land, and 'tis little he cares, with his hurling an' fiddling an' his versifying an' his confounded nonsense.'[6] In Colum's *The Fiddler's House*, 1907, the musician rejects the narrow life of the small farm for the freer life of the roads. And in his unpublished play, *The Kingdom of the Young*, the girl rebels against her father in favour of that joy in life that he and his generation missed.

The choice facing the children of such harsh, authoritarian fathers, short of killing them with the blow of a loy, is to knuckle down to the brutalising servitude of the small farm, or to leave home. The basic irony of Colum's play 'The Land', in which the action takes place on that great day in 1903 when the land is finally reclaimed and when men can walk upright at last, is that the victory turns to ashes in the mouth, that the conflict is now between slavery to the land and freedom for the self. The test of love and manhood is made in that context. Murtagh Cosgar is a hard man whose ten children have all emigrated, rejecting the farm in favour of opportunity elsewhere, just as Christy's brothers and sisters in Synge's *The Playboy of the Western World* have run from old Mahon. His remaining son, Matt, declaring his love for Ellen, and finding that marriage to a girl who has neither land nor fortune is opposed by his father, first of all decides to seek freedom of action in America, but on reflection feels the pull of the land into which he has put so much of his strength. As a result he loses Ellen, who goes off to the new world with the other boys and girls, to 'Streets and streets of houses and every house as crowded as the road outside the chapel when the people do be coming from Mass'. Their images of America define what is missing from their lives in rural Ireland: fine clothes, crowded streets, great houses, money, marriage, opportunity, theatres, fine things, and above all – personal freedom!

The dominant issues in late nineteenth- and early twentieth-century Irish writing about the peasants are land hunger, loneliness, repression, individual freedom of action, family, and personal pride. Carleton had written of a huge and impersonal tragedy and of events sometimes so anarchical as to be almost melodramatic. The later writers focus on issues of individual choice and the pressures of a tight society. Possession of the land brought economic and social stresses, which in turn affected personal decision. But in late nineteenth-century Ireland the way back was much harder.

Maurice Harte, in T. C. Murray's play of the same title, in what is the typical modern instance, found the whole experience traumatic. His honest realisation that he has no vocation is disastrous for him, for his brother, who has made a good match and whose wedding ceremony is to be performed by Maurice, and for his family, who have gone deeply in debt to pay for his education on the strength of one day having a priest in the family. Act One ends with their determined effort to dissuade him from his decision to leave Maynooth.

> Mrs. Harte. Will you be talking wild, frightening, foolish talk about your conscience, and not think at all of them, nor of us, and all we done for you?
> Maurice.   (*distressfully*) Mother! Mother!
> Mrs. Harte. You'll go back? 'Tis only a mistake?

Maurice.	Great God of Heaven!... you'll kill me.

Maurice.   Great God of Heaven!... you'll kill me.

Michael.   You'll go back, Maurice? The vocation will come to you in time with the help o' God. It will, surely.

Maurice.   Don't ask me! Don't ask me!

Owen.   'Twould be better for you, Maurice. 'Twould surely.

Mrs. Harte.   (*passionately*) If you don't how can I ever face outside this door or lift up my head again?

Maurice.   (*piteously*) Mother!

Mrs. Harte.   How could I listen to the neighbours making pity for me, and many 'o them only glad in their hearts? How could I ever face again into the town o' Macroom?

Maurice.   Oh, don't.

Mrs. Harte.   I tell you, Maurice, I'd rather be lying dead a thousand times in the graveyard over at Killnamartyra –

Maurice.   (*with a sudden cry*) Stop, mother, stop!
(*There is a tense pause.*) I'll... I'll go back – as – as you all wish it.

He sinks into a seat with an air of hopeless dejection.

Mrs. Harte.   (*drawing a long, deep breath.*)
God, bless you, boy, for that! I knew you would.[7]

Not unexpectedly, Act Two ends with the final return of Maurice from Maynooth, broken by this terrible conflict. Murray's dramatisation of the conflict is superbly accurate in its insight into the mixture of ignorance, pride, love, and determination in the family that compels the sensitive young cleric to go against his own conscience. Significantly, his role in this scene is reduced to anguished cries, since there is no way that he can hope to explain his inner torment to his peasant family and since he himself knows only too well the force of respectability that drives them to oppose him. Ironically, his parents offer prayers of praise and thanksgiving to a God whom they see on the side of the small farmer.

The issues of respectability and social status have become central: in T. C. Murray, in Lennox Robinson's *The Clancy Name*, in which another dominating parent fights to hold both land and honour for her son, in Padraic Colum's fiercely proud possessors of land. Once sounded, the theme echoes forward to O'Connor and O'Faoláin and into all those novels, stories, and plays in post-revolutionary Ireland that deal with the middle class. Not that it has been entirely absent from Carleton, as, for example, in that harsh story of greed and cunning that comes after his essay on 'The Geography of an Irish Oath', but it is essentially a product of that social revolution by which men, finding secure possession of the land, turn to other goals for themselves and their children – respectability, position, wealth, the good match, the secure profession, and the drying of the marrow from the bone.

To move through the work of George Moore, Padraic Colum, and T. C. Murray toward J. M. Synge is to see how central Synge was to the prevailing mood. His work is not so much the rushing up of the buried fire, as Yeats had declared, nor even that he was in advance of his time, as Yeats also said – seeing him mainly within the context of nationalistic conflict and narrow-minded opposition – but that he had the capacity to portray more deeply and with greater clarity the essential psychological and social problems of the time. To place his work beside any of these contemporaries is to see its greater vitality and imaginative force. His first play, [*In*] *the Shadow of the Glen*, 1903,[8] takes the familiar custom of the made marriage and shows the utter loneliness of the spirit to which it may lead. It is to be free of this kind of bargain that Colum's young people in 'The Land' empty out of the countryside and it is in obedience to its harsh law that the less spirited couple, Sally and Cornelius, accept the marriage compact in return for the farm for themselves and their children. Cornelius's final words provide an ironic curtain: 'Men of Ballykillduff...stay on the land, and you'll be saved in the man and in the nation. The nation, men of Ballykillduff, do you ever think of it at all? Do you ever think of the Irish nation that is waiting all this time to be born?'[9]

It is tempting to pursue an answer to this question as to the kind of nation born out of such peasant practicality and compromise, or from a society from which the best have fled. The consideration would lead us right into the gombeen paradise of post-revolutionary Ireland and through the realisation that, although the Easter Rising of 1916 was led by poets and schoolteachers and that although romantic nationalism gained the day in the immediate aftermath, it was the peasants in the towns and cities who won the social revolution as they flooded into the jobs and took over.

Here, more immediately, we may note the judgment of the final scene in *The Shadow of the Glen*, after Nora Burke has chosen the freedom of the roads, in which her old husband sits down with her spineless young man who had hoped by his death and through marriage with Nora to get the money and the land. Of the two choices made, Nora's is the more attractive, even though it perhaps leads to bad health and a short life. Furthermore, it is in line with the choices made in *Birthright*, in Moore's stories, in *The Fiddler's House*, and in *The Kingdom of the Young*. What the restrictive life of the made marriage and the small farm may involve is projected all through *The Shadow of the Glen* as sexual deprivation and imaginative loss. It is the kind of existence that the young people in Colum's 'The Land' want to avoid.

Carleton saw the huge and general catastrophe of the whole people. Synge, Colum, Moore, and Murray see the tragedy of the individual and the particular. 'No man at all', Maurya concludes sadly and firmly in *Riders to the Sea*, 'can be living forever and we must be satisfied.' The application is universal, but Synge has moved toward it through an austere and classical discipline so that the individual instance becomes representative of all. Perhaps the most fundamental aspect of Synge's best work is his ritualising ability. In his hands the issues of the made marriage, the doomed existence, the rebellion against the old, and the familiar figures of the spineless young men, the spirited girls, and the crusty old men, are transformed into a ritualising and ritualised existence in which every gesture and every action become formalised and are made part of a myth.

The triumph of Synge's art and its illusion of absolute realism and fidelity to peasant life is that it translates reality into the mythical. Pegeen Mike and her transforming Christy Mahon speak of love's experience with pristine wonder and delight. In the glorification of the potential hero, resurrection is a poetic fact, a comic correlative for a life-giving spirit by which the play itself, its language, its action, and its central figures transcend themselves and are lifted out of the here and now. The social reality remains the impoverishment of the Congested Districts, a world of emigration and purposelessness, of the made marriage, and of a desolation grimmer than anything in Colum or Moore. That Christy may go romancing through a romping lifetime to the dawning of the Judgment Day only means that he exists in the myth created by the play. In that world, redeemed by the imagination, the killing of one's da is as acceptable and as real as Pat Frayne's enthusiastic celebration of murder by faction. Ultimately it may be said that what makes Carleton and Synge the great artists they are is that in their best work imagination triumphs over reality and the inherent calamities of life are transcended.

Synge penetrated the peasant culture, but Carleton possessed it, and for both the individuality of Irish life was diminishing. Carleton's consciousness of this decline stimulated him to be the memorialist of his people and in this he resembled his contemporary poets and antiquarians and anticipated the various movements of cultural and literary renewal of the Revival period. For whether we discuss Irish writing in terms of the east–west dichotomy or the present–past division, the central impulse in the majority of the writers is to create out of loss, in the face of the steady erosion of that network of values, responses, and customs that make a distinctive culture. Because of this inherent anaemia, Yeats felt his isolation within a tradition that was broken. From his romantic viewpoint rural Ireland was 'a community bound together by imaginative possessions, by stories and poems which have grown out of its own life, and by a past of great passions which still waken the heart to imaginative action'.[10] The words echo Carleton's evocation of life in the Clogher Valley at the end of the eighteenth century, although they conveniently ignore what had been lost in the meantime.

Even Joyce, repenting in Europe, could send Gabriel Conroy's thoughts drifting westward across the Shannon to where Synge had found a 'popular imagination' that was 'fiery and magnificent, and tender',[11] and to where

Douglas Hyde had found 'one of the most valuable heritages of the Irish race – its Folk Songs' among 'the Irish-speaking peasantry – a class which is disappearing with alarming rapidity'.[12] Even for later realistic writers, peasant Ireland has been a region of the imagination and of the spirit through which they sought contact and tried to come to terms with remnants of the old Gaelic way of life and the lost childhood of the race.

Affronted by the middle-class world of post-revolutionary Ireland and later still by the mid-Atlantic culture that further threatened and diminished the individuality of Irish life, they made imaginative pilgrimages on the long road to Ummera, to the silence of the valley in Gougane Barra, to Clonmacnoise crossed with light, to the chosen island of Granuaile, to the allegorical waters at Ballydavid Pier, to the shards of a lost culture in the rough field. George Moore's artists, although resentful of local irritations, knew that imaginative nourishment lay in what Paddy Durkin and Father Pat would say to them on the roadside. 'One explores an inheritance to free oneself and others... But one must start from home – so the poem begins where I began myself, with a Catholic family in the townland of Garvaghey, in the country of Tyrone, in the province of Ulster'[13] – which is where the story began with Carleton.

Notes

1   Sections of this essay appeared first in *Views of the Irish Peasantry 1800–1916*, eds Daniel J. Casey and Robert E. Rhodes (Hamden, CT: Archon Books, 1977) and as 'Aspects of the Peasantry in Anglo-Irish Literature from 1800 to 1916', *Studia Hibernica*, 1975, pp. 105–27.
2   *The Works of William Carleton* (New York: P. F. Collier, 1881).
3   *A Short History of Irish Literature* (New York: Capricorn Books, 1968), pp. 196–8.
4   *Traits and Stories of the Irish Peasantry, 1830–33* (London: William Tegg and Co., 1876).
5   *Three Plays* (New York: Macmillan, 1925).
6   (Dublin: Maunsel, 1911), p. 14. Page references are provided where dates refer to first performances.
7   *Maurice Harte* (Dublin: Maunsel, 1911).
8   *The Complete Works of John M. Synge* (New York: Random House, 1935).
9   Padraic Colum, 'The Land', *Three Plays*.
10 'The Great Plains', *Ideas of Good and Evil* (Dublin: Maunsel, 1907).
11 'Preface', *The Complete Plays*, p. ix.
12 'Preface', *Love Songs of Connacht* (Dublin: Gill and Son, 1905), p. v.
13 John Montague, 'Note to the Rough Field', *The Rough Field* (Dublin: The Dolmen Press, 1972).

2
THE ENIGMA OF SAMUEL FERGUSON[1]

Harmon treats Sir Samuel Ferguson as a nineteenth-century Irish prose writer in an essay published in Irish Writers and Politics, *1990. In this edited version he has added a discussion of Ferguson's poetry. The interest here is partly in filling the gap in the period before W. B. Yeats's appearance, and in contrasting their two careers. For many readers Ferguson's work might be unfamiliar and, therefore, the essay defines both the state of Irish poetry during this time and Ferguson's contribution to its development.*

WHEN Sir Samuel Ferguson died on 9 August 1886, his funeral service at St Patrick's Cathedral was conducted by Lord Plunkett, the Archbishop, and attended by dignitaries of Church and State, by scholars and literary people. In his address the Archbishop spoke of him as 'a man of general culture and of varied learning', who had achieved renown in antiquarian research and who was a poet and a scholar.[2] At his death Ferguson had achieved a position of eminence in Ireland. He was at that time President of the Royal Irish Academy, had received an honorary degree from Trinity College in 1874, and, in 1878, had been knighted for his public service. He had been educated at the old Belfast Academy, at the Belfast Academical Institution, and at Trinity College. He was called to the bar in 1838 and became a Queen's Counsel in 1859, but retired from the profession of barrister in 1867 to take up a position with less pay but also less stress as first Deputy Keeper of Public Records in Dublin. In 1848 he married Mary Catherine Guinness and they lived at Number 20, North Great George's Street in Dublin. They had no children.

Obituary notices seem to confirm the Archbishop's high opinion. John Pentland Mahaffy, Professor of Ancient History and Provost of Trinity College, stressed Ferguson's patriotism. Ferguson was, he wrote, 'a man who loved his country from pure affection and as a moral duty', who saw 'the social defects and the dullness of the average English character' but was a loyal British citizen. He was also, according to Mahaffy, a loyal friend, a genial host, and a man of practical charity.[3] Margaret Stokes's article in *The Academy*[4] praised the originality of his scholarship and gave his poetry a careful appraisal. Written in 1886, W. B. Yeats's estimate of Ferguson as a poet now seems excessive: 'Sir Samuel Ferguson, I contend, is the greatest Irish poet, because in his poems and the legends, they embody more completely than in any other man's writings, the Irish character. Its unflinching devotion to some single aim. Its passion.'[5] Later, in defining his own place in Irish literature, Yeats said that he wanted to be counted one with Davis, Mangan, Ferguson. When Yeats asked to be identified with Ferguson, it was Ferguson the precursor of the Irish Literary Revival that he had in mind, the man who showed the uses that could be made of Irish poetry and early Irish saga.

During his lifetime, however, Ferguson's literary reputation was by no means as secure as these notices might suggest. Outside of Ireland he was virtually unknown.

William Allingham noted in his diary (10 August 1886) that the *Times* obituary did not even have one word about Ferguson's poetry or other writings. 'No London paper', he notes, 'speaks of Ferguson as a man of letters',[6] despite the publication of his first collection of poems, *Lays of the Western Gael*, in 1864, *Congal*, his long epic poem, in 1872, and, in 1880, his last collection, *Poems*. The one review that *Poems* received in England is worth quoting:

> Sir Samuel Ferguson's volume of verse may possibly give pleasure to a few intimate friends, but it would have been much better to print it privately, and issue copies as presents only. There is absolutely nothing in it that reaches even to the low-water mark of poetry.[7]

Clearly this anonymous reviewer had no idea who Ferguson was or of the literary traditions within which he worked. Over ten years later another anonymous reviewer in the *Saturday Review*[8] cannot understand why Yeats praises Ferguson so highly in the Introduction to *A Book Of Irish Verse, Selected from Modern Writers*.

The high point of Ferguson's literary fame in Ireland came about 1894–95, when Dublin newspapers published a controversy between those who sought to rate him higher than Homer and Edward Dowden, Professor of English at Trinity College, who rightly refused to countenance such nonsense. In 1896 Yeats recorded John O'Leary's story about the reaction of a Fenian friend whose opinion of Ferguson he sought: 'a better patriot than I am; he [Ferguson] has done more for Ireland than I have done or can ever hope to do'.[9] In that same article Yeats recalled that enthusiasm for Ferguson was common among Irish writers and students when he was a young man in the mid-1880s. Even in Ireland, despite Yeats's attempts to identify his importance as a precursor of the Irish Literary Revival, his reputation declined in the twentieth century. He is read today only by serious students of Irish literature and remembered by a few poems, such as 'The Burial of King Cormac', 'Cashel of Munster', 'Deirdre's Lament for the Sons of Usnach', or his untitled poem on the death of Thomas

Davis in 1845. Indeed to turn to his literary career is to be confronted even more forcibly with the enigma of the man who might have created a national literature, but did not, and who had the right ideas about how it might have been done, but failed to put them fully into practice.

Ferguson the family man is almost completely hidden. The best available evidence is the memoir *Sir Samuel Ferguson in the Ireland of his Day*, 1896, written by his wife, in which he does no wrong, suffers no setbacks, has no self-doubts, writes admirable letters to the best people, and receives gratifying replies.[10] He and his wife shared an interest in antiquities and travelled much together in Ireland, England, and the Continent. His marriage to a member of the Guinness family was on condition that he restrained his sympathies with Irish culture and this hindered the development of the interest in Irish poetry, which he had expressed strongly in 1834 in his famous long review of James Hardiman's anthology, *Irish Minstrelsy*. Certainly his marriage to a member of the Guinness family affected his social position. He became part of the Establishment. His prose writings reveal the complex nature of his political allegiances, and more than any other nineteenth-century Irish poet he showed how one could effectively reach across the cultural division between the two traditions.

The first important essay is 'A Dialogue between the Head and the Heart of an Irish Protestant',[11] published in 1833 when Ferguson was 23 years old. It reveals the ambivalent nature of his relationship with Catholic Ireland. He is a Protestant Loyalist yet is drawn to Irish history and culture which are inextricably part of the Irish Catholic heritage. The 'Dialogue' dramatises the conflict.

The Heart knows that Irish Catholics have had to endure great hardship for their religion. 'They have fasted for it, fought for it, suffered confiscation, exile and death for it; ... and the human heart cannot deny some charity to such devotedness.' The Head wants the Heart to repress such '*apologetic, compromising, prurient, rebellious sympathies*'. The Heart, however, will not abandon them: 'I love this land better than any other. I cannot believe it a hostile country. I love the people of it, in spite of themselves, and cannot feel towards them as enemies.' The Head, growing heated in the exchange, points to benefits brought to Ireland as a result of English occupation:

Arguments for the blessings and benefits of English rule, however, do not convince the Heart that Irish rebellion is not justified when it is specifically directed at English 'misgovernment'. The Head argues that the Irish had ample time before the English arrived to establish just government, to 'make a nation', but failed to do so, and, therefore they needed the English. Without them they would have remained a lawless, fragmented society. The Heart, persuaded by this, agrees; they agree too that the means of control is the printing press, the persuasive force of argument. The Christian Heart can still love the Irish Catholics and out of love may even be the persecutor of their error so that eventually it may 'love them absolutely as free, loyal, and united Protestants'. Ah, yes, the Head dryly concludes, such have been the feelings of all men who have been called Ireland's misgovernors; it is those feelings that all Irish Catholics hate. The argument ends as one might expect – with Protestant certainty of the rights of Protestantism and with the ideal of the conversion of Irish Catholics which, as Ferguson makes clear in a later essay, is a moral charge not a religious one. Irish Catholics have to learn to behave like Protestants.

The 'Dialogue' lays the ideological foundation for Ferguson's four-part review of James Hardiman's *Irish Minstrelsy*, 1834, an anthology of poems in Irish with verse translations in English. Hardiman himself felt that Irish literature was destined to emerge from obscurity, but the appeal of the poetry was not the same for Catholics as for Protestants. For Catholics it confirmed a sense of loss after the collapse of the old Gaelic order in the face of English aggression. For Protestants it was a reminder of injustice done to fellow-Irishmen by their ancestors, of territorial dispossession, and of linguistic and cultural repression. It showed, too, that behind contemporary sectarian and social division lay a rich heritage of poetry and song that was stunningly different from the sweet melodies of Thomas Moore and the preoccupations of Wordsworth and Byron, different not only in subject matter but in form and feeling.

Ferguson's ability to understand Irish society, already apparent in the Heart's allegiances, is even more evident here. Since he had begun to study the Irish language with fellow Northerners George Fox and Thomas O'Hagan, later the first Catholic law officer of the Crown in Ireland since the time of James II, he was able to see that the translations in the anthology failed to capture the spirit, forms, and idiom of the originals. His alternative translations, introduced in prose form throughout his review and some then assembled in verse form as an Appendix, are not only better than those in the anthology but show how perceptive Ferguson was becoming about Irish poetry. His critical faculty is remarkably well developed; he can write about Irish history and literature with authority and confidence, challenging his Protestant readers to cast aside racial and religious prejudice, to open their minds to the different nature of Irish poetry, its subjects and values.[12]

When he appeals to Protestants to open their minds to Irish Catholic culture as presented in Hardiman and asserts his belief in the importance of the two races existing together, he maintains that such tolerant coexistence may be based on mutual understanding: 'Let it first be our task', he writes, 'to make the people of Ireland better acquainted with one another.'[13] The Protestants have position, wealth, and influence but their intelligence has not encompassed a thorough knowledge of the 'genius' of their Catholic fellow-citizens. The history of centuries, he declares, must be gathered, published, studied, and digested before the Irish people can be known to the world and to one another as they ought to be. He sympathises with the much-abused peasants whose sufferings he bluntly enumerates. In order to influence his Protestant readers he creates images of the Catholics on the evidence of the anthology and on evidence drawn from his own reading. He emphasises cultural activities, family affections, and the liberality and splendour of their lords. The Anglo-Norman lords, examples of lapsed allegiance to the British Crown, provide him with the best evidence of domestic manners. They may, he knows, be criticised for disloyalty, for having become more Irish than the Irish, but his purpose is to use them to illustrate a distinctive culture. Through his portrait of David O'Murray, the blind harper, playing 'the sweet, plaintive, passionate melodies of Ireland', Ferguson compels his readers to see Irish song and culture in a sympathetic light. From one perspective Lord Mayo is despicable: an Anglo-Norman lord who adopted Irish customs and has in Sir John Davies' contemptuous phrase 'drunk of this Circe's cup', but Ferguson's literal translation of 'Tighearna Mhaigheo' (Lord Mayo) brings out the dignity and restraint of the original. The harper pleads for reconciliation with his lord and gives him the praise and respect that would be given with equal formality to a Gaelic chieftain: 'Henceforth do not reject me, / Oh, branch of the blood most noble – / (I pray you) by all that are of the great bells / Of the saints in Rome.' The contrast between stereotyped views of Irish life and character and these fervent and simple lines lends weight to Ferguson's appeal for an unbiased response.

Similarly when he quotes from Sir Josh Bodley's enthusiastic account of a Christmas visit in 1602 to the home of Sir Richard Morrison, governor of Downpatrick, he is creating a more favourable image, one based on a sophisticated life-style. On the second evening the guests sat down to a banquet fit for royalty: 'a great and fair collar of brawn, with its garnishings, mustard, to wit, and wine of Muscadel; geese, with puddings in their bellies'. Before he faces up to 'the tippling references in Irish love songs' Ferguson reminds his readers that before tea became fashionable English girls also drank with their men and that Spanish ale was an acceptable beverage. The combination in Irish poetry of references to drinking and to lovemaking he goes on to argue is not a sign of debased living. He translates some of O'Carolan's best known drinking songs and love songs, pointing out their uneven quality, some forced and unnatural, others fresh and dignified. Ferguson's translations of love poems are particularly effective. His aim is to provide literal translations so that his readers who cannot read Irish and have no conception of Irish poetry may read them as poems in their own right.

Those accustomed to Thomas Moore's fashionable mode and to the neoclassical balance and decorum of his poems will have to adjust their notions of poetry, if they are to appreciate the 'uncouth' style of Irish poetry, which appeals directly to the heart. Two of the love poems illustrate the integrity of Ferguson's work. First, 'Ellen A Roon':

> Oh, with love for you, there is not sight in my head!
> > Ellen a Roon:
> To be talking of you is delight to me,
> > Ellen a Roon:
> My pride very just you are,
> My pleasure of this world you are,
> My joy and happiness you are,
> > Ellen a Roon.

Then the magical 'Cashel of Munster':

> I'd wed you without herds, without money, or rich array,
> And I'd wed you on a dewy morning at day-dawn grey;
> My bitter woe it is, love, that we are not far away
> In Cashel town, though the bare deal board were our
> > marriage – bed this day!

Ferguson's recognition of the unique characteristics of this poetry – 'simple sincerity, exact verbal positioning and freshness of imagery' – enables him to strive for a translation that will be as true as possible to the original.

His belief in the connections between history and literature, apparent in his placing of poetry in historical contexts, is even more evident in the third essay, in which he explains and illustrates the various kinds of loyalty in Irish society: that of fosterage, seen in 'Torna's Lament', that between bard and chief, seen in 'O'Hussey's Ode', and that of the clans. He regrets that the loyalty and bravery of the clan wars were not used in united attempts to preserve the country and that Catholic Ireland supported the cause of James II, but he insists that such loyalty is an aspect of Irish life and character that Protestants should respect and understand. Finally, his discussion of various types of loyalty expressed in Irish poetry turns to love of country, as exemplified in 'The Fair Hills of Holy Ireland', in both the prose and verse translations.

> A pleasant and a hospitable place is Ireland to dwell in,
> > Uileacan dubh O!
> In which is the fruit of health in the top of the barley ear;
> > Uileacan dubh O!
> There is honey in the trees in the valleys of mist,
> And streams in summer are along the verge of every road:
> There is water in the rills there, and dew at high noon,
> On the fair hills of holy Ireland.

Finding an appropriate style is crucial. The classic language of Alexander Pope will not answer to the homely phrase of O'Carolan; but the slang of Donnybrook is equally inconsistent with the Bard's legacy. The translator must reconcile 'measure and sentiment'. Ferguson views this as the supreme challenge. In Irish poetry, he says, the rhythm and music may 'breathe the most plaintive and pathetic sentiment' but the words, no matter how translated, do not seem adequate and the syntax may be 'absurd'. It is the fundamental problem. English cannot reproduce the melodic patterns of Irish poetry without lapsing into jingling.

If the four articles on Hardiman give early indication of the directions of Ferguson's thinking in 1834, the six historical narratives in *Hibernian Nights' Entertainments* that appeared in the *Dublin University Magazine* between December 1834 and May 1836, while less well known, also indicate his political ideology. Like William Carleton's *Traits and Stories of the Irish Peasantry, 1830–33*, Ferguson's tales are told on successive nights but with one narrator. Turlough O'Hagan tells these stories to while away the time before the planned escape of Hugh Roe O'Donnell and the two sons of Shane O'Neill from Dublin Castle in the winter of 1592. They are political narratives aimed at simulating a sense of identity and purpose in the impressionable and high-minded young men. While their moral and political purposes detract from their artistic freedom, the stories reveal Ferguson's intentions and values. The first story, for example, 'The Death of the Children of Usnach', had the obvious appeal of the tragic romance of Deirdre and Naoise, but it is the impact of this story of division among Ulstermen that is important. Just as Ferguson regretted the fragmented nature of Irish society in his Hardiman essays so here the young princes see the political foolishness of Irishmen fighting against Irishmen when there is a greater, common enemy. Hugh Roe O'Donnell reflects on the 'chief truth' of the story: 'In God's name, my cousins, let not the old quarrels of our houses hinder our hearty union!...let us first join in keeping the country, and let us settle its division after.'[14]

It is not Deirdre's moving song of exile as she leaves the glens of Scotland, not her dignified lament for the deaths of Naoise and his brothers that move Turlough's three companions in the tower, but the romance of 'noble deeds and generous division', the moral power of unity over division, and the atavistic attraction of place. Even references to St Patrick's connection with Irish topography cause O'Donnell to remember his own connection with particular places. The imagination, stirred by storytelling and song, encompasses different periods and in the process binds the generations and the clans together. The evidence of Ferguson's topographical affinities with Ireland east of Lough Neagh, which is a strong element in motivating him to write the epic narratives *Congal*, 1872, and 'Conary', 1880, based on early Irish sagas, is already apparent in these earlier stories; in the Irish mind it is inescapable from genealogy because of the tribal nature of Irish society up to the end of the sixteenth century. The next story, 'The Return of Claneboy', that is of Clan Aedh Buidh, tells how Yellow Hugh O'Neill regained his territory from Norman control. Ancestral pride and topographical identification are also evoked in the story of Shane O'Neill. But in the three stories 'The Captive of Killeshin', 'Corby Mac Gillmore', and 'The Rebellion of Silken Thomas', Ferguson pursues the theme of trans-tribal allegiance.

Although these stories are marred by their moral and political purposes, they reveal Ferguson's historical sympathies. It could be argued that his response to the past is more easily expressed than his belief in the reconciliation of Catholics and Protestants in his own time. Nevertheless, within four years of completing *Hibernian Nights' Entertainments*, he formulated an impressive belief in the creative possibilities of a realistic engagement with present reality and history:

> There can be no true romance, no real poetry, nothing in a word, that will eventually touch either the heart or the imagination, that has not its foundation in experience of existing facts, or in knowledge of the acts, opinions and conditions of our ancestors... It is this enlarging of our portion of space, of time, of feeling that is the true source of intellectual pleasure.[15]

His prose writings document the directions his mind was taking. In his review of his friend John O'Donovan's *Annals of the Four Masters*, 1848, he called not for a general history of Ireland, but for 'particular and local' histories... such as will enable us to know one another and the land we live in... such knowledge would beget mutual confidence, because it would be based not on received opinion, but on objective, verifiable evidence'. A man inspired by such sympathy with Irish culture had little difficulty in understanding the aims of the poets associated with *The Nation* and in feeling close to the spirit of the young nationalist leader Thomas Davis. 'They awoke the whole country', he wrote, 'to high and noble aspirations through their fine enthusiasm...'. His own enthusiasm and commitment are apparent in his review of O'Donnell's *Annals*. 'It is the very time, he wrote, 'for men of a large and noble ambition in letters to live in Ireland... A new root of society has been planted, and a new flower of civilisation is yet to bloom, in this western world.' The new civilisation will grow downwards from the Protestant mind. In a letter written to the Catholic poet Aubrey de Vere in the same year, Ferguson makes this clear:

> I rely more on the slow but certain effect of a national literature operating among the heads of society and thence downwards than

on any instruction or organization of the populace. It has for
many years been my great object and ambition to promote a
literature of this kind, and I have the satisfaction of seeing the
foundations laid in our Royal Irish Academy Library and
Museum, and the materials already in part supplied by our native
scholars and poets'.[16]

At the same time Ferguson's sympathies are always challenged by
distrust of priest-craft and his dislike of the crudities of the Irish peasantry.
In the final analysis Catholics are only acceptable when they behave like
Protestants, which, given the post-Tridentine nature of the Catholic
Church in Ireland, they were unlikely to do. This prejudice, transcended to
some degree in his enthusiastic advocacy of what Hardiman brought into
the public consciousness, was not exorcised in the course of that long
engagement. While he could argue for an honest and open-minded
recognition of the unique qualities of Irish literature and culture, he could
not overcome his deep-seated suspicion of things Catholic. This conflict is
seen clearly in his portrait of Thomas Davis.[17]

Ferguson's portrayal of Davis as an educated Protestant gentleman, poet,
scholar, and lover of art and literature is almost a mirror image of himself.
While in later life he would distance himself from the poets of *The Nation*,
he clearly admires and respects Davis, the leader of a movement called
Young Ireland, and was drawn into political sympathy with him. Davis, he
declared, 'sounded the intellectual *reveille* of a whole people, and if they
had slept, they awoke refreshed'. In any question of national independence,
he writes:

> The Protestant, or we should say the true Irish Catholic, stands
> on a very different footing from those whom, with every respect
> for their conviction, we must designate as Italians. This is
> politically a free country... self-contained and absolutely inde-
> pendent of all external authority. In whatever change may take
> place within our union, that independence must be preserved, or
> the Irish Protestants must perish or disperse...we will continue to
> maintain and propagate these principles of national
> independence till all the Irish once again rejoice in their ancient
> freedom.

Ferguson's argument has a number of elements of which the assertion of
the rights of the Protestant Ascendancy is central; they have as much right
to be considered Irish as any of those who have arrived in previous periods.
But the overriding idea is the importance of the Protestant virtue of private
judgment. That moral superiority is never in doubt and Catholics would be

well advised to model themselves on it. The argument is both a challenge and an invitation to Catholics to draw the line at 'ecclesiastical despotism', that is, to interference from Rome in matters other than the 'dogmas of abstract faith'. He notes with satisfaction that intelligent Roman Catholics in Ireland have begun to distinguish between areas where Rome has a right to intervene and those areas involving 'the principles of morality and social duty' in which Catholics claim 'a very Protestant freedom of private judgment'; they are, he concludes, 'virtual Protestants'.

Between 1830 and 1840 Ferguson was actively involved in the question of the relationship between the two traditions of Catholicism and Protestantism and with the issue of the relationship between Ireland and England. He was drawn to the Young Irelanders, to Thomas Davis in particular, defended Richard D'Alton Williams, the Young Ireland poet from a charge of treason felony in 1848, and founded the Protestant Repeal Association. Ferguson's speech in favour of an Irish legislature ended with the declaration: 'We are not a colony of Great Britain – we are an ancient kingdom, an aristocratic people, entitled to our nationality, and resolved on having it ... '.[18]

But his political interest, his support, though brief, for Repeal, his passionate advocacy of Irish culture decreased after 1848, when he became part of the Dublin Protestant Establishment and took no further active role in politics. Unfortunately his poetry suffered. The enigma of Ferguson's literary career is the most puzzling of all. In the 1830s it seems clear that he intended to broaden his involvement with native Irish material. He wrote several prose narratives from Irish history; in reviewing Hardiman he demonstrated real feeling for and appreciation of Irish culture; he reviewed Carleton favourably, and advocated the creation of a national literature. But from about 1837 to 1845, when he wrote 'The Welshmen of Tirawley' and the lament for Thomas Davis, he seems to have written little. It was a time in his life when he was trying to work again as a barrister, concentrating on the North-East circuit. Solicitors with briefs to give were not sympathetic to writers of patriotic verse.

Ferguson's best-known poem is probably the elegiac lament on the death of Thomas Davis, untitled by Ferguson, but variously titled as 'Lament for Thomas Davis', 'The Lament for the Death of Thomas Davis', and 'Thomas Davis: an Elegy, 1845'. It is unusual in its repeated use of the first-person pronoun and its expression of grief. The poem is carefully organised through a series of metaphors of the sower, the salmon, and the eagle, which are then gathered up in the final stanzas. Each stanza has the same parallel structure, each addresses Davis, each defines him by means of a single, elevating metaphor, and each is set at different corners of Ireland.

> I walked through Ballinderry in the springtime,
>> When the bud was on the tree;
> And I said, in every fresh-ploughed field beholding
>> The sowers striding free,
> Scattering broadcast forth the corn in golden plenty,
>> On the quick, seed-clasping soil:
> 'Even such this day, among the fresh-stirred hearts of
>> Erin,
> Thomas Davis, is thy toil!'
>
> I sat by Ballyshannon in the summer,
>> And saw the salmon leap;
> And I said, as I beheld the gallant creatures
>> Spring glittering from the deep,
> Through the spray, and through the prone leaps striving
>> onward
>> To the calm, clear streams above,
> 'So seekest thou thy native founts of freedom, Thomas
>> Davis,
>> In thy brightness of strength and love!'

It is an ennobling, idealising poem that moves beyond lament to a stirring prophecy that God will avert civil war in Ireland and that the brave young men associated with Davis will make Ireland a nation yet.

When Ferguson turned his attention to writing poems based on early Irish literature and wrote versions of Irish sagas, such as 'Mesgedra', 'Conary', and *Congal*, Victorian values interfered to such an extent that the very faults that he found in the translations in Hardiman's anthology – versification for the drawing rooms of Dublin or London – affected his work. But his poems about Deirdre, including her lament for the sons of Usnach, based on Ulster Scots' sympathy for Border ballads, have a particular simplicity and dignity.

> The lions of the hill are gone,
> And I am left alone – alone –
> Dig the grave both wide and deep,
> For I am sick and fain would sleep!
>
> The falcons of the wood are flown,
> And I am left alone – alone –
> Dig the grave both deep and wide,
> And let us slumber side by side.

His poem on the burial of King Cormac is a narrative about the conflict of pagan and Christian forces in which the River Boyne carries the king's coffin to the Christian burial place at Rosnaree and not to the pagan site at Brugh na Boinne. And 'The Welshmen of Tirawley' is a vigorous account of revenge, when the Welshmen, choosing blindness in preference to castration, rear sons to bring retribution on those who had blinded them. With 'The Forging of the Anchor', perhaps the most original of his successful poems, 'The Fairy Thorn', published in the *Dublin University Magazine*, 1834, was much admired by poets of the Revival period; it evokes a supernatural experience in its tale of the seduction of a girl by the fairies. Here the rhythms and tone combine to create the eerie feeling of otherworldly influence. Four girls are dancing a highland reel around a thorn tree when they sense a strange power exerting its influence over them.

> They sink together silent, and stealing side to side,
> They fling their lovely arms o'er their drooping necks so fair,
> Then vainly strive again their naked arms to hide,
> For their shrinking necks again are bare.
>
> Thus clasp'd and prostrate all, with their heads together bow'd,
> Softly o'er their bosoms' beating – the only human sound –
> They hear the silky footsteps of the silent fairy crowd,
> Like a river in the air, gliding round.

By 1874 Ferguson valued his Irish sources principally as raw materials: 'there is matter enough', he declared, 'for the creation of a wholly new, fresh and ennobling school of epic and dramatic literature in these despised sources'.[19] His prose writings alternate between a broadminded response to the hidden Ireland and an ineradicable distrust of Catholicism. Yet Dublin in the 1830s and 1840s was an exciting place for a man of his interests and talents. Thomas Moore was compiling the final volume of his *Irish Melodies*, Carleton published his authoritative *Traits and Stories of the Irish Peasantry*, various new journals appeared – the *Dublin Penny Journal*, *The Nation*, *The United Irishman*. Much scholarly work was in progress, including George Petrie's *Ecclesiastical Architecture of Ireland*, John O'Donovan's *Annals of the Four Masters*, and William Reeves's *Ecclesiastical History of Down, Connor, and Dromore*, which Ferguson also reviewed. Ferguson was friendly with fellow antiquarians and scholars – O'Donovan, Petrie, Reeves, Eugene O'Connor, Whitley Stokes, and Dr James Henthorn Todd – all involved in editing and translating Irish texts. His Hardiman essays fit easily into the ambiance of renewal and discovery that was part of the period and his scholarly antiquarian interests were part of a general movement of exploration of the Irish past. It is a pity that he moved so far away intellectually and socially from the milieu that he enjoyed prior to 1848. His belief in the superiority of the Protestant conscience may have been the rock on which his imaginative sympathies foundered or conversely schooled him in the poetic exegesis of the texts edited by Stokes, Reeves, Todd, and the others. It turns up again in his highly laudatory review of Todd's *War of the Gael with the Gall*, 1867, where his anti-Catholic position is virtually taken for granted.

> The expediency of encouraging the Irish mind to dwell on the past has often been questioned; but the educated classes among whom these tastes prevail have carried the pursuit too far to be now arrested, even were that course desirable... It is worthy of observation that this sympathy with the native traditions and recollections exists mainly among men who have been nourished on the principles of civil and religious freedom; and that the most persistent efforts to discountenance the cultivation of a national literature have proceeded from a school of economists and politicians, supported by the power of that influential body to whom mental liberty has at all times been distasteful.

He was stirred again to poetry in 1882 by the Phoenix Park assassinations of Lord Frederick Cavendish, the newly elected viceroy, and Under-Secretary T. H. Burke, and by the Maamtrasna murders. While he condemns the latter in one poem, his poems about the Phoenix Park murders, 'At the Polo Grounds' and 'In Carey's Footsteps', are dramatic monologues in blank verse written in imitation of Robert Browning. 'At the Polo Grounds' concentrates with moderate success on the inner reflections of James Carey, who identifies the victims for the assassins. Carey is surprised by his own coolness and this quality of detached reflection characterises the poem.

> How cool I feel; and all my wits about
> Are vigilant; and such work in hand!
> Yes: loitering here, unoccupied, may draw
> Remark and question. How came such a one there?
> . . .
> They've taken from us who have the right to it,
> For these select young gentry and their sport.
> Curse them! I would they all might break their necks!
> Young fops and lordlings of the garrison
> Kept up by England here to keep us down.

Ferguson's dream for the creation of a national literature persisted. In all his statements about it there are recurrent emphases: he is against rudeness and barbarism, wishes to raise the native element to a dignified level, wants men of noble vision to be involved; the literature must be lofty and moral, must bridge the gap between the two cultures. Literature could marry the rudeness and vitality of Irish culture with the idealism and rationality of the Protestant tradition, and scholarship by concentrating on the facts could bring truth into the contemporary understanding of Irish history. In his presidential address to the Royal Irish Academy in 1882 he advocated 'a characteristic literature rising above the conventional Irish buffooneries'.[20] It is idle to speculate on what might have happened sooner had Ferguson been more single-minded about his literary career. In a blunt way one can say that modern Irish literature began when a man of genius came along. Ferguson was not a genius; he had talent and enthusiasm, he was intelligent but had too many interests and in the long run his scholarly work and his professional career hindered his creativity. Behind that dichotomy lies the fact that he had to make a living. He never forgot the fate of James Clarence Mangan and he feared poverty.

Perhaps more than anything else he was an eminent Victorian who fitted readily after his marriage into a social and political context that kept him at too great a remove from the source of his imaginative strength in Irish culture. From that perspective he could call for the creation of a national literature but could not devote himself whole-heartedly to the task. His conservative principles and moral sensibility made it difficult for him to respond to the full range of Irish literature; but he showed what could be done. Some of his ideas about the two cultures remain valid, as does his emphasis on local history and his insistence on the importance of factual evidence. His rediscovery of the Irish past enabled the people, as he said, 'to live *back*, in the land they live *in*'.[21]

In the year of his death he wrote: 'We will have to make a literature for this country whatever be the fate of this or that policy... It must be lofty, moral and distinctively Irish... The Poets will save the people whom the rogues and cowards have corrupted. I shall not live to see the salvation, but I shall die believing in it.'[22]

Notes

1   Sections of the essay are repeated from Harmon's article in *Irish Writers and Politics*, eds Okifumi Komesu and Masaru Sekine, *The Irish Literary Studies Series*, 36 (Gerrards Cross: Colin Smythe, 1989), pp 62–79

2   Lady Mary Catherine (Guinness) Ferguson, *Sir Samuel Ferguson in the Ireland of His Day*, 2 vols (Edinburgh: Blackwell, 1896). Hereafter cited as *Life*.

3   *The Athenaeum*, 14 August 1886.

4   21 August 1886.

5   'The Poetry of Sir Samuel Ferguson', in *Uncollected Prose by W. B. Yeats. Vol. One. First Reviews*

and Articles 1886–1896, ed. John P. Frayne (London: Macmillan, 1970), p. 87. The article was the first published prose piece by Yeats which has survived and first appeared as 'Irish Poets and Irish Poetry' in the *Irish Fireside*, 9 October 1886.

6   *William Allingham: A Diary*, eds H. Allingham and D. Radford (London: Macmillan, 1907), p. 348.

7   *The Academy*, 24 July 1882, p. 60.

8   *The Saturday Review*, 23 March 1895.

9   *The Bookman*, May 1896.

10 More recently,Gréagóir Ó Dúill's biography, *Samuel Ferguson: beatha agus saothar* (Baile Átha Cliath: An Clóchomhar, 1993), gives a fuller account. Harmon notes, 'I am indebted to him throughout this essay.'

11 *Dublin University Magazine*, November 1833.

12 It seems clear that Ferguson was assisted by a number of friends whose knowledge of Irish exceeded his.

13 *Dublin University Magazine*, April 1834.

14 *Hibernian Nights' Entertainments*, First Series, 1887.

15 *Dublin University Magazine*, 1848, pp. 31, 359, 571.

16 See Gréagóir Ó Dúill, 'Sir Samuel Ferguson, Administrator and Archivist', *Irish University Review*, 16 (Autumn 1986), p. 121.

17 *Dublin University Magazine*, February, 1847. Barrister and journalist Thomas Davis, with Charles Gavan Duffy and John Mitchell, co-founded *The Nation* in 1842. Ferguson's article was published eighteen months after Davis's death as part of the series 'Our Portrait Gallery'. The article concluded with the poem lamenting the death of Davis, which Ferguson had composed on the day Davis died, 16 September 1845.

18 *Life*, I, p. 254.

19 Letter from Ferguson to Thomas Larcom, quoted in Gréagóir Ó Dúill, 'Sir Samuel Ferguson, Administrator and Archivist', p. 127.

20 *Life*, II, p. 307.

21 *Life*, I, p. 47.

22 *Life*, II, p. 248.

3
THE REJECTION OF YEATS:
THE CASE OF AUSTIN CLARKE AND
SEÁN O'FAOLÁIN

W. B. Yeats cast a long shadow over Irish writers. Some work against it, others adapt aspects to their own poetic needs. Harmon's anthology Irish Poetry after Yeats *with its comprehensive Introduction has become a definitive study. First published in 1983, the essay that follows is a distillation of the effects of Yeatsian influence upon the following generation of Irish writers using the poet Austin Clarke and the fiction writer Seán O'Faoláin as exemplary prototypes.*

FOR Austin Clarke, born in 1896, raised and educated in Dublin, Yeats was by far the most influential literary figure throughout his early years. He himself emerged as a distinctive writer only when he developed a mode of writing and a vision that were demonstrably different in style and subject matter from Yeats's.

For Seán O'Faoláin, born in 1900 in Cork, Yeats was not so much a literary influence as the voice of romantic nationalism. It coincided with and confirmed the nationalism that O'Faoláin had absorbed from other sources. Later O'Faoláin approached Yeats as an academic subject; he gathered material for a proposed biography and for a bibliography of Yeats's writings, published in the *Cambridge Bibliography of English Literature* (Vol. III, 1940). As a young man, with Yeats in mind, he disliked 'arty' writers, but when he began to think about his position as a writer in Ireland that emerged on the heels of nationalistic revolution, Yeats was the only significant model available, as inevitable an influence for him as Yeats had been for Austin Clarke ten or more years earlier. And just as Clarke asserted his individuality as a writer through a development greatly and deliberately different from Yeats's, so O'Faoláin asserted his individuality, and the different requirements and claims of his generation, through a conscious rejection of the Yeatsian way of addressing modern Ireland.

The lives of Clarke and O'Faoláin are similar in so far as home, education, religion, and early cultural and political influences are concerned. To rehearse these similarities is to define the nature of Irish experience generally at the time, roughly 1900 to 1940, and to reveal the differences between their lives and their Ireland, and the Ireland that shaped the character and imagination of William Butler Yeats. His birth in 1865 into a Protestant, merchant, educated, and artistic family made him different from young men born into post-Vatican I, Catholic, lower middle-class homes. Their Ireland was transformed by the emergence of political violence and revolution. They, too, were transformed.

The major similarities in the upbringing of Clarke and O'Faoláin are easily identified. Both responded enthusiastically to the Gaelic League. Through it Clarke entered the imaginative world of the Irish Literary Revival, learned to speak Irish, searched in the countryside for places associated with legendary beings. Other factors, a nervous, sensitive disposition, the sudden death of his father, a disastrous and frustrating love-affair, the effects of a Jansenistic Catholic upbringing, together with an over-stimulated imagination, propelled him into such a nervous condition that he had to be treated in St Patrick's Hospital, a mental institution founded and endowed by Jonathan Swift. For Seán O'Faoláin, also, the discovery of a Gaelic culture and a countryside where people spoke Irish liberated him from the restrictions of a home that was in virtually every way as rigidly conservative and narrowly moral as Austin Clarke's. Clarke witnessed revolution and was sympathetic to the Republican cause, but O'Faoláin's involvement was direct. He joined the IRA, took part in the Civil War, was appointed a Director of Publicity for the Republicans, and became deeply disillusioned with their cause when he realised how inadequate their thinking was about the kind of Ireland they sought to create. That awakening to the blindness of the idealists was a shock from which he struggled to recover for years. If they were blind, he had blindly followed. Their emotionalism had found a receptive echo in his heart. Henceforth he would be wary of emotion, would use his mind to investigate and understand the forces that had drawn him, and many like him, into irrational, shortsighted, culpable insurrection. To discover himself he had to examine the forces that went into his formation – his family history, his education at the hands of the Presentation Brothers, his training at home, and the impact of revolution. For him the Gaelic League, revolution, and first love were powerful, inextricably entwined ingredients of a dream that drove him to rebel against his father's house, to become an old-fashioned Fenian anti-clerical, and to be driven into demoralising defeat at the hands of the Free State Forces. A lesser man might have crumpled at this stage, but O'Faoláin – proud, intellectually vigorous, passionate, and idealistic – wanted answers.

Between them Clarke and O'Faoláin, men of vastly different tempera-ments, gave witness to what it was like to be Irish, Catholic, and artistic in the Ireland that one had watched coming into being and the other fought to create. Both men spent years away from the fledgling Ireland, the one in uneasy disillusion and flight, the other in pursuit of learning, mental discipline, and detachment. Both returned, O'Faoláin in 1933, Clarke in 1937, in the years in which a new, primarily native, Catholic middle class began to make its presence felt. How they coped with a repressive, isolationist, and sectarian environment is in itself a story of great interest.

They often targeted the same subjects. More fundamentally there was the task of handling their own lives so as not to become soured in an Ireland that had little understanding of the needs or contributions of the writer. Clarke fell silent for a long period, but re-emerged in the 1950s to a final achievement without which his stature would have been greatly diminished. O'Faoláin suffered alternating periods of hope and despair. He joined battle with the new Ireland, was its most courageous critic during the six years in which he edited *The Bell*, 1940–46, but freed himself from the chains that bound his generation by a liberating discovery of Italian culture. He returned to the Roman Church, leaving a nation to join an empire. He was, he declared, born spiritually in Italy. From the beginning of his literary career he had advocated the importance of the European connection as a means of maintaining standards in literature and a necessary counter-force to becoming too inward looking. Now, confident in his ability, he began to journey to Europe, to write about it, to set some of his stories there, to find ease and pleasure in its varied and attractively complex life. As editor he strongly advocated the dynamic ways in which European countries developed: 'this terrible evolution of European civilisation which is and always may be a recurring series of periods of achievements and defeats, of full living and hard enduring, of rebuilding and new starts, of Peace in which men create splendidly, and interruptions of every kind which they struggle to control' (*The Bell*, January 1945).

Austin Clarke put on Yeats's singing robes as a young man, accepting the programme under which the Irish Literary Revival had created a modern, indigenous literature by drawing upon the vast heritage of Irish myth and legend. Like Yeats he began his literary career by retellings of Old and Middle Irish material. His short poems written during the same period, 1916–25, relate the visible and invisible would, reality and myth, in rhythms that are close to what he admired in Yeats's early poetry: the delicacy of music and nuance, the wavering suggestiveness. 'The Musician's Wife' makes the two main figures 'shadows' of the unhappiness that surrounds them. The details are turned in upon themselves, becoming part of the sad mood that is the poem's central achievement and that makes it resemble the mood of sadness so prevalent in the early Yeats.

> They hurry, forever,
> Where forests are felled
> By lake-water, they
> Have no rest from the fluting
> And though they are shadows,
> He dreams of strange beauty
> And she weeps to herself
> As they fade in the dew

But it was all too imitative. Almost by accident Clarke found a different period in the Irish past from which he could draw, through which he could reflect personal experience and comment directly on his own Ireland. The title poem of the collection *Pilgimage*, 1929, celebrates the Celtic-Romanesque period when Ireland was renowned as a place of learning, sanctity, and artistic achievement. The poem is an imaginative pilgrimage to places associated with the early Irish Church, such as Clonmacnoise. Clarke creates the sense of its achievements through harmonies of sound and image.

> O Clonmacnoise was crossed
> With light: those cloistered scholars,
> Whose knowledge of the gospel
> Is cast as metal in pure voices
> Were all rejoicing daily,
> And cunning hands with gold and jewels
> Brought chalices to flame.

The light of God's blessing combines with the delicate tracery of sounds that are marks of spiritual and artistic accomplishment. In this idealised, unified world all action serves as spiritual worship.

By now Clarke has taken a stand in relation to Yeats and the Irish Literary Revival. There are three main elements in what he wants to achieve. In the first place he saw that the Revival ignored the question of the racial conscience. For a poet who had suffered from the over-zealous training of his mother and the hell-fire sermons at Belvedere College, and one whose imagination had been over-stimulated by the stories of judgment and damnation, literature had to give voice to the Catholic conscience. In *Pilgrimage* and in fiction and drama, he investigates characters who have been wracked by the conflict between personal longing for sexual fulfilment and the unyielding admonition of the Church.

His stance was deliberately anti-Yeatsian. Not only did he, unlike Yeats, imitate the forms and prosody of native Irish poetry, but he revealed the casuistical mentality that was the creation of the post-Tridentine Church whose influences, in the emphasis on the sacraments, devotions, and mathematical definitions of error, had blighted his upbringing. In an important sense his work is of compelling interest because it so deliberately reflected this all too frequent experience of his generation of Catholics. This was, as Clarke rightly said, a subject foreign to Yeats for whom Catholic guilt was not an issue.

The second element in Clarke's formulation of a distinctive anti-Yeatsian poetic was to write poetry that was classical, formal, and objective in contrast with the subjective, romantic poetry of the Revival. Again he emphasised what could be learnt through the study of Irish poetry and criticised Yeats for not learning the language even though he advocated creative appropriations from the Irish past.

The third element was Clarke's attempt to free poetry from the iambic stress pattern of English poetry. Yeats had shown how this could be done in his earlier phase, but had gone on to write a less 'Irish' kind of poetry. By becoming a world poet, he had, in Clarke's view, left the Irish Revival baby on the doorstep. Unfortunately, the next generation of poets, who might have developed a distinctive Irish mode and expressed the Catholic issues, had been executed for their part in the Rising of 1916. The question for Clarke was what to do with the abandoned baby. *Pilgrimage* was one answer. So, too, was *Night and Morning*, 1938.

'Night and Morning' faces the problem of the conflict of faith and reason. Clarke supports his dramatisation by introducing the pre-Tridentine debate between advocates of intellectual freedom and adherents of clerical authority. The presence of this philosophical and theological framework gives depth to the poems. But the work has a more immediate impact. The speaker in 'Night and Morning' is divided between his longing to participate in the Church's ceremonies and his inability to give intellectual allegiance to what the Church ordains. For him 'thought still lives in pain'; he is one 'in whom God's likeness died'. His isolation resembles that of the scholastic 'heretics' who sought God through argument despite the rulings of councils and decrees.

> How many councils and decrees
> Have perished in the simple prayer
> That gave obedience to the knee;
> Trampling of rostrum, feathering
> Of pens at cock-rise, sum of reason
> To elevate a common soul;
> Forgotten as the minds that bled
> For us, the miracle that raised
> A language from the dead.

This small book of religious lyrics was Clarke's response to Yeats's omission of the Catholic conscience.

When he began to write poetry again, in 1955, he spoke out in direct, satirical, reflective confrontation with post-Yeatsian, post-revolutionary Ireland, in which the pious Paudeens at their greasy tills had become an influential middle class happily guided by a dominant Church. Short poems identified incidents of social justice and clericalism. Longer autobiographical poems tell the story of one man's experience of Irish life in the knowledge that what happened to him represents what happened to many. The direction, emphasis, and style of Clarke's later poems, 1955–74, are markedly different from what one finds in Yeats. Clarke is no longer a maker of myth and has never been a symbolist. A literalist of the imagination, more Joycean than Yeatsian by background, temperament, and training, he recorded what he saw. When he writes of people, events, or creatures, they are in the real world: 'real bits of life console us'. The poetry is both public and private, occasional and commemorative.

The question that pervades Clarke's work is the effect of early experience on the imagination. If 'there is nothing left to sing/Remembering our innocence', how can the imagination do its work? He is sometimes grimly persistent, as though wrestling poetry out of a reality almost too horrible to handle. So much has been blighted – early innocence, romance, sexuality, nationalism, Irish life, religion, reason itself – that it is a struggle even to deal with reality. He can record, but not celebrate and sometimes the act of recording is so laboured with topicality and historical allusions that they fall short as poetry. Poems such as 'Martha Blake at Fifty-One' and 'Burial of an Irish President' shear away encrustations of history and shine in the light of the unencumbered imagination. His major long poem, *Mnemosyne Lay in Dust*, 1966, the story of his treatment in St Patrick's Hospital, is essentially about the loss of memory, without which the poet cannot write. Mnemosyne, goddess of memory, lies in the dust and must be recovered. The poem memorably describes his alienated sensibility, and registers the shock of the treatment. Clarke's return to normality, self-possession, and creativity comes in his recognition of the 'goodness' of the actual. The disordered imagination yields to the rational, creative imagination.

Clarke was not on good personal terms with Yeats. In one of his portraits of the older poet he describes his aloofness. Seán O'Faoláin found Yeats's aloofness inappropriate, but valued his insistence on standards of taste. He worked with him in the Irish Academy of Letters, which was Yeats's creation, and when he died, it declined, despite O'Faoláin's efforts to keep it going. Yeats gave dignity to those occasions at which he presided, such as the dinner in honour of the Academy's benefactor, Dr Patrick MacCartan. O'Faoláin left a record of the occasion in *Vive Moi!*, 1963. Yeats had insisted that he must be allowed to tell his friends and associates of this personal gift.

> You are those friends and associates, and I tell you that I shall be given for the next few years enough money for dignity and ease. Standing amongst you, I thank Dr. MacCartan, but I do not yet thank these others, I have not yet got all their names, and, when I have, I may still have to wait a little time. I think, though I cannot yet be sure, that a good poem is forming in my head – a poem that I can send them. A poem about the Ireland that we all served, and the movement of which I have been a part.
>
> . . .

> For the moment I could think of nothing but that Ireland: that great pictured song. The next time I go, I shall stand once more in veneration before the work of the great Frenchmen. It is said that an Italian mystic, when he has taken a certain initiation on a mountain in Tibet, is visited by all the gods. In those rooms of the Municipal Gallery I saw Ireland in spiritual freedom, and the Corots, the Rodins, the Rousseaus were the visiting gods.

The speech evokes an era and an attitude that had gone, blasted away by revolution, civil war, the emergence of meaner minds and lesser men. Close to Yeats, or remembering the past, the younger writers felt the passing of their literary idols. Their gods – Yeats, Lady Gregory, Synge, Edward Martyn, George Moore, AE – were already part of the tapestry of a different world. Even some of the events that Yeats noted in that grand manner had for them a personal and now much less inspiring relevance. Recording the occasion O'Faoláin admitted that all the young writers put together, Frank O'Connor, Liam O'Flaherty, Austin Clarke, Kate O'Brien, Elizabeth Bowen, F. R. Higgins, Padraic Fallon, Brian Coffey, Denis Devlin, Peadar O'Donnell, Francis Stuart, himself, and many others could not represent literature with anything like Yeats's achievement and authority.

When O'Faoláin had made his early visits to Dublin, meetings with Yeats were part of his image of the capital as a place where literature had been born. It was the city where sixteen men, commemorated by Yeats, had been shot and it had been those executions that had transformed O'Faoláin into a rebel. Because of them he had confronted his policeman father in angry rows, made his mother weep at such division, and went off in quest of another Ireland in the Irish-speaking regions of West Cork. Yeats's nationalistic poetry and drama fitted in well with what O'Faoláin was experiencing. When he began to take his place as the intellectual leader of the following generation, Yeats was his model; and he was, like Yeats, an indefatigable organiser – in *PEN*, the Academy of Letters, the Dublin Drama League, several intellectual discussion groups, the AE Memorial Committee, the Thomas Davis Centenary Committee, the Association of Civil Liberties, and others. Through articles, historical biographies, and fiction, he persistently sought to understand and explain the developments – social, cultural, political, and economic – that were taking place in a democratic, one class society in which Yeats's Olympian detachment seemed greatly out of place. Yeats lacked the common touch. Many of O'Faoláin's comments see Yeats as 'Johnny Forty Coats' with attitudes bordering on the phoney – 'the pose, the silly side of esotericism, the pompous poetic cloak, the business of being a Poet'. In a radio discussion he said that Yeats had put a barrier between himself and others. He had lived a remote and isolated life.

By contrast O'Faoláin had a different principle: he accepted the circumstances of his own time, and was determined to see them as clearly as possible. To some degree this was an antidote to the high idealism that had marked and blinded him as a young man. To some degree it was an antidote to the anger, disillusion, and bitterness that seared him with the defeat of the Republicans in the Civil War, a determination to avoid the kind of uncritical glorification of things Irish, Catholic, and nationalistic that characterised Irish life in the 1940s and 1950s. He hated its isolation, he lamented that the Sinn Féin ideal that had once inspired the people to be proud, self-reliant, and adventurous had been replaced by timid self-protectionism and by the wish to isolate the country from self-examination and change.

To be the investigator of such a society, he had to have the common touch. In truth, that did not sit easily with one whose home had been narrowly respectable and snobbish. The camaraderie of revolution made up for that loneliness. He was essentially private. But he knew that in his changed Ireland, Yeatsian arrogance, aloofness, or fakery would get him nowhere. His life of Daniel O'Connell, published in 1938, the same year as Clarke's *Night and Morning*, accepted O'Connell as he was, with all his coarseness and cunning, dishonesty and ambivalence, and showed in turn that O'Connell worked with the people as he found them – the dispossessed remnants of the eighteenth century, unorganised, excluded from advancement, and with no political clout. He accepted them and shaped them, gave them a vision of the future and a sense of their democratic strength. And he learned from abroad. He was not isolationist. It is, to be sure, a hero-sized portrait, but to write it O'Faoláin had to overcome his instinctive antipathy to the unattractive aspects of O'Connell's character. In an unpublished play on Parnell he complained that Parnell was lazy. This, he made clear, could not be said about O'Connell, who drove himself mercilessly in the service of his people. It was a model dear to O'Faoláin, who had a crusading, Messianic streak. All his heroes, O'Connell, Wolfe Tone, Hugh O'Neill, have a practical sense of what is possible. They are not narrow-minded, not puritanical, not isolationist. They have an inclusive and generous sense of society. Those whom he dislikes, Yeats, Eamon de Valera, kept their noses in the air.

O'Faoláin ran *The Bell* for six gruelling years on the principle of acceptance. He encouraged young writers, published documentary articles on slums, hospitals, law courts, prisons, dance halls, shops, family incomes. He kept a tight rein on Frank O'Connor, who fancied the Yeatsian role. 'It is a great temptation', he told him in 1940, 'to behave like a genius in public – the Yeats touch, the grand performance' – but circumstances have changed. There was no Coole Park now. If he can get the Dublin printer J. J. O'Leary to give a prize to the Academy or the Cork businessman William O'Dwyer to give £50 for *The Bell* or if he can get Joseph McGrath of the Irish Sweepstakes to give money for literary purpose, that is all to the good. 'The main point is that an Irish businessman becomes a patron of the arts... It is not the Yeats atmosphere –

there is no grand manner hanging around. It is just Jacky O'Leary... replacing Edward Martyn.' He is not ashamed of that. 'I am making the Academy get recognised and breaking down the arrogant ivory wall which Yeats built about it.' He was there for the long haul. 'Take the long view... Bit by bit we can spread ideas, create REAL standards, ones naturally growing out of life and not out of literature and Yeats and all that.'

'Those who examine nothing and question nothing', O'Faoláin declared in his first extended editorial (April 1941), 'end up knowing nothing and creating nothing.' Political nationalism, he believed, for too long absolved the country of the need for constructive thought. He frequently pointed out in *The Bell* and in other writings that the generation that had planned and carried out the revolution had failed to think out the kind of society they would try to create once independence had been achieved. Now in the 1940s, hyper-nationalists and hyper-moralists resisted change and opposed the free exchange of ideas. In the intellectual vacuum *The Bell*, he thought, could be a positive, receptive counter-force, a place where ideas could be freely deployed and issues examined in a dispassionate manner.

He worked quietly to introduce new thinking, to bring readers to an awareness of the actual conditions of Irish life. As a matter of policy and strategy he explained present developments in the light of history or by comparisons with developments elsewhere. He had a different approach to the past from Yeats, examining it for evidence of events, figures, and ideas that had gone into the making of modern Ireland. Before he gave up being editor, he had begun to condemn the excesses he had so often deplored. His most-inclusive statement came in 1945, when he gathered together the main components of the Irish society that had developed since the revolution and flung them, in accusation, at the one man whose 'reflex' they were – Eamon de Valera.

> The truth is that the people have fallen into the hands of flatterers and cunning men who trifle with their intelligence and would chloroform their old dreams and hopes, so that it is only the writers and artists of Ireland who can now hope to call them back to the days when these dreams blazed into a searing honesty – as when Connolly told the wrecked workers of this city that he found them with no other weapons but those of the lickspittle and toady and that his job and theirs was to make men of themselves. Surely these are honourable footsteps to follow? Surely it is not to let the country down but to try to raise it up, to reveal the drab poverty level of life which has sent our youth stampeding to the wartime cities of Europe and now threatens another exodus of their wives and children... Surely it is the duty of our writers to keep hammering at such facts.... (June 1945)

O'Faoláin had become disillusioned, weary of attacking the middle class, the Little Irelanders, the chauvinists, the puritans, the pietists, the Anglophobes, the Celtophiles (April 1946). There is a lot of O'Faoláin in that emotional editorial of June 1945, the passion, the commitment, the sense of betrayal, the anger that so much had been lost and so much wasted.

There was in all O'Faoláin's thinking about Ireland an awareness of the difference between the Ireland that Yeats had enjoyed, when there was a sense of excitement and promise in the air, when the Abbey Theatre was in full swing, when the Literary Revival was at its peak. All that had gone with the deaths of the lions of the Revival. Ireland after Yeats, and in particular Irish writing after Yeats was the subject of a number of his articles. When Cyril Connolly's magazine, *Horizon*, did an Irish issue (January 1942), O'Faoláin contributed 'Yeats and the Younger Generation', in which he summarised the changed position of Irish writers in his time. Their problems, he said, social, political, and religious, were more insistent than they had been in Yeats's time. They had grown up through revolution, were knitted with common life to a degree that Yeats was not. Unlike Yeats, most of them were Catholic, and their Church made life impossible for them. He was thinking not just of censorship but of what lay behind it – the general asceticism or Jansenism within the community, together with a long tradition of penury that had little understanding of luxuries of mind and body and that was suspicious of anything that sounded like intellectual independence.

In 'Ireland after Yeats' (*Books Abroad*, 1950) he defined the revolution as a social revolution, not just the romantic nationalist rebellion that Yeats had commemorated. The new *petite bourgeoisie* had little interest in the intellectual's fight for liberty of expression and had no intention of jeopardising their mushroom prosperity by gratuitous displays of moral courage. They had a vested interest in nationalism and even in isolationism. 'The new, raw, hard faced democracy' did not understand Yeats's noble, aristocratic manner. For the young, disillusioned writer there was no longer any question of dishing up local colour, describing the noble peasant, writing poems about fairies and leprechauns, or old symbols of national longing. 'We have explored Irish life with an objectivity never hitherto applied to it, and in this Joyce rather than Yeats is our inspiration.' The Ireland that O'Faoláin wrote about resembled the American writer Nathaniel Hawthorne's New England in Henry James's famous description: 'Try to be one of those on whom nothing is lost.' It was vastly different from the Ireland imagined by Yeats. The old boy, wrote O'Faoláin to Richard Ellmann (15 December 1953), brought his pre-Raphaelitism trailing about his feet 'like a falling-down nightshirt' to the end of his days. Yeats wanted beautiful images all the time. He also had a desire for beautiful ladies, which he called Life. He could never reconcile the images with the facts of life or, in other words, 'the rather precious 1890-ish idealised *manière de voir* with the common reality that became more and more common as the century wore on'.

It was the attempt to interpret that common reality that characterised the generation of Clarke and O'Faoláin and that drove many of them towards a Joycean acceptance rather than a Yeatsian transcendence. In that, both Clarke and O'Faoláin anticipated the responses of many writers who came after them.

4
WRITERS ON RADIO:
A SEVENTY-FIFTH ANNIVERSARY TALK[1]

One of the Thomas Davis Lectures Harmon has given on Radio Telefís Éireann (RTE 1) in Dublin was the talk to commemorate the 75th Anniversary of the founding of Radio Eireann. It was broadcast on 16 April 2001. In addition to being a valuable summary of RTE's pioneer programmes devoted to writers and their work, by writers, the essay identifies literary contributions from 1931 to the present by less known as well as well-known speakers.

QUITE early in its history Radio Eireann began to develop programmes in which writers could be used. By 1935 the station reported on the introduction of new speakers that included W. B. Yeats, Douglas Hyde, F. R. Higgins, Denis Devlin, Brinsley McNamara, Seán O'Faoláin, Francis Stuart, and Brian O Nualláin. In the same year they had their first impromptu debate between W. F. P. Stockley in Cork and Seamus McCall in Dublin on the merits of the poet Tom Moore. The first broadcast of a play by the Abbey Theatre Company also took place this year and there were original short stories by T. C. Murray, Daniel Corkery, and Francis Stuart.

Radio is a voracious medium and through the years Radio Eireann has tried various ways of attracting writers. In 1935 they held a competition for sketches and plays in an attempt to discover new material and new writers. They had weekly reviews of books and by 1938 reported that the station had broadcast six thousand and eighty-seven talks in English, forty-one debates and thirty-three poetry readings. They became rather proud of the poetry readings, since it was the only radio station to devote time in this way to poetry. When Thomas J. Kiernan, Director of Broadcasting, was asked by the American broadcaster Edward R. Murrow, 'What do you do that no other service does?' Kiernan replied, 'We broadcast a weekly programme of poetry.'

The series on Modern Irish Poets had a simple structure: it told the life of the poet; some verses were read to illustrate the career at various stages; the poet's personality was described by a friend; poems were set to music and sung; and each programme concluded with a critical assessment. The poet then had the right to reply.

Throughout the 1930s and 1940s, plays were a regular feature – all the classical repertoire of the Abbey were broadcast, some repeatedly – J. M. Synge, T. C. Murray, St John Ervine, Lady Gregory, and others. In 1938 they broadcast eighty plays, including several productions of Shakespeare, and held a competition for original material that netted Roger McHugh's *Trial at Green Street Courthouse*, a play about Robert Emmet. They continued to broadcast the Irish classics and, in addition, had recitals by Dame Sybil Thorndike and Anew McMaster. The popularity of radio plays increased and the response of listeners was enthusiastic. By 1941 they devoted seventy hours to them.

In 1943 came Austin Clarke's highly successful *As the Crow Flies*, written especially for radio and memorable for its simple but effective sound effects – the splash of oars on the Shannon, the wind rising, the fury of the storm, rain, thunder, and the voices of monks praying. It was even more memorable for its exposure of evil in its story of betrayal. The sinister Crow of Achill seeks and is given shelter in the Eagle's nest but persuades the Eagle to seek knowledge about the storm from the Salmon of Assaroe. In stark description, the Salmon warns the Eagle against the Crow but it is too late. The Crow of Death has killed and eaten her young. The wise Salmon describes the Crow:

> ... In his boyhood
> Cuchullin was her friend. She croaked
> Three times upon the pillarstone
> Before he died. She was alone
> With him in his last moment. Mist
> Of blood had hid her from his fist.
> She ripped the lashes from each lid
> And blinded him.[2]

The oldest surviving script is of a play by Gabriel Fallon called 'And the Light Shineth in Darkness', a nativity play written and arranged for radio and broadcast on Christmas Day, 1931, with music by Vincent O'Brien. It carries the delightful injunction: 'This play should be listened to in silence and in the dark.'[3] Seeing the star, the Shepherds go to Bethlehem. The script says: 'Music begins again and continues very softly as before leading gradually to the recurring horn notes of the Bass Oboe.'

> *Then (Leading from the music)*
> The Voice (*Recitative*)
> In the beginning was the Word,
> And the Word was with God,
> And the Word was God.
> ...
> In Him was life and the life
> Was the light of men
> And the light shineth in darkness.

There is a 'prolonged fanfare of trumpets' followed after a pause by a joyful hymn of praise and welcome, beginning with the words 'Sing joyfully to God, all the earth' and concluding:

> O, Praise the Lord all ye nations:
> praise Him all ye people.
> For his mercy is confirmed upon
> us and the truth of the Lord remaineth
> for ever.

Another frequent contributor to radio drama in the 1930s was P. L. McCann. I like in particular his 'Santa Claus Says, No!' The cast includes Peter the Postman and Santa Claus himself, who speaks with a Dublin accent, complaining about chimney pots.

> Santa: Do you know that nowadays I have to make a survey of the district before I chance making a call at all?
> Peter: Do you tell me that now?
> Santa: They don't take me into account, when they're building these modern buildings. Fourteen houses I visited tonight, and fourteen times I nearly broke my back trying to squeeze through the poky little spouts they call chimneys nowadays.

He has other troubles, such as a letter he got from his daughter, giving a list of the presents she wants, but then says in a PS, 'This is the last time I'll write a goofy letter like this. I know it's you, Daddy, all the time...I think, Daddy, you should be old enough now to give up the playacting, at least have some respect for my age as I'm nearly seven.'

In 1940 the station arranged for T. S. Eliot to give a talk on 'Verse-drama' and Frank O'Connor contributed some humorous monologues. The following year saw broadcasts by Donagh MacDonagh, Joseph Campbell, and Roibeárd O Farracháin. Seán O'Faoláin, Maurice Walsh, Lynn Doyle, and Francis MacManus read short stories. New writers this year included Padraic Fallon, who became increasingly involved with radio work. In 1945 Benedict Kiely gave six talks on 'Writers of Irish Fiction'. In 1946 Samuel Beckett sent in an account of his experiences with the Irish Red Cross in Normandy after the war, 'The Capital of Ruins'. In 1950 Bryan MacMahon talked about Listowel. In 1952 Brendan Behan spoke about his childhood on Dublin's northside and about 'Galway – My Capital'. In 1953 Patrick Kavanagh gave his views on the art of poetry under the title 'A Goat Tethered outside the Bailey'. The next year he spoke about his home-place in 'Return to Inniskeen'.

Writers became aware of the possibilities of the Mobile Recording Unit that went to different parts of the country. Seán O'Faoláin wrote 'End of the Record', a haunting short story about the Unit's interview with an old woman, the widow of the tailor from Gougane Barra. Patrick Kavanagh regretted that the Unit had not been with him in a pub in Dundalk to record some of the sayings he heard. 'It's curious,' he wrote, 'how almost everything good comes casual.' That day he had heard it said of a certain family that they 'gambled the plates on the dresser'.

The importance of radio in the life of the country continued to grow. The station's *Annual Report* for 1942 sums it up as follows: 'The microphone continued to be the chief "mixer" in Irish life, bringing to each other the public and the scholar, the writer, the disputant, the actor, the dancer, the journalist, the cleric, the globetrotter, the spokesman, the hobby-rider, the doctor, the lawyer – some out of every class of Irishman and the guests of Ireland.' This statement gives a sense of what was being accomplished and how those who made programmes saw their work.

Radio had a vast cultural and educational function. Listeners throughout the country and in cities and towns were given a wide range of imaginative and intellectual entertainment. For most people talks, plays, short stories, reviews, and other material – historical talks, travel talks, musical programmes, features – made them aware of their cultural heritage in literature and the theatre. Discussions of novels and stories were a constant element. There were writers such as Padraic Fallon, who not only wrote plays and did books reviews but discussed stories by The Banims, William Carleton, George Moore, W. B. Yeats, AE, James Stephens, Joyce, Liam O'Flaherty, and others.

A people, as Yeats had said when he proposed the founding of a national theatre, accustomed to an oral culture, naturally inclined to anecdote and storytelling, to the use of imaginative detail and enlargement, had a natural affinity with a medium that relied on the imagination of the listener. This cooperation with the listener who is an active participant not a passive recipient is perhaps radio's most exciting element.

Radio plays created and gathered an audience of *aficionados*. The Sunday night play became an event in many homes. I can remember how we gathered round the radio to hear the latest production, how the voices of the actors and actresses, particularly after the founding of the Radio Eireann Players, became familiar, their names well-known, their styles anticipated, their interpretations understood. Even the sound effects – a door opening, footsteps approaching, cups and saucers rattling, a drink being taken, sounds from the countryside animals, the pony and trap, thunder, lightning, rain – were part of what we expected and enjoyed. Radio was part of everyday life. I remember too when a neighbour's daughter sang in a school choir from the old studio in Henry Street. It was an event. Mrs Carton walked from Hampton to our house in the Ardgillan woods, pressed an ear against the side of the radio, listened in rapture, and, when the choir had ended, solemnly declared that she could hear her daughter's voice!

Poetry programmes were less widely appreciated but for those who liked poetry, who wanted to hear how poems were spoken, and who appreciated the sound of the poet reading his or her work, they were invaluable. Austin Clarke broadcast a programme every week, assisted at times by his Verse-Speaking Society. James Stephens read his own work, as did Louis MacNeice. There were competitions that discovered new poets, including W. R. Rodgers and John Hewitt.

Readings by short story writers similarly gave the flavour and the imaginative feel of the story. In January, 1942, Frank O'Connor read his lovely story 'The Long Road to Ummera', which evokes the distant magic of West Cork from where the old woman has come and to where she is determined to go after her death. His reading of 'The Bridal Night' in which the old woman, speaking in dialect, tells the deeply moving story of her son's infatuation with a young teacher, the madness that made him want to sleep with her, and her goodness in allowing the unfortunate boy to rest by her side before men came from the asylum to take him away. The country's affinity with oral narrative made such listening a natural extension of ordinary life.

In a reflective piece called 'The Mind in Irish Radio', written in the 1974 *Annual Report*, Roibeárd O Farracháin points out that the 'first people within radio were all known for their connection with ... Irish traditional music, drama, variety, classical music and the Irish language'. In literature and drama, he wrote, radio 'fostered native and natural talents. Many an Irish writer, of short stories, of poetry, of plays, and of the other genres found a major outlet for his work, which did not formerly exist. The spoken word, once more an Irish thing, has been fostered, in both languages.'

But the financial reward for radio work was poor. Even the competitions did not draw in as many writers as was hoped. The prizes were small. In 1947 the new competition for short story writers offered prizes of £15, £10 and £8. A verse competition in 1949 offered 6gns and 4gns for a reading. In 1948 a competition for a sixty-minute radio script offered a prize of £25. It was difficult to get writers to do even a short programme. But they were not affluent times. It is revealing that in order to defray expenses for a trip to Dublin to see a rugby match Louis MacNeice offered to record some poems. Last time he got 15gns. That would be satisfactory again, although he would he glad to get more. He did not. Hilton Edwards offered to do six talks at the going rate of £12 per talk.

In the early years of the war Seán O'Faoláin became a regular contributor, did book reviews, took part in discussions, gave the 'Book Talk' almost every month, usually at 5gns a time. He complained when T. J. McKiernan reduced fees from the traditional payment in guineas to payment in pounds.

In a letter to O'Farracháin, dated 25 June 1941, he sums up what is involved when a writer prepares a talk.

> I want to put in on record with you that this is a typical talk by a typical script-writer. I have been working at it full belt since 3 pm on Monday afternoon until this morning Wednesday at 12.30 . . . I turned over all my old American notes, consulted two books of reference, and ran through a history of the American novel. I skimmed swiftly through six novels. From 8 am on Tuesday to 11 p.m. that night I was soaking in it, so that I could not sleep last night, and was up early this morning again.

Prepared under proper conditions, he writes, the talk would have taken at least four or five days. He presumes that the usual fee of 5gns will be paid. Such a fee he says is shocking and he makes a plea for all writers to be paid more. The reduction in fees from guineas to pounds, Roibeárd O Farracháin recalls in the 1974 *Annual Report*, caused 'bitter resentment'.

By the 1950s, the golden years, Radio Eireann had built up a list of regular contributors including Mervyn Wall; Gabriel Fallon; the novelist Phillip Rooney; Lennox Robinson, the playwright; and Kate O'Brien, Brinsley McNamara, Donagh MacDonagh, Maura Laverty, Patricia Lynch, Padraic Colum, Monk Gibbon, Padraic Fallon, and H. L. Morrow.

Larry Morrow had a natural gift for radio and gave talks on a vast number of different subjects: Mendelssohn and Dublin, Paganini in Ireland, Oliver Goldsmith, Charles Dickens, John Banim, and Edward Bunting. His autobiographical piece about old Dublin moves effortlessly through a series of memories: his father on the Abbey stage, himself there at the age of twelve, and then being taken out to dinner with real poets, real playwrights, real statesmen, and real High Court judges. He met Paul Henry in his studio, Seamus O'Sullivan took him round the bookshops, Joseph Campbell read a new unpublished poem to him, and Susan Mitchell took him to tea with AE at Plunkett House. Dublin was his dream city. Most dream cities crumble and change but Dublin has a secret. The truth is, he says, that no one who has ever lived in Dublin has ever really died. They are kept alive in memory; they keep returning in conversations. It is a city of ghosts.

The good radio-journalist has the ability to produce fine descriptive writing, to create atmosphere, to bring characters and moments alive, in the days before television writers had to provide visual images. The novelist Phillip Rooney was another skilful contributor. His *Connemara Journey* begins with 'Pony in the Sky'.

> There he was . . . a pony in the sky . . . We sighted him first when the car stopped at a crossing of the Connemara roads where the

signpost, leaning a little awry, seemed unable to make up its mind which way to direct us.

Then the listener hears the sound of hooves approaching, and the voice continues.

> Now, no one in all this Connemara country can say with accuracy how many descendants of the Arab and Berber horses are running wild amid the lonely peaks and hidden valleys of the Twelve Bens...Since we came west of Oughterard we'd been seeing them in every field, on every hill, still as statues in the rushy margins of the lakes about Recess, nimble as cats on the slopes of the hills around them.

The narrative goes on to the races at Omey island – with voices of countrymen and music, with the voice of the Bellman who starts the races, with a description of the sights and sounds – the bar and the beer, the covered wagons, the booths and shooting galleries, the roulette wheels, the women who sell dillisk and sugar-stick and currant buns, all the noises, bustle and voices, the melodeon playing, the fiddler, and finally one of the races, concentrating on a slight, dapper lad.

> All about him the other riders in the race were making ready, tightening a belt, stripping off coats, adjusting the buckle of a legging...Coolly the chestnut's rider made his brief preparations ...he folded the ends of his flannel slacks and tucked them neatly into the tops of his socks...An instant later he was pounding across the sands to the starting point ... He wheeled into line and once a gap shows in the pack of horses he forges to the front – His blue coat peppered by the spray of white sand thrown up by the galloping hooves of the leaders, he had settled down to ride with hand and heel...His whip swinging in time to the striding rhythm of the chestnut, he lifted his mount through the gap in the line of galloping horses and strode on to win, cool and calm and dapper as ever....

This kind of vivid and colourful writing was a source of wonder; it evoked the magic of the West, it was carefully founded on select and exact detail. Other talks were serious and had a different impact. When Seán O'Faoláin gave three practical talks on the 'Art and Craft of the Short Story', they were rated 'excellent' within the station and at least one aspiring writer listened avidly. 'I remember it', Eilis Dillon wrote, 'the way an outcast member of the Foreign Legion would remember his first drink after he had crossed the desert on foot. I had been waiting for it all my life, at least all my conscious life, and here it was, unmistakably.[4]

The 1950s in which Phillip Rooney, Padraic Fallon, and Gabriel Fallon were at the height of their powers saw the revival of the Cork radio station, an important contribution to Munster and regional programmes; and the start of the Thomas Davis lectures that have become part of Irish culture. Inclined more to history than to literature they have nevertheless included talks on 'The Irish National Theatre', on 'Irish Nineteenth-Century Novelists', 'The Decline of the Hero in Fiction', 'Turgeniev', 'Early Irish Poetry', 'The Permanence of Yeats', 'The Art of the Short Story', 'Jonathan Swift', 'Sean O'Casey', 'Modern Irish Poetry', and 'Modern Irish Fiction'.

Padraic Fallon was the supreme radio dramatist of the time, his work deeply imagined. As poet and journalist Anthony Cronin pointed out, it was in the 1940s that evening radio for serious listeners came into its own as a source of intellectual and aesthetic pleasure. By then people began to believe that there was a way of combining the possibilities of radio and the richer and more poetic possibilities of words together to produce an effect on the imagination which was peculiar to radio alone. Fallon's plays, for him, were the more lasting assertion of this belief.[5]

Usually Fallon set his plays in the early Irish period, as Yeats had done. Among Fallon's mythological plays is one called *The Green Helmet*, which deals with the same subject that Yeats treated in his play of the same title which is about the challenge given to the Ulster heroes by an unusual visitor who says that if one of them cuts off his head, he will return and do the same for the Ulsterman. Fallon wrote a play about Diarmaid and Grainne, one called *Deirdre's King*, and his best-known play, *The Vision of MacConglinne* – a subject Austin Clarke had handled in his play *The Son of Learning*. When the King of Munster is possessed by a hunger demon, he consumes the food and produce of the entire province. He can only be cured if the demon can be lured out of his stomach through the descriptive power of words uttered by the poet MacConglinne. For this purpose the poet conjures up enticing visions of food. As he does so, the demon howls like a wolf.

> I walked in sleep last night
> Into this vision. I was hungry, too.
> I saw a tall well-filled house
> With great pantries of good food.
>   (*Lupine Howl.*)

> A pond of new milk
> In a plain that knows no cow's hoof.
> A mighty pat of yellow butter
> thatched the roof.   (*Howl.*)

The doorpost was white custard
Frozen till it stood,
The windows were white wine.
The doors were cheese, a lovely wood.
                    (*Howl. Howl.*)

The walls were smoked bacon
There was that and more
In the naked cauldron
That bubbled on the fire.
                    (*Wolf Howl.*)[6]

Fallon also wrote plays set in the modern period. I like the one about the blind harper Turlough O'Carolan. Called *At the Bridge Inn*, it deals with an attempted elopement by a young couple. The girl's mother pursues them as far as the Bridge Inn where O'Carolan happens to be. It gradually becomes clear that he had attempted to elope with the woman who now arrives in hot pursuit of her errant daughter. On that occasion his pursuers caught him and beat him so badly that he was blinded. The girl he loved was taken off and he never saw her again. Now in grief and rage at what happened to them that girl, now the pursuing mother, cries out in bitter realisation of her years of loss and suffering. She begins with self-condemnation, when she sees her former self recreated in the daughter's amorous flight ...

                    I was such a chit myself.
The fiddle's not particular whose hand
Picks out the tune.
                    What's what I say.
                    And I
Can prove it.
                    Open that door, young man.
                    No, No,
The door into that common room.
                    (*Harp Music Floods In.*)
Now look.
See all that lives of lovers.
                    That fellow there,
That death's head with the harp,
                    A lady loved
That mountebank.
                    A girl like you, of blood
And place. She ran away with him, indeed.
And in just such an inn as this, mark this,

They halted for the night.
    That fool, that coxcomb, there,
Had quite forgotten to provide fresh horses,
That fool she loved, that coxcomb, on whom
She had depended.
    Luckily for her,
Her father's men caught up.
    They brought her home.
And she lived happily ever after.
    I
vouch the truth of this.
    She lives
Who loved that thing.
        (*Loudly*)
This jingle-jangle man,
Of note in public taverns, cadger of meals,
Who finds a bed in some man's charity,
And cuckolds where he can –

O'Carolan has never forgotten her, her beautiful voice, her beautiful face. Now, as he enters the room where she is, he recognises her by her voice. After some moving scenes the old couple, the blind and dying harper and the old lady of the Big House, are reunited. The delicacy, the rising tension, the complex emotions through which this conclusion is eventually reached are beautifully managed.

The pattern established in the 1940s and 1950s has continued down to the present when we have the Francis MacManus Short Story Competition and the T. P. O'Connor Drama Award. Each is an attempt to discover and encourage new talent, to stimulate interest in writing for radio, and to obtain material for broadcasting. Poetry readings, discussions of literature, and dramatisation of novels are also a regular feature. Interviews with writers are a source of significant information and insight. I remember in 1972 Thomas Kinsella's informative comments on his innovative collection *[Notes] From the Land of the Dead*. His remarks have become part of the life of criticism about his work. Richard Murphy, John Montague, Seamus Heaney, and others have also availed of radio interviews to provide useful insights to their work. The educational side of radio has been a constant feature of Irish life, in particular Irish literary life. There is an understandable tendency to use particular writers to the exclusion of others and residence in Dublin is an advantage. Programmers and directors turn to those they know and can rely on, whose voices or personalities suit radio. But younger writers are also given a chance. Paula Meehan, Rory Brennan, Paul Durcan, Dennis O'Driscoll have become familiar voices as have Jennifer Johnston, Ita Daly,

Dermot Bolger, Val Mulkerns, and Michael Longley.

The effect of radio on listeners may be gauged by a letter from Kate O'Brien written spontaneously to Francis MacManus in May 1957, from her home in Roundstone, County Galway. 'In recent years', she writes, 'I've been getting so much pleasure from R.E. programmes that I burn to write a laudatory article for some newspaper or other... truly, you are giving us in the country so many excellent things that someone should shout a bit... about the programmes... to-night after Toscanini we had the beautiful *Saint Joan* production, and after that we had half an hour of Irish music as lovely as be damned... and the other night there was Mervyn Wall's play, and constantly one is being delighted, amused or roused at least. Truly I think some praise should be loudly accorded to a programme which so constantly produces surprises of pleasure and stimulation.'

That response in the late 1950s by a distinguished novelist could as easily and as fittingly be made today.

Notes

1 Catalogued as 'Radio in Ireland'. I am grateful to Radio Eireann for permission to publish this material from their Archives.
2 *Collected Poems* (Dublin: The Dolmen Press, 1974).
3 Unless otherwise stated all quotations are taken from scripts.
4 Quoted in Maurice Harmon, *Seán O'Faoláin: A Life* (London: Constable, 1994), p. 138.
5 Louis McRedmond, 'Many a Long Night: The Box with the Lighted Dial', *Written in the Wind. Personal Memories of Irish Radio 1926/1976* (Dublin: Gill and Macmillan, 1976).
6 Editor's note: And Maurice Harmon howled vigorously.

Part II

DEVELOPMENTS IN PROSE

5
SEÁN O'FAOLÁIN: MAN OF IDEAS[1]

Born in Cork in 1900 Seán O'Faoláin was a member of Aosdána and elected Saoi[2] *in 1986; he died in 1991.* Seán O'Faoláin: A Critical Introduction, *1967; rev. 1985, was Harmon's first book and the first book-length study of O'Faoláin's fiction. It was followed by several articles and, in 1994, an authorised biography,* Seán O'Faoláin, A Life. *His most recent essay on O'Faoláin, included here, was given as a keynote lecture on 7 April 2000 at Turin University, Italy, for 'Seán O'Faoláin – A Centenary Celebration, 7–9 April 2002' and published in the Conference Papers. He has written the O'Faoláin entry for* The Dictionary of Irish Biography.

'THOSE who examine nothing and question nothing', Seán O'Faoláin once declared 'end by knowing nothing and creating nothing' (*The Bell*, April 1941). He was an intellectual at a time in Ireland when there were few intellectuals and when their role in society had neither been defined nor established. One of the remarkable things about him is that the ideas we associate with him as an editor and social analyst emerged early in his life. As a young man he had been involved in the nationalist movement: he joined the IRA and was an active supporter of the Gaelic League. But after the disillusion brought about by the Civil War he began to assess the nature and effects of nationalism, the ideological basis of Republicanism, the integrity of the Gaelic League, and the directions Irish education and Irish literature might take. On all of these major issues of the time he took positions that were opposed to those of his Professors of Irish at the university and of his mentor and friend, Daniel Corkery. He objected to Corkery's study of eighteenth-century Irish poetry, *The Hidden Ireland*, 1925, because it lauded the culture of a defeated Ireland and sought to identify modern Ireland with that period.

What is striking about O'Faoláin's response at this early age is that in opposing Corkery he was deliberately taking on one of the most influential literary figures of the time. It is worth noting also that although he had supported the Republican side during the Civil War and had personally experienced their demoralising defeat he was able to transcend political divisions and to take a more inclusive view. He argued that what others, including those on the Free State side, had done to bring about an independent Ireland should be recognised; he mentioned AE (George Russell), Michael Collins, W. B. Yeats, and referred to engineers, craftsmen, gunmen, and writers. He believed strongly in his own generation. Their attitude, he said, was not based on a perception of national defeat, as was that of the older generation, but was courageous and positive. It was not isolationist but fearlessly embraced ideas from abroad.[3] He takes issue again and again with Establishment figures. In *Sinn Féin*, the Republican periodical, he attacked leading Republicans because of their uncritical, reverential approach and attacked Sinn Féin itself on the grounds that it lacked intellectual standards and failed to deal with facts. Even this early he noticed signs of an emerging middle class and warned that the combination of this class with an uncultivated Catholic Church could be dangerous for the new democracy, the Republic he had fought to create.

These early articles contain virtually all of O'Faoláin's central ideas. At the age of twenty-four and twenty-five, on the rebound from romantic nationalism, he had discovered that the Republican movement was deficient in social and political ideas. This meant, he realised, that he and many others had been led into revolution by men and women who had little political or social conceptions of the way ahead. Their aim had been to achieve independence from British rule, but apart from James Connolly no one seemed to have given serious thought to the kind of Ireland they would create once freedom had been won. O'Faoláin himself had become a rebel for emotional reasons; joining the national movement liberated him and other young men and women from the restrictions of home and gave him a sense of comradeship with fellow rebels. It was fuelled by his discovery of the Irish language and culture and with the landscape of the Irish-speaking districts of West Cork, that wonderland of Ballingeary and Gougane Barra that would always be one of the touchstones of O'Faoláin's sense of Irishness. But the divisions and cruelties of the Civil War and his discovery, when he was Director of Propaganda for the IRA, of the paucity of ideas behind the movement opened his eyes to the deficiencies of emotional nationalism. The question as to why he and others had been emotionally overwhelmed by romantic nationalism was one he had to face. It was tied in with the larger issue of the consequences for the country as a whole. In O'Faoláin's case personal and national issues tended to be deeply intertwined.

Being away from Ireland from 1926 to 1932 gave him time in which to become more detached and more objective about his country, to search for some balance between emotion and reason, and to counter the romance of rebellion with the realism of social and political analysis. Although intellectual challenges were not among the attractions that drew him back, within a very short time of returning he was expressing dissatisfaction with the absence of ideas and his failure to find anyone with whom he could hope to have an intellectual conversation. Within a few months he was sick of politics and dismayed that Ireland was so isolated from the world of ideas, that nobody was European in outlook. The source of this apathy and isolation, he argued, were the influential Gaelic Revivalists and Catholic Actionists who did not accept that they were European and did not accept that they were descendants of the poor whom Daniel O'Connell led out of the poverty and dispossession of the eighteenth century.

Daniel Corkery's book on J. M. Synge, 1931, which rejected Anglo-Irish writers, was wholly at odds with O'Faoláin's inclusive response. Behind it he detected a fear of the possible emergence of an Anglo-Irish nation. Corkery's argument, espoused by Eamon de Valera, was that the Irish Celt, suppressed by Tudor invasion and the Anglo-Irish aristocracy, was about to reappear in the twentieth century. It was joined to the political notion that Irish language and culture, so long suppressed by the British, would again be strong and vital. Such glorification of the past, as O'Faoláin had argued almost ten years previously, was not logically sustainable. As he recurrently pointed out during the 1930s it ignored the fact that modern Irish life came not from the celtic past but from Catholic Emancipation and the Land Purchase Acts of the nineteenth century. Corkery's and de Valera's appeal across the historical realities of the eighteenth and nineteenth centuries had, he knew, a kind of mystical quality; it became a popular, unexamined ideal. He regretted that the habit of critical engagement with tradition was not part of Irish life.

O'Faoláin's intellectual examination of post-revolutionary Ireland was paralleled by an imaginative engagement in short stories and novels. One of the most satisfying things about his life as a writer is the ways in which his intellect and imagination were deeply engaged with Irish life. The rhythm of that engagement takes him repeatedly and in a coherent manner from short story to novel, from novel to biography, from biography to article and editorial. His anti-romantic nationalist response already visible in his articles is also evident in the first collection of short stories, *Midsummer Night Madness*, 1932, which casts the behaviour of Republican activists in a pointedly different light from Daniel Corkery's ennobling portrayal of them in *The Hounds of Banba*, 1920. Many of O'Faoláin's rebels are lecherous, treacherous men, arsonists, sacrilegious kidnappers, and executioners, not romantic idealists. In the final story, set in the Civil War, the Republicans are defeated and demoralised, the young rebel just wants to get back to his beloved, and only the orator, obsessed with abstractions, remains true to the cause of full freedom. It is a sympathetic portrayal, but clearly O'Faoláin has had his fill of fanatic idealists.

In his first novel, *A Nest of Simple Folk*, 1934, which also examines nationalist rebellion, revolution disrupts family and individuals. While most people are concerned with making a living, the rebels throw family values to the winds as they follow the demon of revolution to sporadic violence, imprisonment, and social rejection. Revolution is a kind of mystical presence, an emotive force passed down from generation to generation.

When O'Faoláin's alter-ego, Dennis Hussey, in turn follows the rebel cause in the Easter Rising of 1916, the causes are many and irrational.

Central to *A Purse of Coppers*, 1937, his second collection of short stories, is the belief that Irish society has experienced a radical disruption. Years of revolution have produced a society in which the individual is unable to reach his potential because he is inhibited by the forces of conservatism, puritanism, and national inertia. In 'Admiring the Scenery', Hanafin declares: 'Every man lives out his own imagination of himself and every imagination needs its background.' If, O'Faoláin is saying, you deny someone a context of living, a society, in which he can reach his potential as a human being, you condemn him to a state of frustration, failure, and disappointment. He becomes, in the image that dominates the collection, a damned figure, beyond redemption. Since society is unchanging the individual cannot be redeemed. The idea is also found in the novel *Bird Alone*, 1936, where O'Faoláin uses the rise and fall of Parnell, including the bitterness, division, and national collapse of the Parnell Split, as metaphors for the rise and fall of nationalism in the early twentieth century. In the shame and desperation of the young girl Elsie Sherlock, who has become pregnant, O'Faoláin shows the effects of a puritanical family, the failure of sympathy, the absence of compassion. In the rage and rebellion of the young man Corney Crone against that society he shows its effects on the potential artist. Corney Crone may reject this Scarlet-Letterish society and its codes but the freedom he gains thereby is barren. He is at odds with the material from which he creates. The task, O'Faoláin believed, was to be able to live in a creative and receptive relationship with society. This was a cornerstone of his beliefs: the writer must not allow himself to become soured by the conditions around him. Corney's failure resembles the successive failures in *Purse of Coppers*. In this novel O'Faoláin explores a question that continued to perplex him: how does the creative artist function in a society that frustrates him, in which he feels alienated, and in danger of becoming embittered or veering into fantasy? It is to his immense credit that he succeeded in remaining creative, in remaining compassionate and understanding. In his later years his stories are delightfully relaxed and open, guided entirely by the aesthetic imperative.

The narrator in the introductory story to *Purse of Coppers*, titled significantly 'A Broken World', longs for a redeeming power, 'an image that would fire and fuse us all'. None appeared in the stories that followed, nor did it appear in *Bird Alone*. The Irish leader, Daniel O'Connell, was the closest O'Faoláin came to a redeeming figure. In his biography of O'Connell, called *King of the Beggars*, 1938, O'Faoláin examines the life and times of a powerful, creative figure who took a defeated and disenfranchised people and forged them into a mass movement. He gave them freedom to vote, to political representation, to the possibility of education and advancement in the professions. O'Connell is O'Faoláin's model leader – liberal, non-sectarian, inclusive of all creeds, European-minded. If the Ireland of O'Faoláin's day was timid, puritanical, backward looking, and isolationist, then in O'Connell and what he stood for there was the example of someone who introduced ideas from abroad, who had a vision of possibility and worked hard and tirelessly to achieve it. It is a powerful book and behind its heroic portrait lies the less attractive figure of Eamon de Valera. The biography reiterates what O'Faolain has often said: modern Ireland comes from O'Connell, from the nineteenth century not from the eighteenth. O'Connell did not seek a fake ideal of the Gaelic past. He saw that English was the language of the future and abandoned Irish. He was a realist who saw clearly and accepted what he saw – Anglo-Ireland, the mixed racial strains.

O'Faoláin's methods in articles and biographies were direct; one analysed and explained, the other gave dramatic embodiment to specific truths. The biographies, while based on research, are also imaginative works. And they are polemical. The O'Connell biography, a vigorous creation of a complex man, is another attempt to define and illustrate how Irish society might be changed for the better. It shows how with a dynamic and creative leader the lives of characters in *Purse of Coppers* and *Bird Alone* could be transformed, how the negation and failure of individual life could be made positive and fulfilling. O'Faoláin's O'Connell challenges leaders in the twentieth century; he displays attitudes and attributes that O'Faoláin thinks could operate effectively in his own time.

But when he undertook the editorship of *The Bell* in 1940, his approach was less confrontational, tactically more subtle, and long-ranged. This more cautious approach emerged in *The Great O'Neill: A Biography of Hugh O'Neill, Earl of Tyrone, 1550–1616*, 1942. O'Faoláin interpreted O'Neill's relationship with the encroaching pressures of a centralising Tudor power as a sequence of pretended avowals of loyalty followed by strategic assaults which in turn were followed by further obeisance. He stressed the disciplined and controlled manner with which O'Neill handled the difficulties of his situation, his clear understanding of the fragmented, tribal nature of Irish society, and his awareness of the advantages of the unifying ideal of the Counter-Reformation already potent on the continent as a force that might bring the tribal chieftains together.

As editor, O'Faoláin adopted similar tactics. We know where he stood on the major issues – nationalism, the nature of Irish society, the Gaelic League, the middle class, sectarianism, censorship, isolationism, liberalism. We know he had his own ideas as to what was required to move the country out of the apathy in which he saw it. He had written those requirements unmistakably in the O'Connell biography. Yet as an editor he did not move into an assault on what he found inhibiting or damaging to the health of the emergent democracy.

He viewed his role as an editor not from the angle of the polemicist but from the perspective of the constructive thinker. *The Bell*, he announced, was a creative journal; it would reflect life as it was really lived, not some idealised version of it and not in terms of a glorious past. Given his belief that Irish life was stagnant, that a new Ireland as it emerged from the years of revolution needed to find expression, and given his belief that there was too much uncritical adulation of the past, he would concentrate on the here and now. Avoiding 'Abstraction', he would allow 'Life' to speak by opening the pages of the periodical to the ordinary and the quotidian. It was entirely in keeping with his perception of Irish life and culture that he insisted that contributors must write about what they knew, what they had experienced. He wanted the new Ireland to express itself and to become visible. One of the things least remembered about *The Bell* is the wide range of topics which appeared in its pages, informative and factual articles on prisons, censorship, theatre, concerts, teaching, nursing, libraries, the legal system, women in politics, the North, Irish literature, poverty, orphans. These reflected O'Faoláin's editorial purpose – to give voice to people and professions, to all creeds, classes and occupations, to social and economic conditions that had not found voice before, that had not been examined before. All of this was revolutionary; it was new; it was basic; it opened windows on reality; it had the dynamism of change.

O'Faoláin's performance as an editor was remarkable. When one follows it through, month by month, year by year, and when one tries to see the tactics behind what he did, the overall picture requires a more complete analysis than I can provide here. But I want to draw attention to the quiet, ongoing manner with which he worked. It was not based on exaggeration, it was not colourful, but it was highly intelligent, perceptive, and creative. At all times he was careful to explain what he was doing; he defined the principles by which he would operate. The basic principles were that he accepted the situation as he found it, the magazine would be inclusive and tolerant, and he was opposed to vague and woolly thinking. He knew exactly what he was doing. He was engaged in measured, constructive thinking, stirring people to reflect, question, and examine. In a country without a tradition of intellectual analysis or investigative journalism he wanted to question assumptions, to change perceptions. To see his work only as polemical is to miss the overall pattern and to undervalue the effectiveness and the strategy behind what he did. It is easy to fly off the handle, to be explosive; it is harder, requiring more discipline and a long-range strategy, to maintain a steady pattern, to chip away at specific targets.

In his first extended editorial he appealed for realism and urged readers to free themselves from the Glorious Past and the Great Future, those dreams that clouded realistic perception. Tradition, he said, needed to be challenged; it must be questioned and analysed to be kept productive. The

Civil War, he argued, helped to wake people up from their hypnotic dream
of nationalism.

> It set us asking questions about political institutions,
> international relations, financial reform, economics, education,
> about the pre-sanctified dogmas of our history. Our dilemma to-
> day is surely this, – that we are living in a period of conflict
> between the definite principle of past achievement and the
> undefined principles of present ambition. We are living, that is to
> say, to a great extent experimentally, and must go on doing so.
> (April 1941)

There is so much in this single eight-page editorial: O'Faoláin quietly states
ideas about Tradition and Talent. Given his sense of an apathetic Ireland in
which there is little change, the editorial insists on the necessity of change.
Given his sense of little intellectual debate, it stresses the need for questioning, the need, indeed the duty of having a creative engagement with
tradition, to escape from sentimentality, nostalgia, and wishful thinking, to
see the social and political realities.

It is difficult today to understand and to appreciate what O'Faoláin was
doing, and why it was necessary, because the country and the culture have
changed so much. These days we have investigative journalists, we have
intellectuals who make it their business to question and analyse, to ask
questions, to challenge politicians and churchmen. But not in his time. He was
virtually on his own. Just how alone and what the forces ranged against him
were have been made clear in John Cooney's recent biography of John Charles
McQuaid, Archbishop of Dublin, who tried to put his Catholic and
authoritarian stamp on virtually every aspect of Irish life and who enjoyed
almost total obeisance from the people, Church, politicians, lay men and
women.[4] The absence of an intellectual tradition meant that O'Faoláin hardly
ever had an adversary with whose ideas he could wrestle. Occasionally one
presented itself, as when Michael Tierney gave an address on 'The Origin and
Growth of Modern Irish Nationality'. O'Faoláin's response was masterly.
First, he set out the importance of Tierney's address, as 'nothing else than a
representative specimen of a sort of theorising that the last generation affected
considerably; as a very clear example of the destructive power of all such
theorising; and above all as a representative example of one still very popular
line of thought that is produced – the Gaelic line – about the nature of modern
Irish life' (November 1941). Then he identified the sources and effects of the
theory that he calls 'Delphic Nationalism' which, as he had argued years
before, seeks to avoid the facts of history by going back to the cultural unity of
the Old Irish past and arguing that modern Ireland has been created from that
source. He takes Tierney's paper step by step to demonstrate that the notion

of cultural unity ignores the lack of political cohesion that prevailed in Ireland since the Middle Ages. O'Faoláin's argument is robust but he is also fair, showing the commendable reason for Tierney's argument. We know, he says,

> that the reason is a natural, and indeed a commendable fact – one has but to look around and listen – that we are now an English-speaking people, and that we have only the broken shards of folklore, and no Gaelic literature at all, because we broke, or were broken from all these things in the Eighteenth century and came up smiling in the Twentieth. This, obviously, is a sort of mystical faith. It cannot be disproven, not even when every visible (and audible) fact rebuts it, but if you deny it you have lost the Faith. Neither can it be proven. But always, one thing has to be done to support the Faith: everything from 1750 or even 1650 to 1850 must be belittled. (November 1941)

His is a vibrant, challenging, reasonable voice. It has substance, it is based on knowledge, it is not mystical, nor sentimental, nor nostalgic for a lost culture. At the basis of his outlook was a warm humanism, which was antagonistic to Eamon de Valera's idea of frugal and simple living and to the Jansenistic strain in Irish life. The humanist concept, he argued, again instructing as he went, included 'man's natural ambition to participate in all that can enrich him in nature and in history, with man's efforts to exploit all his human potentialities... to develop his reason and employ his creative powers to the utmost' (April 1942). In these words he reiterates the imaginative faith expressed in *Purse of Coppers*.

The true measure of O'Faoláin emerges – qualities of mind and heart that have been discernible in earlier writings, but that now are given fuller vent as he speaks to an entire people. He becomes in effect the spokesperson for his time, its intellectual leader, whose principles are clear – liberal, non-sectarian, politically inclusive, European, Irish, Catholic, and nationalist. He spoke warmly at times about the importance of the Irish language, recalling the 'enlargement of mind and soul' he and many others had experienced on visits to the Gaeltacht. After acknowledging that, he could express his dismay at what had been done to that inspiration through the introduction of compulsory Irish in the schools and the requirement of a knowledge of the language as a prerequisite for certain jobs: 'The Gaeltacht, the language, the Revival, everything associated with what was once so honoured and so nourishing, is now a bitter taste in the mouth, sometimes positively nauseating. The once precious things are associated in the mind of the average man with jobs, with money, with dishonest speeches from public men...' (February 1943). O'Faoláin not only uses the occasion to pour scorn on the hyper-nationalists, but praises the richness of the language as a positive force in the country, thereby making his criticism more telling and less offensive.

O'Faoláin's humanism had a deeper element. His approach to the excessive interference by the Church in individual lives was based on the belief that if you deprive human beings of their freedom to choose, you undermine them. On a number of occasions it was an argument he relied on, but with particular force in his reflections on the behaviour of the government during Dr Noel Browne's proposal to introduce a free health scheme for mothers and children. When the Archbishop of Dublin opposed the scheme on moral grounds, the government refused to support the Minister. The manner of the Church's interference became public knowledge when Noel Browne released the correspondence to the press.

O'Faoláin's analysis of the situation was a model of dispassionate objectivity. He saw the controversy over the scheme, the sudden demise of the bill, the dismissal of Browne, the obsequious response of the Taoiseach, and the secrecy behind which the elected representatives of the people and the Archbishop behaved as a clear illustration of how Irish democracy works. The basic factor was the authority exercised by the Church in a predominantly Catholic country. 'The Dáil', O'Faoláin trenchantly remarked, 'proposes; Maynooth disposes' (June 1951). What particularly concerned him was that the Church had shown that it did not trust the people. For, he pointed out, had the scheme gone ahead it would have been administered by an almost entirely Catholic government, Catholic doctors, and the ordinary Catholic layman. The Church's distrust of the people was damaging. For, O'Faoláin argued, 'If you shatter a man's pride – by, for example, shattering his belief that he is worthy of trust – you shatter his personality as a Christian: for as a Christian he is a whole man or he is nothing. If people are treated as children, and all that is asked of them is that they go here, go there, do this, do that, and are never left to act as whole Christians, why, then you are left with children and childish morale' (November 1951). This is at the heart of O'Faoláin's response to many of the faults he described – clericalism, puritanism, censorship, the negative attitude towards outside influences and ideas, the injunctions against normal pleasures. They were all over-protective, all fearful that the individual would be unable to exercise a wise choice. In them the Sinn Féin ideal of self-reliance had become cruelly thwarted. It made Ireland, he once said, a dreary Eden.

Ultimately, he knew, ideas would seep in – through radio, books, newspapers, travel. Literary censorship, film censorship, the stifling of even faintly liberal ideas would all be in vain. Isolationism, as he argued in his 'One World' series, was impossible in the modern post-war world; mutual interdependence between countries would be the norm. In these articles he was holding up a vision of a new world in which national barriers and divisions would break down. Eventually, in this and in so many other things, he was proven right. Ireland has become more closely connected with Europe and society's values became those he had advocated. In his last attack, on the Ireland that had emerged under de Valera, his idealism, passion, social conscience, and indignation find eloquent expression. It is his apologia – for himself, for Irish writers, for the people of Ireland.

> It is the nature of writers to have a passionate love of life and a profound desire that it should be lived in the greatest possible fullness and richness by all men: and when we see here such a wonderful raw material, a nature so naturally warm and generous as the Irish nature, so adventurous, so eager, so gay, being chilled and frustrated by constant appeals to peasant fears, to peasant pietism, to the peasant sense of self-preservation, and all ending in a half-baked sort of civilization which, taken all over, is of a tawdriness a hundred miles away from our days of vision – when we see all that we have no option but to take all these things in one angry armful and fling them at the one man who must accept them as his creation, his reflex, his responsibility. In a nutshell, we say that this is surely not the Ireland that Wolfe Tone would have liked to live in, or Dan O'Connell, for all his peasant coarseness and cunning, or the aristocratic Parnell, or any man like that old eagle John O'Leary, or the warm-hearted James Connolly, or any man who really loved men and life, and we accuse it. (June 1945)

Seán O'Faoláin was a new kind of Irish writer. Unlike James Joyce he did not dedicate himself to literary innovation. Unlike W. B. Yeats he did not devote himself exclusively to aesthetic pursuit. Unlike them he had a stake in his country. He had fought for independence, he was emotionally and intellectually engaged with his society. From an early age he was the spokesperson for his generation, its intellectual leader who analysed what was happening, who clarified the forces that threatened the freedom of the artist and the dignity of the individual, and who fought them on several fronts – articles, editorials, biographies. To his credit he held an equilibrium between emotion and reason, did not become embittered, and as a creative writer remained true to aesthetic truth. In the totality of his achievement he is greater than his contemporaries – the novelists and short-story writers Mary Lavin, Kate O'Brien, Elizabeth Bowen, Liam O'Flaherty, Frank O'Connor, Francis Stuart, Peadar O'Donnell; the poets Austin Clarke, Padraic Fallon, Thomas MacGreevy, Brian Coffey, Denis Devlin; the dramatist, Denis Johnston – it is not an insignificant generation. He stands tall because he achieved aesthetic mastery as a creative writer and at the same time was more fully engaged with society than any of them.

Notes

1   In *Seán O'Faoláin: A Centenary Celebration*, ed. Donatella A. Badin (Turin: Trauben, 2001).

2   Established 1981, Aosdána, an association of living artists in Ireland, is funded by the state through the Arts Council. Membership is limited to 220 members, nominated and elected by their peers. The title of *Saoi*, held by only five members at one time, is awarded for original and outstanding contribution to the arts, and is conferred by the President of Ireland for life.

3   See Harmon, *Seán O'Faoláin: A Life* (London: Constable, 1994), pp. 67–8.

4   See *John Charles McQuaid: Ruler of Catholic Ireland* (Syracuse, NY: Syracuse University Press, 2000).

6

MARY LAVIN: MORALIST OF THE HEART

Maurice Harmon had a long association with Mary Lavin. His essay examines her unique achievement mainly as a short-story writer in a generation that included Liam O'Flaherty, Seán O'Faoláin, and Frank O'Connor. During the preparation of the Mary Lavin Special Issue of the Irish University Review *(Spring 1979), he talked with her many times. The record of their conversations is in the Appendix. Then at the height of her powers, she spoke with conviction and authority about her own work and about the nature of the short story. She was a member of Aosdána and was elected* Saoi, *its highest honour, in 1992. She died in 1996. Harmon has written the Mary Lavin entry for* The Dictionary of Irish Biography.

MARY Lavin was born in East Walpole, Massachusetts, in 1912, the only child of Tom and Nora Lavin. Her mother returned with her to Ireland when she was nine years old. She lived for a time in Athenry, County Galway, with her mother's family and later in Meath and Dublin. In 1936, at the age of twenty-six, she completed an MA thesis on the novel and Jane Austen at University College Dublin, and began writing fiction. Her first story, 'Miss Holland', was published in *The Dublin Magazine* in 1938. Since then she has published about a hundred stories and sixteen volumes of stories as well as two novels and other miscellaneous works.

When Mary Lavin looks back over her work, she mentions the fourth or fifth story she wrote as the one in which she first said something that was important to her. That story, 'The Will', 1944, was based on an aunt who married against her mother's wishes, did not have a happy life, and was left out of her mother's will. She had, Mary Lavin has told us, 'a great depth of spirituality and also the strength to make her own moral decisions...She became for me a prototype of all wild and restless people who followed their own impulses even at a grievous cost to themselves'.[1]

'The Will' asserts the moral superiority of Lally Grimes who married for love, had a hard life hereafter, but retained a glow of happiness and independence. As she herself says, 'You were always yourself, no matter where you went or what you did. You didn't change...Nothing you did made any real change in you.' That conviction is reflected in the narrative style of this story. It accounts for the dramatic objectivity of her clash with her middle-class family when she returns home for her mother's funeral. A fundamental difference in values breaks through the grief of the occasion.

When her family try to change her impoverished way of life, they come up against her resolute will. Kate, the eldest member, is speaking:

> 'It's not a very nice thing for us to feel that our sister is a common landlady in the city. Mother never forgave that! She might have forgiven your marriage in time, but she couldn't forgive you for lowering yourself to keep lodgers.'
>
> ...
>
> 'I can't say I blame Mother!' said Nonny, breaking into the discussion with a sudden venom. 'I don't see why you were so anxious to marry him when it meant keeping lodgers.'
>
> 'It was the other way round, Nonny,' said Lally. 'I was willing to keep lodgers because it meant I could marry him.'

That taut style, tense with opposition, is occasionally offset with more relaxed images of Lally's girlhood – the blue feathers in her hat on the day she told her mother she was getting married, the white dress she wore for her first dance, the leafy trees. The language in the story alternates between such visionary images and the family's gloomy sense of physical deterioration in her and in them. Where she is generous and open, their feelings degenerate into personal abuse; they criticise her 'old clothes', her dirty hair, her 'disgusting' teeth. Her tawdriness of dress and appearance, however, are transcended by the radiance of her spirit, whereas their social pretensions are diminished by their spiritual impoverishment.

The emotionally charged conclusion reveals a woman who is harried by the fear that her mother will suffer in Purgatory for her bitterness towards her daughter. Her emotional distress is signaled in a succession of parallel statements: 'She tried to remember... She leaned her head back... and clenched her hands tightly as she thought of the torments of Purgatory. Bright red sparks from the engine flew past the carriage window, and she began to pray with rapid unformed words that jostled themselves in her mind like sheafs of burning sparks.'

'The Will' dramatises Lally's moral superiority, but its sequel, 'A Happy Death', 1946, gives a devastating portrayal of moral disarray. Whereas Lally had a coherent grasp of the values by which she lived, Ella has a distorted sense of purpose. Twenty years after their elopement, she and Robert live in squalor and rancour. Their tragedy arises from their inability to live according to the realities of their situation. Both live in illusions: he in a dream memory of what she calls their 'outworn romance'; she in a distorted vision of a time when he will be renewed, as though by sheer willpower she could bring back the man she married: 'He would be a gentleman again.' In bitter disappointment that that dream has not lasted she seeks to restore it. Her pursuit of this aim is monstrous, an illusion adhered to despite appalling degradation, disappointment, and cruelty. Ella thrashes against reality, flinging herself after three unattainable goals: to restore Robert, to cure him when he goes to hospital, and to obtain the grace of a happy death for him.

Such women are vulnerable. To adhere so radically to false hope is to incur disappointment proportionate to the intensity with which the illusion was pursued. Ella will not accept what is real: the shabby man whose appearance denies the notion of renewal, the sick man whose hospital table she loads with useless gifts, the death of a man who dies with a 'look of rapturous happiness' on his face as he relives their earlier intimacy. For her 'it was utterly incomprehensible... that God had not heard her prayers, and had not vouchsafed to her husband the grace of a happy death'.

The style of the story emphasises Ella's extraordinary energy – she moves in 'a fever of energy'; she 'rushed', 'ran', 'dragged', snatched'. These terms also emphasise the absence of serenity and stillness, of mental calm, of physical peace. Ella's 'furious energy' churns up the space around her and it is this energy that determines the length of the story and that pursues it with a corresponding vigour. Her portrait is achieved by exaggeration, in particular by the exaggerated, self-deceiving claims she makes for herself: 'She had been so proud of him. She would have worn herself to the bone working for him if he had kept his looks, and stayed the way he was long ago when she used to steal out of the house and meet him in Long Meadow back of the churchyard.' Everything that Ella touches is contaminated by this kind of exaggeration and distortion – 'She'd gladly have worn herself out... She'd have broken her back... she'd have worn her fingers to the bone.' The clichés only mark the obsessive nature of this drive to translate an unacceptable reality into a self-excusing illusion. Her stress on appearances – the white shirts and white collars, the mirroring shoes – is another manifestation of her unwillingness to see the squalid conditions in which they live. Instead of relating what is actual – Robert as he really is, his need for his job as a mark of self-esteem, the fact that people change over twenty years – or, most likely of all, making some effort to analyse and understand her own behaviour, being honest about herself, she rushes into unproductive action. She is baffled and tormented by the chasm between the dream and the reality and learns nothing from experience.

Self-deception is a persistent theme in Mary Lavin's fiction. A number of stories in the collection *The Long Ago*, 1944, treat it with increasing depth and complexity. In 'The Nun's Mother', Mrs Latimer cannot understand why her daughter has become a nun. There is an attractive, but deceptive honesty about the mother's reactions: bewilderment, disbelief, anger, disappointment, irritation with her husband and with Angela, self-criticism. It is one of the main achievements of this story that it enters so clearly into the woman's complex reactions, showing her in such an honest engagement with her own motives and responses, while also causing us to see ultimately that she has been affected by forces hidden within the self. The style is attuned to her sensibility, which is refined, intelligent, perceptive, capable of delicate discrimination in evaluating her own feelings and motives, but also capable of self-deception. She recognises, for example, that she has always had a fear of bringing another person into the world, a fear of the physical. It finally emerges that she has never had a frank talk with Angela about sex, not even when she said she was going to become a nun. The story closes on her frightening image of the madman, the flasher at the roadside, whose breath in Mrs Latimer's imagination fouls the chaste water-lily image of her daughter.

The story moves by a process of gradual revelation of the hidden areas of Mrs Latimer's psyche. The tone is mildly exasperated and self-critical. It is replaced later by darker nuances. Her interactions with her husband and daughter result in a form of isolation; she cannot speak directly to Angela about sexual pleasure and she cannot admit that inhibition to her husband. She is therefore thrown back upon herself, upon her own self-questionings and doubts. Unconsciously, Mrs Latimer's thought processes reveal a sensibility that finds it difficult to cope with what she sees as the unpleasant side of reality. She has a preference for orderliness, neatness, good taste, and personal modesty; and even though she enjoys sexual love she lacks a language for it and cannot bring it into the realm of normal life. In a way one begins to suspect that she herself is more nunnish than her daughter. There is, it would seem, good reason for Mrs Latimer's anxious reflections.

The intricacies of the mind fascinate Mary Lavin. In 'A Happy Death' she approaches them from the outside; in 'The Nun's Mother' she works through direct and intimate involvement with the mind of the main character. In Mary Lavin's stories people suffer the consequences of such failures to assert themselves. Nothing, one might say, nothing fails like a failed *exemplum*. When Mary Lavin herself resorts to that method, the results are precise. 'The Widow's Son', 1946, is a story with two endings. In one the widow loses her only son when he is killed trying to avoid killing her hen; in the other she loses him when she abuses him for killing her hen. 'Perhaps', Mary Lavin concludes, 'all our actions have this double quality about them; this possibility of alternative, and that it is only by careful watching, and absolute sincerity that we follow the path that is ordained for us, and, no matter how tragic that may be, it is better than the tragedy we bring upon ourselves.'

'Careful watching' and 'absolute sincerity'. On reflection we might see these as comments on all those who fail to act in accordance with private conscience, all those failures brought about by self-deception, wishful thinking, evasion, or a too easy dependence on others. In practice, of course, the choice is not as clear-cut as it is in that fable of the widow and her son. In practice, too, when dealing with Mary Lavin's stories the make-up of the individual person is so complex in some cases that it is not easy to determine whether the character has brought tragedy on herself or himself, or has simply experienced something that has been ordained. For it is of the essence of a Mary Lavin character that life provides almost endless opportunities for choice and consequently for deception and evasion. The standard of judgment is the honesty with which the choice is made. It is also fundamental to her method of characterisation that the individual character has the capacity for myriad decisions and indecisions. The techniques of the fiction accommodate this kind of character and this mode of characterisation. Style is a measure of character. Thus, in 'Frail Vessel', 1955, another story about the Grimes sisters, Bedelia and Liddy, the narrative point of view is Bedelia's; the style reflects the dry complications of her calculating temperament. Everything in the story moves from her or towards her, motivated by her, reacting to her or through her, even though the inexplicable mystery of Liddy's love lies outside of her control and beyond her comprehension.

The portrait of Bedelia Grimes in 'The Little Prince', 1956, shows an even more closed and unreceptive consciousness and one that deliberately suppresses natural instinct. The writer's task is not so much to unravel the complexities of the individual temperament as to bring Bedelia through a kind of purgatorial process in which she is punished for exiling her brother, Tom. That initial injustice, like Lear's, is fairy-tale-like in its folly, and, like Lear, Bedelia must undergo a process of self-discovery. The matter-of-fact style reveals the harsh efficiency of her temperament; nothing interferes with her plans. Bedelia's hardness is reflected in the forceful precision of her language: 'He will listen to me, I know he will,' she said. 'I know him like a book.' That confidence, however, is undermined by the consequences of her plan. By driving Tom away, she denies the love she has for him in her heart. That stifling of natural feeling blunts the heart's potential. When, forty years later, she journeys to America in search of Tom, the little prince of her memory, 'Her heart was filled with love for her brother – her little brother that she had cared for like a mother when he was a child – her brother, who at one word from her, had severed all ties of home and family, and come away to this alien land!' Such dishonest sentimentality is appropriately shattered by her inability to see any trace of Tom in the dead man, 'the stranger' she finds in America. 'She laid her heart open to him', but 'it was too old and cracked a vessel' to hold love.

Dishonesty is a form of death; it shrivels the heart, blunts the sensibility, and undermines one's sense of what one should do or say. Widowhood is also a potential death. Mary Lavin's widows find their identity and their individuality threatened. Marriage involved love and companionship, but it also involved dependence and the giving up of a separate identity. The primary task then is to recover, to avoid going into the tomb. The risk of being entombed is mentioned in a number of these stories. At the beginning of 'In the Middle of the Fields', 1961, the woman speaks of anxieties and fears: 'These were the stones across the mouth of the tomb', preventing her release, threatening to bury her as well as her husband. In 'In a Café' the woman crouched at the door of the artist's studio is asked to identify herself. That blunt request has a salutary effect. Why is she behaving in this foolish way? The answer, she realises, is loneliness; it is Robert she really seeks. That truth is confirmed by her complete vision of him that follows.

The style of these later stories, expressive of this mature kind of character, becomes more balanced in registering several points of view. It is detached in its observations, mellow in its apprehension of external details. These women contrast favourably with the fury of Ellen in 'A Happy Death' or the bland superficiality of Hallie in 'The Long Ago'. They have an all-round decency, compassion, and common sense. In none of these stories is there a question of naïveté or inexperience. On the contrary the widow knows what she is doing, has known love and passion, feels a keen sense of loss, but is determined to 'take hold of life'. The woman in 'In the Middle of the Fields', practical and capable in dealing with Bartley Crosson about farming matters, is equally able to deal with him when he tries to kiss her and does so with understanding and sympathy. Vera Traske in 'The Cuckoo Spit' handles the relationship with young Fergus with deft understanding and mature judgment. The widow's ability to cope is given a shaping context within her memories and experiences of lost love, and the narrative, while weighted towards her point of view, flows objectively and smoothly between the different characters, moving easily from description to dialogue to interior monologue.

The narrative ease may be seen also in the open-textured style of 'In the Middle of the Fields', in the imagery of the grasslands of County Meath, its birds and beasts, its satisfying presence:

> Like a rock in the sea, she was islanded by fields, the heavy grass washing about the house, and the cattle wading in it as in water. Even their gentle stirrings were a loss when they moved away at evening to the shelter of the woods. A rainy day might strike a wet flash from a hay barn on the far side of the river – not even a habitation! And yet she was less lonely for him here in Meath than elsewhere... It wasn't him *she* saw when she looked out at the fields. It was the ugly tufts of tow and scutch that whitened the tops of the grass and gave it the look of a sea in storm, spattered with broken foam. That grass would have to be topped. And how much would it cost?[2]

Even in these few sentences the woman's nature is indicated: the deep awareness of surroundings, the reflective manner, the clear analysis of her own state of mind, the rejection of superficial consolations, the sound practical sense. The style is compact, flexible, and capable, adjusted to her character.

These stories of widowhood are written from a comprehensive point of view. All the elements – characterisation, theme, imagery, structure, style – are brought together in the service of the larger over-view. Even the pace of the narrative matches the sense of wisdom and experience embodied in the main character. There is, for example, the leisurely manner of the opening sentences of 'The Cuckoo Spit'.

> Drenched with light under the midsummer moon, the fields were as large as the fields of the sky. Hedges and ditches dissolved in mist, and down by the river the thorn-bushes floated loose like severed branches. Tall trees in the middle of the fields streamed on the air, rooted by long, dragging shadows.

Or there is the expansive, mockingly indulgent opening sequence of 'A Memory', which delights in its shrewdly deflating portrait of the smug academic. Indeed the relaxed manner of the later stories is one of their attractive features. The strains and stresses of the earlier work have been transcended, exorcised in the process of the writing itself. Even those stories that return to earlier themes and previous narrative methods retain the pace and linguistic expansiveness of their later contemporaries. 'Happiness', for example, revives the figure of the harried woman; 'A Memory' re-examines the issue of individual honesty and its correlative – the destructive nature of illusions; and 'Asigh' re-creates the figure of the impulsive girl who retains her happiness despite misfortune.

One of the earlier stories, 'A Woman Friend', 1951, showed that the male mind also has the capacity for self-deception and for selfish insensitivity to the emotional needs of another. 'A Memory', 1972, returns to this theme. Once again we meet the self-centred man. 'His work filled his life as it filled his day', except when the mood forsakes him and he has to go to Dublin to spend the evening with Myra. James's self-regarding complacency infuses his relationship with Myra and helps to destroy it. The story reveals the price Myra has paid for this relationship. While he appreciates 'the uniquely undemanding quality of her feeling' for him, she knows her femininity has been eroded. There is often a tension between our perception of what Myra says and his misinterpretation of what she says. We are prepared for the row that occurs, the explosion that annihilates the cosy world they have built on illusions, although he is taken by surprise. Why, she asks, does he never telephone to say he is coming?

'Wouldn't it be a very small sacrifice to make, James, when one thinks of all the sacrifices I've made for you? And over so many years?' Her words, which to him were exasperating beyond belief, seemed to drown her in a torrent of self-pity. 'So many, many years', she whispered.

It was only ten.[3]

At this point the story shifts to her, its narrative rhythms determined by her responses and turmoil of feelings. The fact is she has sacrificed herself. Lived a lie, let herself be 'denatured' in order not to disturb the carefully contrived cocoon in which their relationship exists. For once she has been true to herself and speaks 'with passion, real passion'. James, however, keeps his composure and leaves in disgust. One of the interesting developments in this story is that James is punished severely for his evasion of responsibility. Not only have his pretences and illusions been mercilessly stripped away, but on his return journey to his rural retreat he is sent blundering into a dark wood where he falls dead from a heart attack. 'Under a weight of bitterness too great to be borne his face was pressed into the wet leaves, and when he gulped for breath, the rotted leaves were sucked into his mouth.'

Both characters are punished, both have indulged in an illusion in which he has selfishly taken advantage of her willingness to live according to his ideals, and she has denied her natural instincts. In Mary Lavin's fiction relationships that diminish those involved are false and harmful. That is true of Isabel and her father in 'A Single Lady', it was true of Hallie and her friends in 'The Long Ago', it was true of Ellie and Robert in 'A Happy Death', it is true of the wife in 'Trastevere', where the strain is so great that she kills herself. In the widow stories the bereaved woman has to be resolute against those, both living and dead, who would diminish her individuality and the opportunity to achieve self-realisation. In 'The Will' Lally has to assert her independence of family interference, as does Liddy in 'Frail Vessel' and Tom in 'The Little Prince', who maintains his long silent rejection of Bedelia's financial sop. The instances are many. Here in 'A Memory' is the powerful example of two people who destroy each other, whose contrasting natures are balanced in the story's structure and tonal orchestration.

A final example of a late story that returns to an earlier issue is 'Asigh', which is related thematically to stories such as 'The Will' and 'Frail Vessel' and that seeks to capture the indefinable essence of the spirited girl. In 'Asigh' she is trapped, her love for Tod Mallon forever denied fulfilment because of an accident. When her father struck her with the buckle of a head collar, the wound became incurable, and that disability made her ineligible to be a farmer's wife. Denied fulfilment, she urges it on her brother Tom in pity for his 'dried and wasted years'. Her own life is a 'long imprisonment', but the passing years do not diminish her need to share it, particularly, 'when the fields were rich and flowering, the hedges flecked with blossoms'. The girl is both expectant and disappointed, rebellious against her fate and accepting of it. She weighs up the reasons for her disappointment and becomes tolerant and understanding. The movements of her mind have the slow rhythms of the Meath countryside. The imagery of the landscape indicates her potential and promise, but it also reflects her condition: 'Closed in by summer, the fields were deeper and lonelier than ever, and the laneway that led out to the road was narrowed by overhanging briars and the wild summer growth of bank and ditch.' She is another of Mary Lavin's memorable victims.

The narrative skill of this story is remarkable. At its centre is the girl's reflecting, observant consciousness that gives it shape and texture. The lucidity of the style, its measured pace and the clarity of its detail, reflects her clear-headed, analytical, and far-seeing mind. Her critical intelligence tries at all times to make sense of life's enigmas and of the values that deter-mine the society in which she lives. There is a firm, even valiant explicitness in her account of experience. She knows, understands, remembers with exact detail, explains analogies and associative links in her memory. Out of this complex weaving backward and forward emerges a deep sadness at the waste of human potential and happiness. The narrator's clarity of mind and of memory and her scrupulous honesty, together with her sense of hope and her openness to love and to nature, are signs of her worth. By her narrative manner we know her.

The sadness grows in the later collections, *The Shrine*, 1977, and *A Family Likeness*, 1985. Mary Lavin will not tolerate sentimental notions about domestic tranquillity or loving mother-daughter relationships. She writes pitilessly honest accounts of complex feelings and moods involved in the relationships between the old and between the old and the young. Love, concern, good intentions exist, but so do irritation, anger, resentment, wounding remarks, frictions of one kind or another, often caused by petty disagreements or misunderstandings. The misunderstand-ings recur from one generation to the next; the pattern of familiar wrangling persists; the tendency to take refuge in self-deception and illusion recurs. Mary Lavin refuses to shirk reality as she sees it as she reveals how vulnerable people are, how prone to hurt, how quick to inflict pain. A simple outing to gather primroses in 'A Family Likeness' becomes an occasion for bickering between grandmother and daughter, with memories of similar disagreements in the previous generation. The family reunion in 'A Walk on the Cliff', happily anticipated by mother and daughter, is spoiled by foolish misunderstandings. 'A Bevy of Aunts' surgically dismembers sentimentalised memories of the past. In 'Senility' the old can be wise and generous in feeling, as Ada, who is better able to cope with the disabilities of ageing than is her less experienced daughter and who prays not that God will make senility easier for her but for her daughter to cope with. But the old priest in 'The Shrine' is vindictively unchristian towards the niece he has loved and who loves him. As often happens in these stories the participants yearn for the love and understanding that they foolishly and unwillingly destroy.

Mary Lavin's stories are deeply concerned with the values by which people live their lives. Problems of choice, the dangers of deception, the possibilities of being emotionally exploited, the need for absolute honesty are some of the preoccupations that pervade her work. Her imaginative treatment of the issues has changed through the years, but her engagement with them had been steadfast and honest. The human mind in her work is wonderfully open, its complexities and contradictions laid bare. In fact it is the closed mind that is found wanting, the mind without sufficient flexibility and depth to deal with experience. Her writing is informed by a belief in the human mind, its capacity to absorb and sift experience, its ability to perceive and to understand, its moral pre-eminence. The human image in these stories is rendered with insight and compassion, and the treatment changes as the writer grows and develops. Furthermore the style of writing is so attuned to and expressive of character that we hardly notice the skills that are involved. When Mary Lavin tells us that she has too much to say to be a novelist, she is being neither frivolous nor boastful. Quite clearly she has important things to tell us about ourselves and does so with sophistication, warmth, and intelligence.

Notes

1   All quotations, unless otherwise indicated, are from *The Stories of Mary Lavin*, 2 vols (London: Constable, 1964, 1974).
2   *In the Middle of the Fields* (London: Constable, 1967).
3   *A Memory* (London: Constable, 1972).

7
THE ACHIEVEMENT OF FRANCIS STUART[1]

Francis Stuart died at his home in County Clare in 2000 at the age of ninety-seven. A member of Aosdána, he was elected Saoi. *Born in Australia in 1902, he published his first book of poetry,* We Have Kept the Faith, *in 1923 and his first novel,* Women and God, *in 1931. In 1996* Writing Ulster *published a Special Issue devoted to Stuart to which Harmon contributed the essay 'The Achievement of Francis Stuart'. His essay, reprinted below, is an assessment of Stuart's place among Irish fiction writers of the twentieth century.*

FRANCIS Stuart belongs to the generation of Irish writers that emerged in the post-revolutionary period. They had been stirred by the romantic nationalism of the first two decades of the twentieth century, by the doomed heroism of the Easter Rising of 1916, by the execution of its leaders, and by the widespread reaction against such treatment of patriotic idealists. But if their emotional involvement with revolutionary nationalism reached a peak between 1919 and 1921, their disillusionment during the civil war that ensued and their disappointment in the aftermath of independence were even more profound. Being young in 1916 and in 1918, they experienced the romance of nationalism with youthful fervour. Their fall into despair was therefore all the more traumatic. The literature that they wrote was consequently realistic and analytical, as they searched within Irish society for clarification of Irish life and character, as they tried to recover from the excesses of feeling and of language that had marked their earlier years, and as they tried to discover a direction for their country and for themselves in a period of stagnation and entrenchment. Post-revolutionary Ireland became predominantly lower middle class and Catholic; it was suspicious of writers who were critical of its values, impatient with its laws of censorship, and advocated greater interaction with other cultures. Not surprisingly, Irish literature in this period is traditional in form, realistic in manner, given to occasional lapses into fantasy, and given hardly at all to Joycean experimentation or radical individual vision. Apart from Flann O'Brien, the fiction was not experimental and apart from Francis Stuart it is not noted for radical quests for personal truth.

Francis Stuart is the outstanding exception: his life and work reflect the period from 1916 onwards; the revolutionary events, the middle-class, claustrophobic society, the forces that threaten the writers' freedom. He is both of the period and detached from it; he reacts to its social, moral, and intellectual restrictions and expresses the writer's vision of an alternative mode of living and thinking. But what gives his work its distinctive character is his persistent belief in the redemptive value of suffering. Such an intense perception of how best to live, being private and spiritual, makes it difficult for him to be a novelist of the traditional, orthodox kind. He cannot easily devote himself to the accurate portrayal of man within society, since the more he seeks verisimilitude the more difficult it is to create a character who is deeply infused with the idea of suffering, or of radical alienation from society as the means to personal fulfilment. Such figures by their very natures are anti-social, indifferent to the values and means by which society exists. Stuart's early phase, from 1931 to 1939, alternates precariously between the necessity of depicting a credible social context and the necessity of creating characters whose search for redemption by means of suffering and isolation can be made credible. Since it is not primarily social contexts that shape their development, the depiction of a realistic social background is in danger of becoming irrelevant. Yet without some outline of an environment the characters are in danger of appearing merely unrepresentative or eccentric.

His first novel, *Women and God*, 1931, anticipated the issues that would preoccupy him: in a world devoid of hope Stuart offers the solution of God's presence. This combination of despair with the belief in the reality of God's power defines his personal vision. In his second novel, *Pigeon Irish*, 1932, a pessimistic view of Irish society is countered by the hero's choice of personal martyrdom. The idea that triumph may arise from apparent failure becomes increasingly dominant in Stuart's fiction in the first phase of his career. *The Coloured Dome*, 1932, shows the directions his work takes. Here he maintains a balance between the realities of place and his religious imagination as he seeks to describe the mystery of human relationships. He offers the story of Christ's suffering and death as a model by which man may gain insight. That Christ spoke in parables makes Him an artistic model for Stuart's attempts to convey the almost incommunicable actuality of mystical experience.

Stuart's most successful integration of social reality with mystical vision comes in *The Pillar of Cloud*, 1948. The setting is Marheim, Germany; the time is immediately after the end of the Second World War; the conditions are extreme: starvation, a city in ruins. In a world without hope a few individuals discover an elemental Christian fraternity. Dominic Malone remains in the ruined city and is drawn into a transforming experience with two young girls. Together they experience a renewed feeling of Christianity, of fraternal, non-sexual love which has been earned through suffering, through the purging of selfish desires. By living with them Dominic finds a profoundly undemanding and generous relationship. Stuart demonstrates the possibility of a new beginning for the world after the horrors of war and the failure of civilisation. Women who have suffered torture, sexual violation, and hunger have, he believes, the capacity to forgive; they have the ability to love their enemies, to enter into communion with others, to be Christlike.

Dominic, who has been in a concentration camp, believes 'That it was in such a place that a new world was taking shape; in the hearts of the tormented a new world was born. A world in which there would be no more victims and no more executioners, without prisons and dungeons.' He puts his trust in Christ and in the reality of the love he experiences with the victims, Lisette and Halka. Although he loves Halka, it is the consumptive, dying Lisette that he marries, at Halka's request, in the hope that he may be able to take her out of Germany for medical treatment. Taking Lisette's frail and feverish body in his arms on their wedding night, he reaches a state of humility and joy. When Halka makes love with him in prison, in the same cell with her torturer against whom she refuses to testify, he is aware of a moment of mystical, inarticulate union. 'Hers was the innocence', Dominic thinks, 'that was on the earth to set over against the monstrous evil.'

It is essential for Stuart's purposes that all the characters should be colourless, without social distinction, without outward distinction. What they are is made visible in how they live. There is a great tenderness at the heart of this novel. Nevertheless, it makes radical statements about human nature, as it insists on values that are unorthodox, such as the innocence of Dominic's life with the two women, the moral rightness of Halka's forgiveness of her torturer, the saintly nature of the two women, the miraculous birth of peace and joy amid horror and suffering. In other circumstances Lisette and Halka might be regarded as prostitutes, as unimportant leftovers of social collapse. But in the circumstances within which Stuart creates them, they are the heroines, witnesses to the truths of Christ's message. Their suffering resembles His, their self-denial and self-sacrifice affirm values for which He died and which He affirmed in His teachings.

The mute style of *The Pillar of Cloud* is replaced in *Redemption*, 1949, by a brooding intensity that invests experiences and objects and people with a more than ordinary significance. The slow-moving style is attentive to its own rhythms of perception; it is a vehicle by which to direct the reader to an alert, measured response. The novel is also more direct in its assault on conventional values. Whereas in *The Pillar of Cloud* the subversion of social and moral conventions was implicit, an indirect consequence of events, in *Redemption* there is a conscious countering of one set of values by another, as though what the Irishman learned abroad, in the catastrophe of war, has to be brought back to Ireland as an aggressive form of personal behaviour, or as a necessary infection that will afflict Irish society and produce changes of attitudes. Ezra Arrigho is the bearer of this redemptive evil: he brings with him a brooding memory of days and nights of violence, social breakdown, and elemental human kinship, the bond of humanity discovered in the obliteration of social isolation, institutions and rules: 'We were a little tribe in the midst of the forest on the edge of death.' Arrigho sets that belief against what he finds in Ireland, neutral, secure, Catholic, middle-class, complacent.

It is this assertive attack on Irish society that is new in *Redemption*. Through Ezra, Stuart articulates the need for a new vision, and through the imaginative life of the novel he embodies its elements. Ezra carries with him a burdened memory of violence. His account fascinates the fishmonger, Kavanagh, creating in him a wish to have lived where great things happen – 'at the beginning of the end . . . in the foreign darkness, among the ruins'. By comparison his vision of darkness is pitifully limited. He therefore urges his mistress, Annie, to daub a holy picture with her blood so that he may enjoy the foolish, superstitious reactions of the people. Altamont must be shaken out of its complacency. Violence must happen, if individual values and attitudes are to be changed. Kavanagh murders Annie; Arrigho violates the priest's sister, Romilly; Romilly, who is about to enter a conventional marriage, seeks out Ezra, willing him to possess her, to 'destroy' and 'spoil' her, and thereby 'save' and 'keep' her. He wants her also to face the horror of contact with Kavanagh, to see something that she has 'never seen before. Take his hand without showing any sign of repugnance.'

Ezra also challenges his wife, Nancy, to abandon the security of her home, a challenge she is unable to meet, disgusted as she is by his way of life and by the 'other woman', Margareta, whom he thought had been buried in the ruins of Germany but who turns up unexpectedly. There is a contrast between Nancy's pride and her disgust with sex and Margareta's humility and instinctive sexuality. Ezra's view of Nancy is uncompromising: 'you couldn't share my follies and irrational enthusiasm, you could only look on in tolerance and patience, and sometimes in irritation and anger'. When she objects that he did not try hard to make her share his follies and that, despite his neglect, she was faithful to him, he replies that she was faithful, but had no faith in him. In its logic of Christian self-abnegation and radical, selfless love the novel disposes of any justification that Nancy may have had for her behaviour. In the novel as parable there is little room for psychological complexity by which individual action may be explained. In Stuart's quasi-mystical vision of how things should be, ordinary incapacities and failings have no function. Nancy is said to be trapped 'in a tower of idealism . . . behind the wall of her own judgment'; she has not had faith in him in the past, she cannot now enter into what he has in mind.

The faith that attracts Stuart is conveyed in Ezra's words about Christ to Father Mellowes: 'He sought the mad, the possessed, and sick and dying, they being in a sense nearest to Him and most likely not to be appalled and scandalised by the extravagance of what He was going to do at the end, when His hour came.' Ezra sees in the priest a true reflection of his own understanding of the Christ who attracted Mary Magdalene, of the Christ who opened his heart to the woman in Samaria, because of her sexual abandonment. But sex was not enough of an abandonment:

> In the last two or three days and nights of His life, He revealed in His body what was to be the final secret of flesh and blood, the new secret beyond sex that had weighed on Him like a guilty secret. From the Last Supper to the Crucifixion, He plunged to the last depths of flesh and blood and tried to pull His disciples down with Him, but they couldn't go very far.

This is the gospel according to Ezra, as Father Mellowes says. Paradoxically, it is the sinner who speaks with mystical intensity to the priest. But the true bearers of truth are women, the Marthas and Marys of the Gospels, and Margareta who returned from the dead and whose first manifestation in Germany he vividly recalls: her 'dumbness and dusty, tawny weariness... annulled all that I had known and been used to'. It is essential to Stuart's purpose that she should thus be insignificant in appearance, a nobody, a stranger, not one whom the world values, but that she should have the capacity to love with infinite compassion, that she should be of the company of the women in the Gospel.

Those who take refuge together in a house in Altamont enter into a life that is marked by forgiveness, openness, and love. Ezra feels one with Kavanagh, now facing trial as a murderer; Romilly marries Kavanagh so that she may be allowed to visit him in prison and share his loneliness; Margareta is content to be near Ezra; Father Mellowes presides over his Christian brotherhood in the 'new life'. The house is in direct contrast with the inadequacies and failures of conventional homes, as Ezra tries to explain to Nancy, speaking of 'all the married couples shut up together in houses and flats everywhere, all the watertight little families bound together more by fear and suspicion of the next world than by love of each other'. So the novel moves to a demonstration of 'a daring and delicate experiment': 'The little group felt the first stir of a life of its own, a tenuous ripple around the table that touched and laved the remotest corners of each single heart.'

These are, as Ezra observes, new modes of communion. Kavanagh, like Christ in the exposed position He held at the end, feels that he is slipping away from his circle of friends. 'But now that the hour had come there was in this letting go of all that he had been holding on to in itself a kind of strength.' At this moment Romilly decides to marry him. She has found the 'miracle' she wanted. Father Mellowes approves of this unselfish love, this abandonment towards one who suffers: this, he tells his small community, is 'true marriage; this purifies the sacrament of misuse'. It is a night of ceremony: Ezra sponges Margareta's crippled body, takes off her old garments, and replaces them with new ones; Father Mellowes hears Kavanagh's confession; Romilly prepares her wedding dress, getting ready for a union that will fill her 'with disgust and love'.

The logic of Stuart's fiction is paradoxical, but then, as he would argue, so is the logic of the Gospels; so too is the story of Christ. Writing of Christ's agony in Gethsemane, he says in *The Abandoned Snail Shell*, 1987, 'This is the historical event with which our own most intense experience of insignificance, failure, loss and an inherent indifference to the environment is far surpassed.' In this work he quotes specifically from *Redemption*, which marks an important stage in his development; in it he firmly articulates a position in relation to conventional society and orthodox values that becomes a fundamental belief in his subsequent fiction. The attacks on Irish duck-pond mentality are direct, even when disguised as parable. Paradoxically, it is the social nonentities, the violent, the cruel, the anguished, the poor, the neglected, who are capable of extraordinary insight and radical experience – just as was Mary Magdalene who entered into the true nature of Christ's mission, who understood instinctively what others failed to comprehend. The war, for Stuart, 'was a traumatic and transforming event'. Thereafter, he applies its effects on him to others. If the experience was transforming, it was not wholly new. After all, he had expressed the same or a similar belief in suffering and death in previous novels. But his wartime experiences confirmed and strengthened what he had previously felt. From now on he had the confidence to trust in his own nature, his own instincts; to recognise not the uniqueness of his essentially instinctive temperament, but its basic human reality. Christ's death and resurrection are the primary examples of the possibility, the truth, the reality of this capacity for change. The resurrection, Stuart argues, was experienced within the consciousness of the disciples, in their new relationship with Jesus. 'A new phase has begun . . . A new set of values came into being as a consequence of the recognition that failure and loss had to precede the new dispensation.'

The difficulty for Stuart as a novelist who believes deeply in this reality is to find ways in which to make it credible. At the heart of these experiences is the creation of a new set of values as a result of events that may be definable as external forces. Ezra's brooding recall of being immersed in and altered by the experiences of war has some degree of objectivity. One may assent to the claim that events changed him. Similarly, but with more difficulty, a reader may be persuaded that the intrusion of similar violence in Altamont may result in the altered perceptions of those who participate in the little community living over the fish shop. When Stuart writes well and infuses his beliefs through significant incidents and recognisable human reactions, his fiction is a powerful testament to what he believes. But when he presents his first sight of Margareta or the unexpected encounter between Halka and her torturer, it is of the essence of Stuart's treatment that the reality is hidden: mere words cannot express the hidden significance, the reverberations of the event. By a quality of absence, of silence, by the refusal even to try to bring the experience into an imaginative reality through language, Stuart affirms its importance. The parallel with his brooding, instinctive, imaginative interpretation of the Gospel stories is clear. Just as there, the simple, unadorned, and understated incident may contain the most far-reaching and most stunning revelation, so in his fiction the simple, understated incident may bear witness to a demanding interpretation. The weight of such an incident in the novel is greater than the amount of literary artifice devoted to it. Characters like Ezra, in their reflexive, intense consciousness, are temperamentally adjusted to benefit from these non-verbal, non-logical events. Their modes of insight are models for Stuart's readers and externalisations of his own artistic vision.

The strength of Francis Stuart's conviction is evident in his most important work, *Black List, Section H*, 1971, which reiterates the familiar narrative of his immersion in the massive European suffering during and after the war, when empires crumble, but joins it with a firmly articulated account of his personal life and artistic development. All Stuart's fiction is autobiographical; he has never been the kind of novelist who creates an imaginative reality apart from the circumstances of his own life and with characters very different from himself. But *Black List, Section H* is more openly autobiographical and more visibly connected with people and events in his own life, even to the extent of calling 'characters' by their actual names – W. B. Yeats, Maud and Iseult Gonne, Liam O'Flaherty. The book is both a manifesto of beliefs, tested in the abyss of post-war dislocation, and an *apologia* for a life lived in accordance with its own obscure laws of intuition and self-belief. It is the means by which these two purposes are related that the book is most challenging.

First, there is the case history or record of H's life, his journey from involvement in local Irish issues – marriage to Iseult Gonne, participation in the revolution, running a chicken farm, gambling, writing novels, visiting London or Europe, reading the work of Christian mystics. All of these ordinary, or fairly ordinary, events are set down with persuasive exactness and precision, with the kind of faithful attention to detail and significance that marks the work of the novelist in command of his medium. The strength that is evident in the change of emphasis in characterisation from Dominic to Ezra, and in the change of approach from the remote and indirect method of *The Pillar of Cloud* to the confrontational morality of *Redemption*, is more pronounced in *Black List, Section H*, in which the density of remembered incident grows and accumulates into a massive narrative of one man's life.

But it is the other part of the work that is problematical. Here the direct 'message' of *Redemption* becomes part of H's interpretation of his own life and its justification. The insertion of a thesis early on in the work and reiteration thereafter gives the book an editorialising quality that tends to undermine its fierce autonomy. H has a distinct concept of the position a poet ought to have: 'Dishonour is what becomes a poet, not titles or acclaim . . . A poet must be a counter current to the flow around him. That's what poetry is: the other way of feeling and looking at the world.' This is what H does, with increasing conviction throughout the novel and particularly at the end when he and Halka wander with the dispossessed. Against authority, he has a preference for poets who have suffered calumny and derision, for people who have been despised and threatened. His radical, nihilistic philosophy is contemptuous of established orders and values. 'He delighted in hearing of riots, no matter where, in civil disturbances, even in bank robberies; also in assassinations and anything that diminished or threw doubt on authority.'

This is Ezra's philosophy pronounced with greater assurance, because it will be shown to have been proven right in the European collapse. Stuart's own life, projected with intensity in *Black List, Section H*, is that the fiction instead of revealing its truth imaginatively, instead of trusting in the reader's interpretative skill, explains its truth. It may be argued that since H is a character in the fiction, a character defined by a set of beliefs, that to show him articulating those beliefs is artistically justified. But what happens is that his beliefs, justified as they will be by the novel's conclusion, are first expressed when he is still seventeen years of age and at a time when he is patently insecure and uncertain of himself. At the best of times H's awareness of what he feels and believes is obscurely present to his mind. Clarity of mind is not what distinguished him. Even his articulation of what he values is awkward and imperfectly realised. What he says about the Irish civil war, for example, stands out of the text, a pronouncement by the later Stuart in justification of an earlier involvement. As the judge of personal motives and of Irish revolution H, at this stage in particular, is accorded a maturity and insight beyond his years.

> The civil war created doubt and confusion . . . And once the process of division had started, H foresaw it continuing, and subdivisions taking place, especially on the Republican side, perhaps creating small enclaves of what he looked on as true revolutionaries whose aim had less to do with Irish independence than in casting doubt on traditional values and judgments.

H is said to be fighting the mould set by 'pious and patriotic Irishmen around the national consciousness'; he seeks 'the dawn of the imaginative and undogmatic mood, that he saw as the prerequisite of true revolution'.

Belief is recurrently asserted as it is validated and confirmed by experiences such as H's perception of a fellow Republican prisoner who is different from 'most' Irish people in what he believes and values. 'What's so horrible,' H says to him, approvingly, 'is to live by established categories.' H's obsessional interests – in mystical writers such as Juliana of Norwich and St. Catherine of Siena, in writers who have been condemned, who do not just reflect social realities (he has little respect for Joyce) – lead him to the New Testament, to a fascination with Christ as one who avoided family and social occasions, who preferred isolated individuals, and who could communicate only in parable. To H, He was someone 'in the grip of new kinds of perception and emotion'. H understands the psychology of Christ on the cross: 'a familiar nightmare, the longing of exposed, tormented beings, stripped of their protective aura, for the coming of darkness'. Christ, he argues, 'had held the most forward position of His time for several hours. And it would fall to the condemned, the sick–unto–death and perhaps a handful of unregarded artists to defend these areas of conscious-ness in the coming days as best they could.'

Not only is Stuart trying to explain his own philosophy, his belief in the creation of new ways of seeing, but he is also trying to explain his way of discovering truth. The explanation becomes his major preoccupation in subsequent fiction. H first explains his belief that reality can express itself as well in fiction as in fact in a conversation at Lourdes. The Gospels, he says, reflect and have the impact of reality 'which is a better way of putting it than asking, are they true'.

Stuart's fiction, more and more, is an attempt to express what is almost inexpressible. Since he is neither a subtle thinker nor a supple stylist, he has to rely on statement, on the authority of narrative voice, on the evidence of incident, which is often given symbolic significance. *Black List, Section H* is an extended documentary, a sustained witnessing of the truth of fiction. H's faith is the driving force; it is, he believes, only 'in surviving perilous situations... that he'd gain the insight he needed to reach whatever degree of psychic and imaginative depths he was capable of, and be able to communicate those in his fiction'. And when he speculates on the new kind of novel he wants to write, since the traditional realistic-naturalistic novel is not suited to his purposes, he thinks of novelists who have written the romance kind of fiction, rather than the conventional 'novel', and is dismissive of his contemporaries, none of the kind of Baudelaire, Poe, Keats, Melville, Emily Brontë, Dostoevsky, Proust, or Kafka.

He pursues an obscurely motivated spiritual odyssey while at the same time he moves in his external life from one miserable relationship to another, from one ill-considered decision to the next, all based on an instinctive trust in the self, on a kind of gambler's instinct, on submission to chance, that is similar to Dominic's or Ezra's yielding to the course of

events, to the inevitable direction in what happens. He will not cling to old
securities when he feels himself being drawn into a 'vortex of painful
experience'. Just as Christ was exposed on the frontiers of human
experience during the crucifixion, so H will find himself exposed at the
place of the greatest cataclysm of modern times. Christ's 'neurological
makeup' appeals to him, as did the 'neurological system' of certain writers.
It is Christ's ability to experience horror, to be receptive and vulnerable, to
have gone deliberately into the depths in order to gain admission to other
minds and hearts that appeals to him, as though Christ too were an artist in
search of extraordinary modes of communication, who experiences the
most trauma in the knowledge that thereby, by the evidence of what He
suffered, He will affect the consciousness of others.

H's life transforms itself into legend. It becomes the myth by which
Stuart's own life is finally justified. The certainty of its truth gives him the
power to pursue his own past, to repossess it and shape it as fictive truth.
In the light of that knowledge he can state his and H's dissatisfaction with
'contemporary ideologies or institutions, religious, national, or social'. His
isolation is both instinctive and achieved: by rejecting the bonds of
marriage, Church, and state; by making Germany his Gethsemane; by
dismissing the whole of modern literature, he magnifies and intensifies his
isolation. It is Stuart's *contra mundum*, which is the only position he can
hold with integrity; it alone satisfies his temperament.

The success of *Black List, Section H* must have encouraged him to write
a more experimental kind of novel. To concentrate on the neurological
truth, rather than the mystical, to try to understand the workings of the
nervous system in the light of up-to-date medical investigation and to use
the terminology of modern science in conjunction with imaginative
evidence, to explore even better the instinctive, obsessive, alogical nature of
certain minds, including his own. In the most recent phase of his career, he
has written novels that show a new direction in his work: *Memorial*, 1973;
A Hole in the Head, 1977; *The High Consistory*, 1981; *Faillandia*, 1985;
A Compendium of Lovers, 1990; and *King David Dances*, 1996. Of these *A
Hole in the Head* best represents what he has been trying to achieve. The
primary vehicle for the new style is the central character whose point of
view controls our understanding of events. Whereas in *Black List, Section
H* the central character was a reliable witness, even if he did over-state the
philosophy by which he lived, in these later novels the central character is
an unreliable witness and the novel is an uncertain 'record' of his
experiences. Having advocated a literature written by obsessive
personalities, Stuart takes the logical step of creating heroes who suffer
from mental and emotional disasters, who undergo breakdown, who have
been treated by modern drugs and who, in addition, are given to sex and
alcohol. Such a central consciousness cannot provide a logical, sequential

account of events, cannot even perceive reality in a reliable or stable manner. Uncertainties of perception, an inability to distinguish between reality and hallucination, a willingness to give credence to imaginary experience are all characteristics of the new hero. The form of the novel itself is necessarily disrupted as a result of the narrator's inability to maintain a 'sane' or sustained control of his material. The result is that the reader is plunged into uncertainty with the narrative; at the same time he is given an immediate contact with the narrator, with his confessional sharing of flux and uncertainty. The reader's trust is in the hidden control of Stuart, manipulating the jigsaw of a consciousness that is compulsive and a victim of its own breakdown.

If flux is that reality, to depict that reality in its complexity and pain, and to show how the creative imagination – for the narrator is also an artist undergoing the stress of failure – copes with it is the achievement of the novel. Stuart moves beyond the notion of the Tiresian consciousness at the heart of T. S. Eliot's *The Wasteland*, beyond the connection of the apparently random consciousness at the heart of James Joyce's *Ulysses* or Thomas Kinsella's *Nightwalker*. His nearest relation is the anguished figure of the self in Austin Clarke's *Mnemosyne Lay in Dust* where the fragmented narrative of the therapy of terror in an insane asylum is also its own reason for being, where the rational imagination recreates a horror and brings its disorders and failures into challenging existence. Stuart presses his fiction into the service of the kind of obsessive mind that he had in the past praised in others and asserted as the source of the kind of literature required in the modern world.

One of the main examples of this kind of writer, for him, is Emily Brontë, about whom he spoke in an unpublished radio talk. There he made a distinction between the writer who remains outside his books, 'concerned with form, structure and characterisation', and the writer who puts himself into his books, into the central character, with all his passions, shame, hope, regrets. Emily Brontë, he said, fictionalises her passionate fantasies, which she has to suppress because of the kind of society that existed about her. She is, he claimed, the doomed, temperamental Cathy and also her violent, obsessional lover, the mysterious Heathcliff. The presence of Emily Brontë, as H's muse figure in *A Hole in the Head*, is therefore significant in relation to the kind of writer he has been and the kind of writer he wants to be; he has, in this characterisation, been a conventional unchallenging writer; he wants to be more like the author of *Wuthering Heights*, to put himself into his characters, to shock the reader with the deeper realities of human nature. The hole in the head has a positive, therapeutic meaning akin to the practice of the Amazonian tribe who puncture the heads of children between the two hemispheres of the brain in order to widen the range of perception by giving them access to both good and evil spirits.

The novel takes place in the transition period in which H recovers from a nervous breakdown. The treatment for a self-inflicted wound in the head involves a visit to a psychiatric clinic in Switzerland, sexual union with the therapist, and the disappearance of Emily Brontë from his hallucinations, but not of what she represents from his imagination. Her presence confirms the directions his writing should take. Her comments on a play that they see together are the voice of his muse: the dramatist, she says, delineates the surface level of his characters. It was when he read *Wuthering Heights* that H knew that his own novels 'were ingeniously concocted instead of being wrung from the heart'. Now the voice of his artistic conscience, externalised as Emily Brontë, urges him not to cling to the sham of preservation, as in the past, to respond to her as 'one fearful and harried creature for another'. To her he can reveal his secret obsessions, however shameful; her understanding and acceptance set 'a counter-current' to cleanse his spirit. He is drugged and crazy, but 'new cells of perception' are developing. The 'extreme exteriorising' of H's fantasies disappears when he is 'cured' which means for him the preservation of 'a dim, wavering frontier between my inner realm and that of outer "reality"'.

In Part II H returns to the northern city of Belgard, which he had earlier visited with Emily Brontë. Here he is faced with conditions that cause extreme stress: he is the intermediary in a siege where he substitutes himself for two children, he is sexually reunited with his ex-wife, he is sexually united with a girl called Claudia, he gives a public lecture on W. B. Yeats, and he is conscious throughout all these activities of the dangerous revolutionary situation. But he also understands that he needs 'complex and even desperate situations' to get his system 'such as it is (neurological, psychological, physical), into top gear', and this includes his writing. The prolonged lovemaking with his former wife carries him in the appropriate direction. She approves of the changes in him, the release of the 'tightly-clenched will', the ability 'to take risks, to do what's possible and then leave it to chance'. In Belgard he shows freedom from hallucination and obsession, and his dissociation from events. The ability not to care is a sign of his freedom. The ability to cope with extreme experience and the capacity to keep in touch with his muse confirm not only that H is 'cured' but that Stuart's artistic vision is right for him.

The structure and organisation of *A Hole in the Head* reflect the unsettled composition of H's mind during his period of recovery, as though it takes place between the two parts of his brain, affected by both good and evil forces. It is at the same time, in his term, a 'record' of that condition and a sign of the completeness of his recovery. To be cured for H is to be able to write exactly the kind of casebook of a 'madman'; it is fragmented and discontinuous in form because that is how experience impinges on H's consciousness. All the apparent incoherence and uncertainty of its component parts – paragraphs and sentences as much as chapters – are artistically justified because they are manifestations of his reality. That they add up to a credible and persuasive portrait of human stress and recovery is a sign, if sign were needed, of Stuart's control. Once again he has taken risks with his fiction, pushed his powers of invention and control beyond the ordered structure of *Black List, Section H* and *Memorial* into the area of organisational fragmentation.

Francis Stuart's fiction is a recurrent, a deepening, and an expanding attempt to understand his own personality and how it functions. It is possible to see it as a critical response to the narrow values of Irish society and to see his life story in terms of an initial involvement with Irish issues followed by a widening of horizons that are as much spiritual or moral as geographical. In essence, however, the struggle is with the self. At its centre is a profound and ineradicable dissatisfaction with things as they are, with society, with institutions, with western civilisation and its values. Dissatisfaction of such scope makes life difficult for the writer; it urges him incessantly to make demands on himself and on his work; it sets goals that are forever beyond his reach, compelling him to do better, to be different. It issues in his work as editorial intrusions, sweeping condemnations, dogmatic claims, and fixations.

The disadvantages with which Stuart works are not hidden. Neither are the persistence and integrity of his exploration of moral values: his dogged, punishing determination to uncover the truth of his own temperament, to demonstrate how it functions, to be true to its insights, and to underpin that discovery with evidence from other writers, similarly engaged, and with the supreme example of Christ's life and work. Stuart could never be the kind of novelist whose delight it is to reveal the complexities and contradictions of social man. He must pursue his daemons. It is to his credit that out of the struggle with himself he has produced novels of real power in which his version of human nature is realised with persuasive force and which are infused with a numinous, paradoxical belief that out of profound loss can come a transformed understanding and that the truths of the creative imagination can be verified.

Note

1   In *Francis Stuart Special Issue, Writing Ulster*, 4 (1996), pp. 19–37.

8
BENEDICT KIELY'S 'GREAT INVENTION'

Harmon first presented the following essay as a talk, 'Benedict Kiely – Master of the Short Story' at The Third Benedict Kiely Literary Weekend at the Silverbirch Hotel, Omagh, County Tyrone, 17–19 September, 2004. Kiely was born in 1919 near Dromore, County Tyrone. He is a member of Asodána and has the title Saoi. *Revised here, the essay has as its principal source the* Collected Stories of Benedict Kiely, 2001, *which Harmon reviewed for* The Irish Times, *7 July 2001: 'Vivid Tales of Life's Losses'.*

IN the short story, Seán O'Faoláin used to say, there is no time for character development, no room for unnecessary details or elaborate descriptions; the beginning and the ending should be brief. The story, he maintained, informs by suggestion or implication, it favours compression, and is usually short. Initially, Benedict Kiely adhered fairly closely to O'Faoláin's conventions. In Kiely's first collection, *A Journey to the Seven Streams*, 1963, the first story is called 'The White Wild Bronco'. The narrator is familiar with the place and with its people; each of his five characters is given a name and a brief identifying activity. The most important of them is Cowboy Carson who, we are told, is 'the only man in our town who lived completely in the imagination'.[1] He keeps a running conversation with Wyatt Earp and other gunslingers as he shoots off his six-gun. Nothing much happens: men gather around the bed of an old fusilier who had been wounded in the First World War and now lives in memory of that experience and in the stories he reads about Tarzan. Isaac, the little boy, listens to the conversation of the old men. He is the first of Kiely's little boys who watch and learn, whose understanding of the town and its inhabitants is part of his education. He wants to be a German when he grows up and ironically is killed crossing the Rhine in the Second World War. In that span of time we have Kiely's imaginative time in which he sets many of his stories – between those who were in the First World War and those who went off to the Second World War. It is an ordinary place but in Kiely's hands, with his observant eye and well-stocked memory, it is rich and specific in detail.

> Alone in the moonlight on the hill that went down to the red-and-white creamery, the brook, the Cowboy's hut, the fields beyond, he pulled and whirled and fired three times. With satisfaction he listened to the echoes dying away at the town's last

fringe of shabby, sleeping terraces, over the tarred iron roofs of Tansey the carter's stableyard, over the railway-engine shed and the turntable.

Two things may be noted about this detailed scene-setting: the sense of reality created by the specific references and the tendency to flesh out characters with relevant information.

In another early story, 'A View from the Treetop', Kiely stretches his wings. The tone of confident narration appears right from the start: 'There were two famous trees in the village: the cork tree and the lime tree. Strangers used to travel miles just to look at them.' The little boy of the story, Paddy Sheehan, likes to climb to the top of the lime tree, because as he says from there you could see the whole world, from there he observes and dreams. The adult narrator of the story looks back at the village, remembering and describing in specific detail its distinctive features, its two famous trees – one exotic, foreign, ugly, and hard to climb, the other local, familiar, beautiful, and easy to climb. Once again Kiely creates credible characters in brief description, in identifying dialogue, or in the stories they tell, and places them within a recognisable setting. They may be given to dreaming, but they exist where we can see and hear them; they are recognisably part of the human race as we know it.

The story expresses the playful, self-delighting imagination of the child who rides an invisible horse, remembers a battlefield, and watches various people – the mad major, the Old Master. The story opens out to a panorama. 'The village', the narrator tells us, 'was alive.' A succession of figures emerge: the Soldier Sweeney, the Badger Smith, an old woman going to mass, the doctor's three daughters as they walk along, a postman, Milly the maid, the mad major races his white horse as the train leaves, the parish priest talks to the doctor, Grandfather Cryan sets off to pick cinders, the Burglar Cryan sets off with his ferret, the Poacher Cryan sets off to his task, two small Cryans collect scraps from door to door, and the Bully Cryan wheels the handcart. There are clearly a lot of Cryans. In fact when one of them dies, it is remarked that he is the first Cryan ever to die. It is leisurely, casual, and animated, a field full of folk as varied and lively as a bunch of characters in Chaucer or Carleton.

Kiely moves characters in and out of the story, plants a clue, returns to it later. Once the narrator creates the tone of confidence and familiarity with his material we are content to be in his hands – he can move the story along in a straight line or, which is more usual in Kiely's case, follow a crooked course, take digressions, go back in time, reminisce, take the main story up again, philosophise. As long as we feel safe in his hands, a Kiely story keeps its control over us. It is only when the digressions and flash-backs, the musings and memories seem to lose a central purpose that we begin to lose interest, or when the voice becomes lost in its own melodies or relies too much on the creation of atmospherics. Kiely can be loquacious at times.

Like Patrick Kavanagh, who also recovered scenes from his boyhood, Benedict Kiely returns over and over to what he knew best and what he remembered, the world of Dromore and Omagh, the unhurried period between the wars, a well-remembered place from which men and women grow up and leave and occasionally try to go back to. He was fortunate, as he knew, in having a capacious and retentive memory. Given that kind of memory it was natural that many of his stories focus on the idea of return, of going back to origins, of retrieving experience, of recreating it in fiction and thereby giving it a permanence it would not otherwise have. Without tenacious recall the past is lost.

Sometimes the end of the road is a happy confirmation, but sometimes it ends in heartache, in the realisation that you can't go home again. The story 'A Journey to the Seven Streams' belongs to the *Dinnshenchas* tradition, the love of place names and of the stories associated with them, that has been part of Irish tradition. The narrator's father was, we are told, 'a terrible man for telling you about the places he had been and for bringing you there if he could and displaying them to you with a mild and gentle air of proprietorship... The reiterated music of their names worked on him like a dream.' It is only natural then, after this explanatory introduction that the entire family should journey back to places the father loves and to the stories that live in places. It is typical of one kind of Kiely story, a spate of description, conversation, one-liners, memories, characterisation, a variety of voices and perceptions, all held together by the central motif of the return. The journey is an outing, an adventure, a release of love. They travel six miles in style and then have the first of many noisy, spluttering, steaming breakdowns. As the story unfolds there are lots of humorous detail and comic dialogue. Kiely manages several voices and descriptions in what is a spreading panorama.

> 'Mother of God,' said my father, 'that's a noise and no mistake. Here, boy, go off and pick flowers.'
>
> He lifted me down to the ground.
>
> 'Screw off the radiator cap, Peter,' said Hookey.
>
> 'It's scalding hot, Hookey.'
>
> 'Take these gauntlet gloves, manalive. And stand clear when you screw it off.'
>
> A geyser of steam and dirty hot water went heavenwards as Peter and my brother, who was always curious about engines, leaped to safety.
>
> 'Wonderful,' said my father to my brother, 'the age we live in. They say that over in England they're queued up steaming by the roadsides, like Iceland or the Yellowstone Park.'

This is Kiely at his best – relaxed, diverting, painting with broad strokes of the brush – peoples, places, conversations, descriptions, and the language suitably heightened without being too fanciful. We realise too that Kiely's affinities are not with the O'Faoláin model of the formal story or even the episodic tale but with tall tales and yarns, folktales, the oral tradition, and lengthy ballads about colourful characters. He needs expansiveness, but within the genial narration he has a delicate touch, as the above passage shows – he is fully in control of a complex narrative, its contrasting voices, its comic elements, its accommodating landscape.

'Homes on the Mountain' is also about a return, but it has a different tone and a different perspective. A couple return from Philadelphia after forty-five years and build a fine house on the bleak side of Dooish Mountain. Their return is an attempt to reclaim the life they once knew. This story has a straightforward development and a three-part structure: the visit to the returned Americans, the visit to the cottage, and the return to the first house. The parents of the boy-narrator regard the return as foolish. 'Dreamers…Living in the past', according to his mother.

They invite his family to a house-warming on Christmas Day. When they left, Aunt Sally O'Neill held an American wake in her house. Now, long after her death, her two bachelor sons who had been at the wake live in that house, in squalor. Thady was not right in the head and followed women; John courted Bessy from Cornavara for sixty years. Now they live like pigs and have, it is said, eight thousand pounds each in the bank. Tommy, the boy's father, decides to visit them. He takes his two sons with him.

Across the countryside lights shine in white cottages, including candles in windows, reminiscent of the scene in Carleton when in a more populous time five thousand to six thousand people came down the mountain to midnight mass. They go through wetland and by runnels in flood and come to the wreck of Aunt Sally's house. Once it was a fine, long, two-storied, thatched farmhouse. Now the roof and the upper storey sag. The description of the two old men reveals poverty and decay. The twelve-year-old boy is remembering the scene years later.

> There was a hunched decrepit old man behind the opening door. Without extending his hand he shuffled backwards and away from us. His huge hobnailed boots were unlaced. They flapped around him like the feet of some strange bird or reptile. He was completely bald. His face was pear-shaped, running towards the point at the forehead. His eyes had the brightness and quickness of a rodent's eyes. When my father said, 'Thady, you remember me,' he agreed doubtfully, as if agreement or disagreement were equally futile.

The conversation the father has with the two old men including the assumed joviality is underlined by compassion. Something very smelly is cooking on the fire for their Christmas dinner. The story evokes decay in the countryside – emigration, lack of vitality, sentimental return visits, romantic Ireland in song and story, waste, years passing, promise blighted. It is a deeply poignant story drawing upon love of a people in decline. Kiely does not try to disguise the way he feels about the theme. The issue which is starkly presented is fundamental to modern Irish life and literature – in George Moore's *The Untilled Field*, in Kavanagh's *The Great Hunger*, in Carleton's reflections on cultural decline in the Clogher valley, in Liam O'Flaherty's 'Going into Exile', in John Montague's poetry. 'Homes on the Mountain' is Kiely's lament for what has gone. If people are, in his estimation, 'a great invention', their disappearance is a deeply felt loss.

'This ground', the narrator says in 'Tonight we Ride with Sarsfield', 'is littered with things, cluttered with memories and multiple associations.' For the writer the task is to bring order to this profusion. For the narrator it is sometimes a question of being drawn by them, going back, facing the pain at the centre. In Kiely's mature stories the complexity of human nature is richly present; the variety of mankind is endlessly fascinating. In 'Near Banbridge Town' the words of the song and their spirit are an accompanying motif, expressing a buoyancy of mood and an appreciation of beauty and love. In the mind of Lisney, the narrator, they stand for 'love and love and more love and bouncing rustic beauties' and not politics, nor dying for Ireland, nor King Billy crossing the Boyne.

The main figure in this story is separated from his mother and his sister. It is the Christmas season and he is going home, for the first time in many years. The spirit of Christmas, of love and forgiveness, of celebration infuses the story from the start but is absent in the ending where it ought to be most clearly present. The story begins with an office party and with the kind of exuberant conversation that attends such festive occasions – jollity, talk about girls, some boasting about romantic adventures, reminiscence – but Lisney's thoughts are never far removed from home and his homecoming. Kiely balances these two elements throughout: one set of experiences, the surface material of the story, acting as a context for the deeper, contrasting concerns of the narrator. In the buffet at Portadown, Lisney meets old school pals. In keeping with the spirit of the season there is much drinking, in the buffet, then in the guard's van, where men and women gather in convivial companionship. Lisney is so full of good feeling for his fellow travellers that he says to himself 'human beings were a great invention'.

In the guard's van introductions are brief and perfunctory but in their state of inebriation and jollity all introductions are unnecessary. Lisney is particularly aware of one of the women – 'She smiled as she passed me by. She is very very very beautiful.' He remembers kissing a girl for two hours on a wooden footbridge over a brawling mountain stream and knows it was 'as good as anything that had ever happened to him since'. Behind the good cheer, the drink, the songs, the loud comments, the old jokes retold, the sexual frisson are these images from the home place to which he is going, its 'lost happy September'. The story is like a Chinese box with one box inside another; it opens out and out, pulling rabbits of memory from the box of life. Kiely's mind is a magic chest in which it seems his entire past is packed and available.

Lisney, remembering the memories of the past now being recalled, thinks: 'These all were part of the furniture of my boyhood.' He remembers a poet he knows in Dublin ' a big, gentle, uncouth, splayfooted man touched by God', who told him he went home for last Christmas, a drink here, a drink there, several drinks at Amiens Street station, seven drinks with old friends in Dundalk, nine drinks with older friends at Blackhorse Halt, then 'out along the lonely road, suitcase in hand, running at the hills like a horse that knows he's nearing home, like a horse, he said'. The touch of desperation in that image is appropriate. The poet in Dublin and Lisney have a lot in common – the instinct to go home again, the uphill emotional struggle this involves, the undercurrent of anxiety that accompanies them.

At the end of the journey Lisney goes to bed with one of the girls from the van. He has a bottle of whiskey for his mother who now and then likes a sip of hot whiskey at bedtime with a spoonful of honey. He runs like a horse at the last hill, kisses his sister, a cold lifeless kiss. He has the whiskey and a Christmas cake given to him by the girl in the van, but he is late and the sister is unforgiving. 'She has found him alone in the cold kitchen by a black dead range, his overcoat still on, a glass of whiskey in his hand, the bottle open on the range, Joan's Christmas cake on the table, it is sleeting outside.' The imagery is a bleak comment on his return. His sister, he thinks, is as cold as the kitchen. He has no explanation for being late; the real reasons he cannot mention. Sorrow, regret and guilt take the place of the emotions of the guard's van. The house, he feels, is a tomb. His mother sleeps. He feels the need to communicate, but can't. So he walks back to the town to see a girl he once knew. She asks him 'How under God did you come to make a mess of your life?' There is no simple answer. The answer lies in the emotional complexity of this story.

Besides Dromore and Omagh in the years between the wars, Kiely has another setting and another time – Dublin in the 1950s and 1960s and the world of journalists in which he worked for many years. The portrait of Lisney is a link between the two. By the end we have a sympathetic picture, but, when he wants to, Kiely can be more critical. The man in the story 'Maiden's Leap' is an affected and unfeeling aristocrat, a successful writer who is isolated in his own snobbish world. He is fastidious to a fault and more distanced from reality than is good for a writer. The bubble in which he lives is unexpectedly burst when a body is discovered in his housekeeper's bed. Instead of telling her employer, the housekeeper has gone to the police station. A policeman comes to tell her employer.

> – She says, sir, there's a man dead in her bed.
> – A dead man?
> – The very thing, Mr. Macmahon.
> – In the bed of Miss Hynes, my housekeeper.
> – So she says, sir. Her very words.
> – What in the name of God is he doing there?
> – Hard to say, Mr. Macmahon, what a dead man would be doing in a bed, I mean like in somebody else's bed.

Mr Macmahon is aware that the guard is smothering his laughter and that the whole town will be discussing the story. Miss Hynes, we hear, has been his housekeeper and his father's before him; furthermore she is a distant relative. She has had her bedroom on the ground floor, its French windows he now thinks – for the first time in all those years – would give easy access for visitors to that bedroom. In this little detail we discover how little he has thought of her through the years, taking her service for granted, never considering her as a human being. When he and the guard go into the room, they note a smell. The guard remarks that he died sweating and is well tucked in, another little detail that leads us to think that she tucked him in after he died and before she slipped out to the police station. As instructed, the guard feels the man's heart and declares

> – Oh dead as mutton, Mr. Macmahon. Miss Hynes told no lie. Still, he couldn't die in a better place. In a bed, I mean.
> – Unhouselled, unappointed, unannealed.

The conversation veers off to other cases of men who died in compromising or unusual circumstances. We hear that when he was eighteen years of age Macmahon had tried to kiss the housekeeper, then a fresh-faced girl from the country and got a stinging slap on the face in return. Now as he rummages through her room he discovers a journal in which she has recorded an unflattering portrait of him in realistic Jamesian detail. Cuttingly she writes a title, 'Reflections on Robert the Riter...By his Kaptivated Kuntry Kusin!!!' The malice is clear, the mockery of the writer who lives in a dream world, who is she sees a literary construct and doesn't know people around him.

In this story Kiely is objective and detached, controlling not only the pace of the narrative but the tone, a mixture of irony, humour, and satire revealing the pomposity of the central figure, the growing contrast between the superficial outlook of this writer and that of the clear-eyed woman whose journal entries have bite. She has bite too in real life when she drops her pose of deferential housekeeper and speaks her mind, before departing from his service forever. The 'maiden's leap' is not only her sexual liaison with her lover, but her final leap to freedom from the humiliation of her relationship with her distant, stuffy, unsympathetic employer. By the end of the story Kiely has stripped away his pretensions and revealed him for what he is.

The ability to write accounts of sensitive and shy young men is found in a story with a different mood. Pike Hunter is a timid civil servant who falls in love with a prostitute in the story called 'A Ball of Malt and Madame Butterfly'. Before that happens he walks through Stephen's Green on a bright sunny day when the girls are lying back in the deck chairs revealing more than Pike, who has been raised by three virginal aunts, is accustomed to seeing. Blushing, he is 'alarmingly aware of the bronze knees, and more than knees, that the young ladies exposed as they leaned back and relaxed in their light summer frocks'.

As a portrait of a self-conscious young man who has been overprotected from the delights of the flesh this is deliciously comic, at once revealing and sympathetic. Before this shrinking violet meets the luxuriant Madame Butterfly, a vision of old-fashioned romance and idealised beauty walks before him down Grafton Street. He refers to the man as 'the poet' and recalls his famous entrances at the Abbey Theatre: 'And there he was now, hands clasped behind his back, noble head high, pacing slowly, beginning the course of Grafton Street.' Pike walks behind him, suiting his pace to the poet's, to the rhythms of the early poetry: 'I would that we were, my beloved, white birds on the foam of the sea.' They walk the literary walk by the statues of Goldsmith, Grattan, Thomas Moore until they come to Westmoreland Street and there the wonder happens – Maud Gonne herself, the woman Homer sung, now with sunken cheeks, lined and haggard, yet still the face of a queen, and dressed all in black. It is a stunning moment for this innocent and idealistic young man whose head is full of poetry. He stands still 'fearing that in a dream he had intruded on some holy place'.

Whatever it is, this cunningly wrought satirical portrait is not a good preparation for what happens to him when he enters the Dark Cow pub and into the real Ireland. There he sees Butterfly – a different kind of vision with her odd slanting eyes, black hair piled high, crossed legs, and knees that outshone the bright globes in the Green. It is all too much for Pike. Moved by a reckless courage he asks Jody the barman to ask the lady in the corner if he may have the favour of buying her a drink. Butterfly checks with the barman, asking if the man has money and on hearing that he does gladly accepts his invitation and in turn invites him to join her. The aptly named Pike is hooked. Butterfly, a fly-fisher of men, reels him in. Pike orders champagne, the only drink he thinks fit for such a queen, who if she didn't come from China at least came from Japan. But things are not what they seem or at least as they seem to Pike. Pike loves her exclusively, she likes him, shares her favours with him, but not exclusively – a girl has to make a living. He sticks to her like a barnacle and that's bad for business. Butterfly, who was a motherly sort of lover to him and a sympathetic listener, found him hard to take. 'Poor Pike, she'd say, he'd puke you with poethry. Poethry's all very well, but.' She had never worked out what came after that qualifying: 'But'.

It is a warm, powerful, inclusive, sad story of the good-hearted prostitute and the molly-coddled man who loves her. The odds are stacked against a happy ending. In the Dark Cow, while Pike and his new-found love sip champagne, he feels that he has found what an English poet had called the long-awaited long-expected spring. But into this idyllic scene comes Austin the fireman. Austin, Butterfly explained, died for Ireland. Be that as it may, he is now alive and well, sipping champagne, declaring that he died for Ireland not once, but several times, when it was neither popular nor profitable. The conversation turns bawdy. Butterfly stands up, kisses the fireman on top of his bald head, and begins to dance as her mother would have danced, up and down the floor, tight hips bouncing, fingers clicking, singing: 'I'm the smartest little geisha in Japan, in Japan. And the people call me Rolee Polee Nan, Polee Nan.' She sits down again breathless, suddenly kisses Pike on the cheek and says: 'I love you too. I love champagne. Let's have another bottle.' Pike is misty-eyed with love. Urged by the barman, Pike and Butterfly go upstairs.

They go on an outing to Howth, which is associated in his mind with W. B. Yeats, Maud Gonne, and others. It's poetry all the way with him spouting about Yeats, Joyce, and Spenser. She wears high heels and a fur coat; he is annoyed at that; she is annoyed she has to walk so much. Something comes over him and he tries to flatten her in the heather in full view of all Dublin. But, unlike Molly Bloom, who said yes, I will, yes, Butterfly says, no, I won't. That quarrel is the end; he leaves never to return.

This is rowdy, boisterous fun, Rabelaisian in its coarse exuberance. It is also a warm portrayal of humanity. All the characters in this story – Pike, Butterfly, Austin, Jody – have a consistent set of responses in keeping with the kind of people they are. But in terms of the conventions of the short story, as described by O'Faoláin, all this is unusual. Kiely not only reveals character through words and action, not only does he provide brief descriptive touches that enable us to visualise or imagine the character, but he describes characters at length, as though they were in a novel. Kiely, in this mode of expansive and inclusive narration, creates characters who are larger than life and who embody human attributes in a more than ordinary manner.

The mind of a Kiely narrator is often alive with allusions to literature, rhymes, poems, ballad, and song learnt in school. In the presence of these expansive narrators all this fits naturally and becomes part of the narrative, as in 'Near Banbridge Town' where the song is a running motif. The furniture of his mind, to use an image from one of his own stories, includes what one might call the normal baggage of someone who has been through an Irish education in Kiely's time. It is generally familiar, even though at times the songs are off the beaten track because drawn locally. The interior monologue, associated with James Joyce's *Ulysses*, fits Kiely's mind and Kiely characters, where digression, recall by association, and anecdotal illustration are natural to the character.

But there is another Joycean technique that Kiely avails himself of and that is the bird's eye view of character and place. We find it in 'A Letter to Peachtree', a story published in 1987 in the collection of that title. It is the final story in the *Collected Stories*, apart from the novella 'Proxopera', published in 1977. Written in the form of a letter to his wife from an American who is in Ireland doing research on the novels of Brinsley MacNamara, it has some of the discontinuity that letters may have, moving from one topic to another, pursuing asides, describing events and places, recording conversations, frankly amused and sardonic in tone, with vignettes of various people, and sharing private observations with his wife, things which, the fiction goes, could not be said in public even though they will be read by the public and with enjoyment of the slice of chaos that is the letter-writer's subject.

Part of the writer's point of view is that the Irish are a colourful lot given to stupendous and prolonged bouts of drinking and non-stop talk and not much troubled by morality. The American sees it with the clarity of the outsider and has the wisdom to recognise that what he witnesses may be thought of as 'a zany folktale from an island that once was, way out in the eastern sea. All parish priests and all that. And drink.' What he records, he asserts, is a genuine slice, or bottle, of old Ireland. The story is Kiely's farewell to what he has recorded in a lifetime of writing, a farewell to a country undergoing rapid change. Kiely is much possessed by life – in its plenitude and vitality, its capacity for colourful action, its delight in companionship, song, feeling, and storytelling. The very nature of his stories, so tumultuous in incident and so exuberant in conversation, so inventive embodies his vision of life. Life, he tells, 'is one long process of loss and attrition until life itself is also lost or worn away'. His middle-aged men who left home and wandered, drunkards, singers, lovers, raconteurs, embody his sense of humanity. This, he says, is the way we are – confused, comical, complicated, sometimes happy, often sad, aware of failings, seeking forgiveness in drink, in song, in love and romance, and most of all in the stories we hear and tell.

Note

1   All quoted selections are from *The Collected Stories of Benedict Kiely*, with an Introduction by Colum McCann (London: Methuen, 2001).

PART III

DEVELOPMENTS IN POETRY

9

AUSTIN CLARKE (1896–1974): AGAINST THE ODDS[1]

Austin Clarke is one of the most significant poets from the Irish Republic to emerge after Yeats. 'The Later Poetry of Austin Clarke', 1964, was Harmon's first published essay. Other studies were followed by an edited Special Issue of the Irish University Review, *1974, devoted to Clarke; by* Austin Clarke: A Critical Introduction, *1989; by more recent lectures and articles, and the Clarke entry in the* Dictionary of Irish Biography.

AS a child Austin Clarke was held aloft to see Queen Victoria on her last visit to Dublin; as a student at University College Dublin, he witnessed the Easter Rising of 1916; as a young man he went into exile as the Irish Free State emerged from the turbulence of the revolutionary period. When he returned in 1937 to live permanently at Bridge House, Templeogue, the middle-class values that would shape his country for the rest of his life were being enshrined in a new Irish Constitution.

Victorian values together with a conservative Catholicism dominated his lower middle-class home. His mother's stern morality compelled him to weekly confession and communion, but his first confession was traumatic: he was questioned insistently, within the confessional and then inside the vestry, about masturbation, until finally, in fear and bewilderment, he admitted to a sin wholly unknown to him. Thus began his long, unhappy relationship with the Catholic Church. His mother had little sympathy for his religious anxieties which increased during adolescence and he quarrelled with her incessantly. He had throughout his growing years a haunting fear of God's punishment and a disabling sense of his own unworthiness. Religious instruction at Belvedere College did not alleviate his worries, but there were happier experiences: stories told to him by his father and elder sister, visits to the countryside, playing the violin, and some of the more comforting rituals of the Church.

When he entered University College Dublin, his interest in literature and in the Irish language was deeply stimulated by Douglas Hyde's enthusiasm for the language and for Irish culture and by Thomas MacDonagh's personal interest in him. He discovered the world of the Irish Literary Revival and its mythological background, and realised he wanted to be a writer. He graduated with a first-class honours BA, went on to take a first-class honours MA, and was then appointed lecturer in English.

But, if his academic interests were advanced at university, his emotional life became unstable. Through a combination of circumstances – the ongoing struggle between the demands of Catholicism and his own growing independence of mind and spirit, his father's unexpected death, his mother's resistance to his intellectual searches, the excitements of nationalism, his imaginative immersion in Irish mythology, and his frustrated love for Lia Cummins – Clarke experienced a nervous breakdown that required over a year's treatment in St Patrick's Hospital. When he emerged, he married Lia, but the marriage was brief and unconsummated. He lost his job at the university, was disheartened by AE's (George Russell) dislike of *The Sword of the West*, 1921, and left Ireland to earn his living as a book reviewer in London.

His literary career had begun auspiciously. His first publication, *The Vengeance of Fionn*, 1917, was generally well received. He met most of the literary figures of the time, often at AE's literary 'evenings', and became friendly with his contemporary, F. R. Higgins. The promise of that first publication was undermined by the loss of control in the next two long narrative poems, *The Fires of Baál*, 1921, and *The Sword of the West*. When he went into exile the country's future, like his own, seemed bleak. The promise and idealism of the years between 1916 and 1922 were shattered in the bitterness and division of civil war. Clarke supported the Republican cause, but the Republicans suffered defeat and in the years immediately after the civil war the new Free State government dealt firmly with extremists.

Gradually, as peace was restored and, aided by the government's policy of encouraging native industry, a new, native middle class began to emerge. Its values were evident in a narrow-minded policy of literary censorship. Clarke's first two novels or prose romances, *The Bright Temptation*, 1932, and *The Singing Men at Cashel*, 1936, were banned. Ironically, they had been vetted under the obscenity laws in England and were found not to infringe them. Almost all of Clarke's early work was written in England, the poetry from *The Cattledrive in Connaught*, 1925, to *Pilgrimage*, 1929, the early plays, and the first two novels.

There can be little doubt that his years of exile were difficult in emotional and financial terms. He felt cut off from his natural sources of inspiration in Ireland. He returned frequently, to see his mother and sisters, to meet with literary friends, such as F. R. Higgins, Seamus O'Sullivan, and Padraic Fallon, to attend meetings of the Irish Academy of Letters, to visit places of historical and cultural interest in the countryside, to go to the Abbey Theatre. On one of these visits he had the good fortune to meet Nora Walker, who agreed to share his life in England. She was an intelligent, good-humoured, and resilient woman who gave him the love and stability he needed. He needed her support when he found himself omitted from W. B. Yeats's anthology, *The Oxford Book of Modern Verse*, 1936, and when his ambitious and highly personal work, *The Singing Men at Cashel*, fell apart in the final chapters. The publication of his first *Collected Poems* in the same year helped to restore his confidence. Life in England, however, became increasingly unsatisfactory, particularly with the signs of the coming war.

But, if life in England was difficult, the years after he and Nora returned to Ireland were even worse. They had three small sons to support and were very short of money, and Clarke, who was prone to recurrent depression, had another breakdown. The war cut off his sources of income from book reviewing in England. With the help of friends he got a regular poetry programme on Radio Eireann and regular book reviewing with *The Irish Times*. But his work suffered. After the agonised poetry of *Night and Morning*, 1938, in which he confronted the issue of intellectual freedom and clerical authority, he wrote no poetry until the 1950s. Together with the poet Robert Farren, he founded the Lyric Theatre Company in 1944 and for the next seven years they produced verse plays at the Abbey Theatre. Their aim was to continue the tradition of poetic theatre begun by Yeats, but their work met with only moderate success.

When Austin Clarke began to write poetry again in the 1950s he emerged as a different kind of poet: he wrote satirical comments on contemporary issues and autobiographical reflections. *Later Poems*, 1961, brought him a wider and more appreciative audience than he had previously had. The strength and vivacity of the later poetry is all the more remarkable when one remembers that he suffered a severe heart attack in 1956 and a slight one in 1958. As he grew older his mood lightened, his comic imagination, much in evidence in some earlier lyrics and plays, reasserted itself. He detached himself from the obsession with the problems of the Catholic conscience and wrote freely and with delight about many topics in a variety of styles. He confronted and exorcised the trauma of mental breakdown in *Mnemosyne Lay in Dust*, published on his seventieth birthday in 1966. He and Nora were familiar figures in Dublin, notably at the various events during the commemorations for Jonathan Swift in 1967 and for J. M. Synge in 1971. Clarke was invited back to University College Dublin by Roger McHugh to give a series of lectures. He received an honorary D.Litt. from Trinity College, a number of literary awards and was able to travel again to the continent, to England and to America.

In 1974 his second *Collected Poems* appeared and for the first time critics could assess the full range of his development as a poet. The Special Issue of the *Irish University Review*, which indicated how significant his work had become, appeared just after his death. When, as the editor, I took a copy to Nora at Bridge House, the birds were singing in the tall trees, the River Dodder sparkled under the stone arches of the bridge, but the kingfisher was nowhere to be seen.

* * *

The relevance of what Clarke wrote has been brought home to us at the end of the twentieth century in revelations in the media about cruelty in schools and orphanages. When people spoke of a silent Ireland in which no one complained publicly about what was being done in institutions run by Church and state, some remembered that Austin Clarke had not been silent. He had spoken out in *The Irish Times* and in his collections of satires. In the 1950s and 1960s he wrote about the inhumane treatment of unmarried mothers, about clericalism, and about unemployment and injustice. When former inmates of the orphanage at Castlepollard, County Westmeath, spoke on radio they might have quoted his poem, 'Unmarried Mothers', which deals with that particular institution:

> In the Convent of the Sacred Heart,
> The Long Room has been decorated
> Where a Bishop can dine off golden plate:
> As Oriental Potentate.
> Girls, who will never wheel a go-cart,
> Cook, sew, wash, dig, milk cows, clean stables
> And, twice a day, giving their babes
> The teat, herdlike, yield milk that cost
> Them dearly, when their skirts were tossed up
> Above their haunches. Hook or zip
> Has warded them at Castlepollard.
> Luckier girls, on board a ship,
> Watch new hope spraying from the bollard.[2]

In its compact lines it evokes the wealth of the Church, the work the girls had to do, and the price they paid. Ironically, some preferred to take their chances by leaving the country.

He voices his anger in 'Three Poems about Children'. When orphans were burnt to death in County Cavan, the local bishop said of them, 'Dear little angels, now before God in Heaven, they were taken away before the gold of their innocence had been tarnished by the soil of the world.'[3] These were heartless words. To emphasise their lack of compassion Clarke recalls how the Penal Church had responded to the 'misery' of its people:

> Better the book against the rock,
> The misery of roofless faith,
> Than all this mockery of time,
> Eternalising of mute souls.

'Those children,' he says, 'charred in Cavan, / Passed straight through Hell to Heaven.' But if certain areas of his work have a particular resonance in these years, his entire career is a record of what it was like to be alive in his Ireland. In one man's ongoing engagement with society we see the forces that were dominant and can determine their impact on individual lives. The need to liberate himself was central to his struggle for identity and self-reliance. His poem 'Ancient Lights' opposes his trust in the reality of this world to the promise of a better life in the next. It contrasts the daylight of personal freedom with the darkness of imposed fear. The images of fear recur: 'darkness / Was roomed with fears'. . . 'My fears were candle-spiked' . . . 'Confided / To night again, my grief bowed down.' At one point the poem recalls his first confession:

> Closeted in the confessional,
> I put on flesh, so many years
> Were added to my own, attempted
> In vain to keep Dominican
> As much i' the dark as I was, mixing
> Whispered replies with his low words;
> Then shuddered past the crucifix,
> The feet so hammered, daubed-on blood-drip,
> Black with lip-scrimmage of the damned.

Then the poem remembers the moment of release when he, 'a child of clay', learns not to be overwhelmed by fears but to rely on himself:

> Still, still I remember awful downpour
> Cabbing Mountjoy Street, spun loveliness
> Veiling almost the Protestant church,
> Two backyards from my very home,
> I dared to shelter at locked door.
> There, walled by heresy, my fears
> Were solved. I had absolved myself:
> Feast-day effulgence, as though I gained
> For life a plenary indulgence.

Clarke does this well. The poem draws upon personal experience, is exact in its use of detail and defines the moment. The note of self-mockery in the description of the confession prepares for the surge of freedom at the end, when, in a great natural baptism, his entire world is washed clear of fear, guilt, and confinement:

> The sun came out, new smoke flew up,
> The gutters of the Black Church rang
> With services. Waste water mocked
> The ballcocks: down-pipes sparrowing,
> And all around the spires of Dublin
> Such swallowing in the air, such cowling
> To keep high offices pure: . . .

Not all of Clarke's early memories are tainted with anxiety. He writes with affection about the Dublin of his boyhood, about Manor Street, Mountjoy Street, and the Black Church; about the sights and sounds of Edwardian Dublin and in particular about the horses that were such a familiar part of the city's life. When he was invited to take part in the Mermaid Poetry Festival in 1961, he read the autobiographical *Forget Me Not*, 1962, full of memories of that time. In it he adapts the well-known 'Horse's Prayer':

> Up the hill
> Hurry me not;
> Down the hill
> Worry me not;
> On the level,
> Spare me not,
> In the stable,
> Forget me not.

As a young man Clarke came under the influence of the Irish Literary Revival and the Gaelic League. His early works – *The Vengeance of Fionn*, the *Fires of Baál*, *The Sword of the West*, and *The Cattledrive in Connaught and Other Poems* – are epic narratives showing the influences of Yeats, Samuel Ferguson, and William Larminie. They are romantic and idealistic in tone, with a lyrical, impressionistic beauty, and reveal a delicate metrical skill. Like Yeats, Clarke went back to Irish myth and saga, to the Cuchullain and Ossianic cycles. But gradually he worked out an important, personal handling of the old material. Where Yeats had formulated a dichotomy between the pagan, aristocratic past and the democratic present, Clarke presented a contrast between the Christian, medieval past and the dogmatic, Catholic present. The most successful was the first, *The Vengeance of Fionn*. Sections of the others, *The Sword of the West* and *The Cattledrive in Connaught*, were moderately effective, but on the whole it was not a good beginning. Within their strange world of escape, wandering, and hallucination we may detect attempts by the young poet to deal with his emotional difficulties. By the time he wrote the more realistic and humorous *Cattledrive*, his style had recovered from the excesses of the previous narratives.

Short lyrics written during the same period are better controlled; they are musical and atmospheric in the manner of many poems of the Celtic Revival. Under the influence of the Gaelic League Clarke learnt Irish and imitated various kinds of Irish poetry, such as the *aisling*, the praise poem, the blessing, the curse, and the itinerary. He also wrote syllabic and assonantal poetry. The high point of this attention to the Irish past came in 1929 with the collection *Pilgrimage*.

Pilgrimage is interesting not only in its presentation of the medieval scene and its dramatic confrontation of Church teaching and natural law, but also because it shows Clarke's personal handling of metrical patterns based on Gaelic assonance and consonance. It was AE who first reminded him of William Larminie's theory that Gaelic assonance could be used in English to modulate rhyme. Clarke explains that in its simplest form Gaelic prosody allows the tonic word at the end of a line to be supported by assonance in the middle of the next line. In some forms only one part of a double-syllable word is used in assonance, providing partial rhyme and muting. Poetry of this kind, he feels, 'can have rhyme or assonance, on or off accent, stopped rhyme, (e.g. ring, kingdom; breath, method), harmonic rhyme (e.g. hero, window), cross-rhyme'. His poem 'The Scholar' illustrates some of these experiments.

> Summer delights the scholar
> With knowledge and reason.
> Who is happy in hedgerow
> Or meadow as he is?
>
> Paying no dues to the parish,
> He argues in logic
> And has no care of cattle
> But a satchel and stick.
>
> The showery airs grow softer,
> He profits form his ploughland
> For the share of the schoolmen
> Is a pen in hand....

He made use also of its denunciations of sexual pleasure in the early Church that paralleled what he heard in his own Catholic Church. The poem, 'Celibacy', portrays a cleric tormented by what Clarke called 'the bright temptation', meaning the female figure that tempts the ascetic who says 'I groaned / On the flagstone of help to pluck her from my body.' Within the broad canvas of his poems, prose romances, and verse plays Clarke drew extensively on the Hiberno-Romanesque period to reflect on his own time and to deal with personal issues. The central question for him was the conflict between individual liberty and clerical prohibition. That what was so natural should be so rigorously denounced was the paradox at the heart of his imaginative and moral life.

His prose-romance *The Singing Men at Cashel* is his major engagement with this issue. It is a deeply imagined exploration of the conflict as experienced by the beautiful, sensitive Gormlai. Married first to the scholar

king-Bishop of Cashel, Cormac mac Cuilleanáin, she is outraged and
ashamed by what she discovers of male, clerical denunciations of the so-
called evil nature of women. His dedication to spirituality finally drives her
from the marriage bed, where their union has not been consummated. Her
second marriage to the grossly physical Carroll, King of Leinster, is a horror
that affects her natural refinement. Seeking advice from the Church, she
comes up against a chillingly, unsympathetic male voice that commands her
to gratify Carrroll's sexual needs or be guilty of the adultery to which she will
drive him. Her third marriage to Niall Glundubh ends prematurely when he
is killed in battle, but it is a happy relationship based on mutual respect.
Unfortunately, the novel, richly sustained and intelligently managed up to
this point, breaks down here; her third marriage is not described.

Clarke's other prose romances, *The Bright Temptation*, 1932, and *The Sun
Dances at Easter*, 1952, are lighter in tone. The former is a lyrical allegory
about what adolescence and love would be like were they not impinged upon
by those who impute evil to them. Its young lovers, based on Diarmaid and
Grainne, triumph over the forces of evil, including excessive moralising. The
later novel, which interweaves a number of medieval tales, delights in love, in
life itself, and in the play of imagination with the material. It is one of
Clarke's happiest works.

The high point of Clarke's engagement with the struggle of the Catholic
conscience comes in *Night and Morning*,1938. Here he faces up to an issue
for which he can find no solution. On the one hand he wants to belong to the
Catholic Church, to share in the communion of the faithful. On the other he
is driven into conflict with its morality by virtue of his natural desires, and
into rebellion against its teaching by his need for intellectual inquiry. No
longer cloaking the issue in historical figures, Clarke draws from his own
experience, from deep within his own perplexities. That he uses the language
and imagery of the Church itself, its sacraments and devotions, its feast days
and religious objects, its theological arguments, its burden of sin and
redemption, its own history of conflict and debate make the poems deeply
authentic. Here Clarke takes his stand as a rebel within the Church and
asserts the right of private judgment. Even the compact, compressed style
reflects the tension between adherence and rejection, the painful division in
a man who wants to belong but is unable to do so on the Church's terms. We
hear the authority of the poet's voice:

> I know the injured pride of sleep,
> The strippers at the mocking-post,
> The insult in the house of Caesar
> And every moment that can hold
> In brief the miserable act
> Of centuries. Thought can but share

> Belief – and the tormented soul,
> Changing confession to despair,
> Must wear a borrowed robe.

He has been through Christ's agony, understands the message of salvation, but cannot give full assent. He may therefore be excluded from the benefits of Christ's death. Ironically, the kind of intellectual freedom he needs was once acceptable. At one time, 'when all Europe was astir / With echo of learned controversy, / The voice of logic led the choir'; in the disputations of the schoolmen one could go to God by the force of argument. Since the Council of Trent, however, the Church has expected submission, not argument, and that makes life difficult for someone like Clarke.

The issue turns up again in one of his greatest poems, the elegy 'Martha Blake at 51', in that deeply compassionate, pityingly honest portrait of a pious woman who gives her life to God, but who has little understanding of the spiritual crisis that others feel, including the mystics whose lives she reads and imagines in an unthinking, adolescent manner. She is an unquestioning Christian, without a doubt in her head:

> Waiting for daily Communion, bowed head
> At rail, she hears a murmur,
> Latin is near. In a sweet cloud
> That cherub'd, all occurred.
> The voice went by. To her pure thought,
> Body was a distress
> And soul, a sigh. Behind her denture,
> Love lay, a helplessness.

In a Church that presents her as the ideal there is little sympathy for the man or woman harrowed by questions. By being authoritarian the Church demeans the individual and creates an impoverished emotional and mental life. A childlike faith makes for a childish morality. The poem is effectively ambivalent in its portrait of a woman whose piety seems admirable, but is in fact meretricious. That her life should be a disappointment is perfectly judged. Clarke's compassion did not obscure his intelligence.

After the traumatic engagements of *The Singing Men at Cashel* and *Night and Morning*, Clarke continued to write plays, not poetry. Clarke's more serious plays also focus on the drama of conscience, and some have the kind of austerity of manner found in *The Singing Men at Cashel*. Several are set in the medieval period. His comedies are more attractive, in particular the trilogy of Pierrot–Pierrette plays written in the manner of *commedia dell'arte*. They are light, fanciful, and theatrical.

When he wrote poems again, in the early 1950s, he emerged as a poet of considerable power and within a few years had begun to gain international recognition. The new generation of poets and critics, at home and abroad, attended to what he had to say in a succession of limited editions: *Ancient Lights*, 1955, *Too Great a Vine*, 1957, *The Horse-eaters*, 1960. The new Clarke wrote an energetic poetry that relied on concrete words, active verbs, and a dramatising mode. Above all it was a poetry of deep and ongoing engagement with Irish society. The issues were often local, or transient, but the value of Clarke's voice at the time was that it externalised and clarified an independent, liberal, and humane response. He spoke for many who otherwise would not have had their feelings and instincts objectified. He was the conscience of his time.

He wrote two kinds of poems during these years: short lyrics about contemporary issues and long, autobiographical poems such as 'The Loss of Strength', 'The Hippophagi', 'The Disestablished Church', and 'Mnemosyne Lay in Dust'. These tell us what it was like to grow up in twentieth-century Ireland. He sometimes contrasts the eighteenth-century past with the Ireland of his own time, the outlawed Church of the Penal days with the powerful Church that he knew, the joyous emotional world of Hyde's Gaelic Ireland and the shame-faced emotional world of the present. Virtually all of Clarke's previous life and work prepared him for this. He knew what it was like to feel alienated, to be at odds with society, at odds with his Church. He knew the pain of isolation and therefore empathised with outcasts and victims. Whereas in the past he had taken refuge in myth and legend, in a reflected picturing, he now grounded his observations on what he saw around him. But he would not be excluded from or denied what he regarded as rightfully his. In legal terms the law of 'ancient lights' asserts the individual's right to light. In Clarke's work that right includes the light of the imagination, of truth, of justice, of God's love, of individual freedom, and the poet's right to artistic freedom.

As one might expect, the long, autobiographical poems are more complex than the lyrics. 'The Loss of Strength', for example, fuses the personal and the political. Clarke has had a heart attack, so that his own loss of strength is joined in the poem with other kinds of curtailment – political, cultural, and moral. The poem moves with great verbal and rhythmic energy, and with superb control of its twelve-line stanzas. It can be quietly reflective as in these lines about his former freedom to explore the countryside:

> Beclipped and confident of shank,
> I rode the plain with chain that freed me.
> On a rim akin to air, I cranked up....

References to the countryside in this poem, to places he had visited as a young man, such as the weirs at Castleconnell, Scattery Island, or Inish Cealtra, or places associated with myth and legend, such as the Falls at Assaroe or Sliabh Mis in Munster, bring another side of his work into focus. Nature is present throughout from the early narratives to the last poems. As a young man he wrote the magical description of Grainne in *The Vengeance of Fionn*:

> Flower-quiet in the rush-strewn sheiling
> At the dawntime Grainne lay,
> While beneath the birch-topped roof the sunlight
> Groped upon its way
> . . .
> Lazily she lingered
> Gazing so,
> As the slender osiers
> Where the waters flow,
> As the green twigs of sally
> Swaying to and fro.

The lyrics of the early period constantly evoke the subliminal presence of myth and legend within their accounts of actual places. The countryside is also a metaphorical element in the prose romances. His later poetry records what he heard and saw close to his home in Templeogue – the kingfisher along the river, the garden robin – 'our robin thinks we'll have rain' – the crow making his observant way across the countryside of south Dublin, the rooks in the trees about the house. He delighted in 'nature at jest in light and shade' and loved to walk along the banks of the Dodder, although they, too, were affected by restrictions:

> I cannot walk by the river now swishing
> The grass, far as the dart of the kingfisher,
> See cress, marsh-marigold, beyond the willow,
> Hazel, wild privet, for the fields are villa'd.

In 'Beyond the Pale' he records a journey with his wife, Nora. 'Pleasant, my Nora, on a May morning to drive / Along the roads of Ireland, going south . . .'. Even his last poem, 'The wooing of Becfola', 1974, turns to what had always attracted his imagination – the concept of the *faeth fiada*, that veil between this world and the Otherworld through which people gained access to the Land of the Ever Young, to a timeless world of beauty, where nothing wasted and died, where there was no sin and the imagination was free.

There are outstanding poems in the later period, such as 'Burial of an Irish President', a low-keyed response to the dishonouring of President

Douglas Hyde, who had been Clarke's teacher at university and whose work he admired. The setting, the event, the participants belong to what actually happened. The tone is subdued, the lines fall quietly down the page, rhymes beat a hollow drum-tap to dishonour and shame in a place where flags attest former courage and dedication, a place where God's 'word' should express an all-encompassing love. That absence reflects Ireland's sectarian, ungenerous state and a Church that forbids Catholics to attend Protestant services, even the funeral of Hyde, who had done the state honourable service. Since he was a Protestant, Catholics, with the exception of Austin Clarke and the French Ambassador, did not enter St Patrick's Cathedral to attend the funeral service. The VIPs waited outside, unresponsive to what Clarke calls 'the simple word from Heaven':

> ... The simple word
> From heaven was vaulted, stirred
> By candles. At the last bench
> Two Catholics, the French
> Ambassador and I, knelt down,
> The vergers waited. Outside.
> The hush of Dublin town,
> Professors of cap and gown,
> Costello, his Cabinet,
> In Government cars, hiding
> Around the corner, ready
> Tall hat in hand, dreading
> *Our Father* in English. Better
> Not hear that 'which' for 'who'
> And risk eternal doom.

The quiet mockery is more appropriate than the satire the occasion might have merited.

But Clarke's major poem of the period is *Mnemosyne Lay in Dust*, 1996, a confessional, psychological narrative which recreates his experiences in St Patrick's Hospital. It connects with other places in Clarke's poetry in which individuals undergo nightmarish experience. Here the individual suffers loss of identity and experiences terror. Maurice Devane enters the asylum, is treated and released. He has suffered from insomnia, depression, and loss of memory, but Mnemosyne, the goddess of memory, can be recovered. The account of his descent into the trauma of disorientation, hallucination, and self-questioning, his suffering and eventual recovery is a psychological narrative that enacts the fits and starts of Devane's progress. The poem's dramatic manner immerses us in Devane's agony, as in this intense description:

Straight-jacketing sprang to every lock
And bolt, shadowy figures shocked,
Wall, ceiling; hat, coat, trousers flung
From him, vest, woollens, Maurice was plunged
Into a steaming bath; half suffocated,
He sank, his assailants gesticulating,
A Keystone reel gone crazier;
The terror-peeling celluloid,
Whirling the figures into vapour,
    Dissolved them. All was void.

His disoriented consciousness engages us; we too, are plunged into the
abyss, we undergo his bewilderment, humiliation, and terror. We feel the
poignancy of his loss, are keenly attentive to the intermittent signs of his
recovery, and eventually walk with him gratefully back to the outer world.
'Rememorised, Maurice Devane / Went out, his future in every vein.' The
main measure of his recovery is his ability to relate rationally to everyday
experience.

The more joyous side of Clarke's imagination that had been much in
evidence in his earlier work, in his comedies, and in *The Sun Dances at
Easter*, re-emerges in his last poems, when the more exuberant side of his
temperament finds expression in a number of poems drawn from classical
and Irish mythology, such as *Tiresias*, 1971, and 'The Healing of Mis'
(*Orphide and Other Poems*, 1970), the former an amusing account of one
who was both a man and a woman at different times. Which, Clarke
playfully asks, the woman or the man, has the greater sexual pleasure? 'The
Healing of Mis' tells the story of the King of Munster's only daughter, who
fled to the forest, and is eventually restored to sanity and cleanliness by the
harpist Duv Ruis. Clarke gives a delightful, sensual and erotic account of
how this is done.

Daily he scrutinised, scrubbed her, rosied all her skin.
    They stayed in the mountain forest twelve weeks or
        more
Hugging his harp at night he lulled her to sleep. Then,
        thinly,
    Tried to serve the longing that woke her.

The story of Clarke's own recovery from the stresses and strains of his
early life may be read in his work, including the autobiographies, *Twice
Round the Black Church*, 1962, and *A Penny in the Clouds*, 1968. Fortunately,
he found an alternative to the constricting world in which he was reared. He
found the faith he needed in the writings of Eriugena, who argued that all

men are redeemed; everyone returns to God. That liberating philosophy underlies and sustains all Clarke's work from 'Ancient Lights' onward. The 'child of clay' in 'Ancient Lights' is able to frighten off the fabled bird. The ordinary individual, in other words, can escape the legacy of fear, if he relies on himself. Throughout his work, we are aware of Clarke's loss of strength, the burdens and deprivations he had to overcome permeate his work; but we are aware also of the persistence, the inner strength, which sustained him.

Notes

1 First given as a Thomas Davis lecture on RTE in 1996 to celebrate the centenary of Austin Clarke's birth, subsequently published in part as 'The Achievement of Austin Clarke' in *Etudes Irlandaises*, 23, 2 (Autumn 1998), pp. 27–37, and edited here.

2 Austin Clarke, *Collected Poems* (Dublin: The Dolmen Press, 1974). Subsequent citations are from this text.

3 *The Irish Times*, 26 February 1943.

10

PATRICK KAVANAGH: TOUCHED BY GOD

Read in Inniskeen, County Monaghan, at the Annual Patrick Kavanagh Weekend, 26–28 November, for the Centenary Celebrations, 1904–2004. The interpretive view of Patrick Kavanagh as 'fool' is first introduced in Harmon's Irish Poetry after Yeats, *and developed here. In the Introduction Harmon notes that Kavanagh's 'rural world added to Irish poetry'.*

BENEDICT Kiely once described Patrick Kavanagh as 'a big, gentle, splayfooted man touched by God'.[1] We say that someone is 'touched in the head', 'not all there', 'a fool', 'a bit of a natural'. Kavanagh portrayed himself as a 'fool', which was in keeping with Irish tradition where people saw the poet as a fool. To be 'touched by God' suggests contact with the spiritual and this, too, is in accordance with Irish tradition in which the poet was seen to be touched by the Otherworld.

When we say that someone is a fool, we mean that he is not fully in control of what he says or does, is different from ordinary people and does not behave normally. It is society, composed of so-called normal human beings, who decides what is normal and what is not. As a result the fool is both in society, yet outside it. He is like us but also not like us. He may be tolerated, looked down on, even feared, but he has freedom to say what he likes and to do what he wants; he has what is called in Shakespeare's time, a 'licence' to behave differently. In the Elizabethan period they made a distinction between the natural fool and the artificial fool, as they did in Inniskeen, when they spoke of an 'iron fool', one who pretends to be a fool in order to protect himself. Kavanagh might have called his memoir 'The Iron Fool', not *The Green Fool*, 1938, had he not felt that the implication in the title would have been lost on many people.

In the classic study of the topic, *The Fool. His Social and Literary History*, Enid Weldsford concludes, 'the fool was the truth-teller whose real insight was thinly disguised as a form of insanity'.[2] He is a truth-teller whose capacity for insight is disguised as a form of madness hidden behind the mask of an assumed foolishness. The mad fool may be a wise fool. Lear's Fool is an 'all-licensed' critic who sees and speaks the truth about others. In giving his property away, the King who ought to be wise behaves like a fool as the Fool tells him in a series of clever observations. 'The hedge-sparrow fed the cuckoo so long, / That it had its head bit off by its young' which is a tellingly exact metaphor.

This Fool is true to himself. He never pretends to be wise but he has insight. We expect him to behave foolishly, but he is wiser than the King. It is he who prophetically says to the King, 'Thou wouldst make a good fool.' Lear loses his wits as well as his possessions, and becomes a fool. It is he who arranges the foolish competition in which the daughters will heave their hearts into their mouths in false declarations of love, except Cordelia, who will not take part. Lear invites her:

> Lear.   What can you say to draw
>   A third more opulent than your sisters? Speak.
> Cordelia. Nothing, my lord.
> Lear.   Nothing?
> Cordelia. Nothing.
> Lear.   Nothing will come of nothing, speak again.[3]

The Fool and the King talk about this 'nothing'. The King, the Fool points out, has divided an egg in two and given both halves away, so is left with nothing. All his other titles he has given away. When the King asks, 'Who am I?' the Fool answers, 'Lear's shadow'; Lear is, in other words, the absence of substance and, therefore, nothing. As Frank Kermode observes in *Shakespeare's Language*, the Fool is both bitter and loyal. 'His master has reduced himself absurdly to a fool's role, and the Fool is now the source of wisdom fantastically delineating a world turned upside down.'[4] Ironically, as his wits start to leave him, Lear begins to see the truth about himself, helped on his road of discovery by the Fool's insights. It is an ongoing, pitiless exposure of foolishness in the rhymes and riddling speech of one who is not altogether fool.

If we go behind this compelling portrayal, we find a long tradition in which the fool is a silly or idiotic person, either a natural fool or an artificial fool. The assumption is that normal behaviour is not foolish and that foolishness is something we should avoid. But it is not that simple. Many writers have explored the shifting complexity involved, and the fool in literature becomes a complex figure, a role-player, a free spirit in a society that could not control him and in a society that also tolerated him. Fools became jesters or clowns. Kings liked to have them at court.

The word fool comes from the Late Latin *follis*, which means a pair of bellows, a windbag, related to Latin *flāre*, to blow. The fool is like a bellows, his words are only air; he looks and acts silly, and what he says is empty of meaning. But he is disturbingly unamenable to normal expectations. The fool's wind, as William Willeford says in 'The Fool and His Sceptre', 'scatters things and meanings yet in the confusion reveals glimpses of a nature which cannot be accommodated to rational understanding'.[5] That aspect of the fool, his freedom from accommodation, becomes a strength. When Kavanagh called himself a fool, he knew what he was doing.

It can be disturbing, this truth beyond rationality, delivered by a being that we think is an idiot; the word idiot itself comes from the Greek *idiōtes*, which means a private person, an ignoramus.[6] It is the essentially private nature of the fool that troubles us. We cannot reach it, cannot reason with it. Therein lies his strength. He is ultimately untouchable. We do not understand him, but he may understand us, as Lear's Fool does. As a result we may fear him.

His language is enigmatic; he speaks in riddles; he is a mystery. Fools babble, seem ignorant or drunken; drunkenness gives licence but it is also a state of possession, a state in which insight may be found.[7] The seeming fool may be wise. There is a huge irony here. The Fool's perception and under-standing seem to us to be uncoordinated and undignified, but he transcends these handicaps in brilliant moments of truth-seeing and truth-telling.

The concept of the Fool in English tradition is similar to the view of the Poet in Irish tradition. In *The Green Fool* Kavanagh portrays himself as the Fool. In the first place, he tells us, 'people didn't want a poet, but a fool, yes they could be doing with one of these. And as I grew up not exactly "like another", I was installed the fool . . . I was the butt of many an assembly . . . At wake, fair, or dance for many years I was the fellow whom the jokers took a hand at when conversational funds fell low. I very nearly began to think myself an authentic fool. I often occupied a position like that of The Idiot in Dostoevsky's novel.'[8]

In *Tarry Flynn*, 1948, the mother's view of Tarry is that he was a 'queer son in some ways. There was a kink in him which she had never been able to fathom.' 'Women thought him a little touched' when he made incomprehensible remarks. Others said, 'that man isn't like another' or 'This son of yours is a perfect fool, Mrs. Flynn. A perfect fool.' '"Who is he?" one asked, and the priest said, "He's an idiot called Flynn."' A clerk in a shop thought he was 'a bit touched'. Although this is fictionalised, we may take it that Kavanagh is drawing from actual experience.

He was different – uncoordinated, impractical, a dreamer, one given to strange expressions, a dabbler in poetry – the kind of person who could attract derision and could be bullied. But he makes the best of his situation. 'Being made a fool of', he says, 'is good for the soul . . . it makes a man into something unusual, a saint or a poet or an imbecile.'[9] It is a complex perception that shifts about as we try to fathom it: the experience of mistreatment and derision may result, Kavanagh says, in one becoming a saint or a poet or a fool. That conclusion keeps all three in the picture. To say that he became one does not totally exclude the others. What he claims is that he came through and gained something. He kept his integrity by turning abuse into something that was good for the soul. There was an area in his being which remained private and unaffected. There is, we may notice, no bitterness in Kavanagh's assessment of the consequences of being treated as a fool. We know that derision and suffering may result in spiritual benefit. The saint can absorb, even welcome, abuse, and turn it to his own advancement. Abuse and humiliation may drive another person mad. Kavanagh's summary encompasses all three possibilities.

His identification with Dostoevsky's *The Idiot* brings in the figure of the holy-fool. In Russian folk tradition, where they also make a distinction between the voluntary and involuntary fool, the holy-fool adopted the mask of idiocy, suffered derision and humiliation in order to achieve sanctity. Dostoevsky drew upon this concept in the creation of Prince Myshkin, the seeming fool who embodies Christian values and experiences ecstatic vision. Kavanagh's identification with him resonates with his claim that the roles of poet, fool, and saint are inextricably mixed. All three are connected with the transformative power of the creative imagination. Fools speak in riddling words, as do poets and saints; fools have remarkable insight, as do saints and poets; all three are associated with a carnivalesque spirit that turns the normal world on its head.[10] When Kavanagh calls his memoir *The Green Fool*, the title is knowingly ambivalent. Green suggests inexperience but also renewal. When we say someone is green, we mean he has not learned to cope with situations or people. The fool is green in the sense of being innocent but also in the sense of having insight, being resilient, transcending difficulty.

In a way Kavanagh was unlucky. They already had a poet in Inniskeen – John McEneaney, the Bard of Callenberg. A versifier and balladeer who focused on local events and local people, he was feared for his satirical powers. They knew that if they annoyed him he might publish a satire on them in the *Dundalk Democrat*. Even more worryingly, his humorous, rhyming satires were easy to remember and could be recited locally. He queered the pitch for Kavanagh, who called him 'a rapscallion, a scandal-monger making rhymes about the neighbours'. Everyone, he said, thought he would turn out like the Bard.[11] When his parents heard that Patrick was writing poetry, 'quite a lot of terror filled their hearts'.[12] Although McEneaney had been to Scotland, England, and America, he used local terms in his poetry and this raises the possibility that as Kavanagh matured he chose his language with an outside audience in mind. When Kavanagh began writing, there was not much difference between some of what he wrote and what McEneaney wrote.

When McEneaney got married, he wrote a poem about the rejected suitor.

> A look of sorrow lingered on Owen's wrinkled brow
> Like rain fell down his tears
> But his offer she had spurned
> For he was advanced in years.

Once when he sued a neighbour, he addressed the court in rhyme.

> My heart with indignation swells
> As I state my case to Mr. Wells
> Alas to tell how I was done
> By Pat the Miser and his son.

Unfortunately, he lost the case. Mr Wells may have been a better judge of poetry than McEneaney realised. Kavanagh also wrote directly about local matters.

> Farrelly climbed in the window
> But Dooley fell back with a shout
> And the singing and ructions were dreadful
> Around the half-barrel of stout.[13]

Believe it or not there is a variant reading of this verse:

> Farrelly climbed in by the window
> But Dooly fell back with a souse
> And the singing and shouting was terrible
> Around the half-barrel of stout.[14]

They did not want another poet in Inniskeen, since they already had the Bard, but could, Kavanagh said, accept a fool. In effect the terms fuse – we have the poet as fool and the fool as poet. 'I have a belief', Kavanagh wrote, 'in poetry as a mystical thing, and as a dangerous thing... poetry made me a sort of outcast. And I was abnormally normal.'[15]

Kavanagh's description of himself as the fool accords well with the many accounts of the poet in Irish tradition, as does the people's suspicion and fear of poets. Traditionally the poet behaved unusually and this in itself set him apart; he had inspired speech, was touched in the head, had contact with the Otherworld, got his knowledge from a solitary fairy woman from the Otherworld or from the fairies. When composing, he was in a state of abnormal mental activity, a frenzy or madness, he had 'ecstatic wisdom' or *buile*, which refers to the vision of the frenzied poet. He also had *fios*, which meant not just knowledge but occult wisdom. His enigmatic speech was a sign of this. People appreciated the poet's ecstatic fervour but also feared it; they did not want their children to be poets, fearing the risk of being close to the spirit world, affected by its powers, but also in danger from them.[16]

Sometimes the poet's gift comes from a visit to the Otherworld or from a meeting with a figure from there, usually a beautiful woman. Turlough O'Carolan was believed to have got his gift while sleeping on a fairy fort. The same was said about Seamus Dall Mac Cuarta from Oriel. It is a mystic experience. There are many stories about this. Seamus Martin from Oldcastle, for example, fell asleep on Loughcrew and when he awoke found a sword, a set of bagpipes, and a book beside him. He picked up the book and knew all languages, was a great scholar and a gifted poet. James Tevlin from Moynalty, County Meath, also got his gift from the Otherworld. As late as 1948 a local man explained what happened: it was after Tevlin met with an accident that he started to make poetry. One night he was coming the road, and he met a black dog. The dog made for him; he tried to strike it with a bridle he had in his hand but it 'wasn't a right dog was in it, for the bridle went through it and hit Tevlin on the knee'. The blow injured the knee, so during the seven years he was in bed he started making poetry and composed most of his songs. Even if Tevlin did have an accident, in the folk mind it was the dog from the Otherworld that caused it and while recovering from this mysterious accident he got the gift of poetry. He was on the edge of the Otherworld, a risky place for him but also the place of empowerment.[17]

This is the kind of material that Kavanagh knows. His awareness of tradition is evident in *The Green Fool*, where he sees Monaghan as a place where Gaelic culture was once strong. The memoir is a literal account of things done and said, the way of life in the rural community and its cultural environment, but with an emphasis on the magical, the mysterious, and the traditional. Incidentally, *Tarry Flynn* and *The Green Fool* are prescribed reading for students of folklore.[18]

When he describes a pilgrimage to Lady Well, he sees it as a tradition that has survived from the pagan past. 'Every year', he says, 'all the neighbours around me went there and carried home with them bottles of its sacred waters. These waters were used in time of sickness whether of human or beast. Some folk went barefoot and many went wearing in their boots the traditional pea or pebble of self-torture.'[19] They take the *Bohar Bhee*, the pilgrim's road that keeps away from the clever villages that scoffed 'at ancient holiness'. There are, he notes, no priests or monks involved. To them the well is a pagan well from which the Fianna drank 'in the savage heroic days'. The people on the other hand believe St Bridget washed her feet in it. The pilgrims around the well are like medieval pilgrims; some making stations, some doing a bit of courting under the pilgrim cloak, some bargaining, some throwing clods at the pilgrims. The well is supposed to rise at midnight; people get excited; they begin to fill their bottles.

Another sense of the past comes in his reference to the 'romantic people of the roads', beggars with distinctive names: Biddy Dundee, Barney the Bottle, Paddy the Bread. 'Those old folk of the roads', he remarks, 'were living records of a poetry-loving people.' The Gaelic world may have passed but the countryside held remnants of story, songs, poems, custom, and tradition. Kavanagh recalls 'the days when there was poetry in the land'.

In 1911, when Kavanagh was 7 years old, the population of Inniskeen was 1,179, down from almost 3,700 before the Famine; of the 199 people over 60, 43 were Irish-speaking, survivors of a generation born during or not long after the Famine which was also known as the Great Hunger. It has also been called the Great Silence, because of its effect on language and culture, song and story. But these things are hard to kill off; they linger in the mind and the memory; tradition-bearers keep them alive and pass on what they know to the next generation.

Inniskeen is part of the old kingdom of Oriel that stretches from Inniskeen to the sea, to Dundalk and Carlingford Lough. In *A Hidden Ulster, People, Songs and Traditions of Oriel*, Pádraigín Ní Uallacháin gives information about eight people from the barony of Farney who contributed to the song tradition in Irish in the early decades of the twentieth century: Owen Byrne, Mrs Goodman, Thomas Meehan, Eilise and Tomás Mac Gruadair, Séamus Ó Cruadhlaoich, Eoghan Mac a' Bhaird, Tomás Ó Corragáin, Mary McMahon. In 1913 Éamonn Ó Tuathail declared that no other place in Oriel had more Irish than Farney, although it was seldom used. Kavanagh mentions two brothers and their two nieces who spoke Irish. There were still Irish speakers in Donaghmoyne and Inniskeen in 1931. The last known Irish speaker in County Monaghan was Dónal Tuite from Inniskeen, who died in 1957 at the age of 82. Tomás Ó Corragáin from Lisdoonan stayed alive so that he could pass on Séamus Dall Mac Cuarta's poem '*An Dán Breac*' to the collectors.

Ní Uallacháin's aim, she says, 'is to enliven the memory of the men and women who lived here the day before yesterday; who carried the songs orally for centuries and who, despite many deprivations and hardship, held fast to their individual and collective voice through song, for as long as possible'.[20] She pays tribute also to the collectors who went about the hills and valleys 'with a desperate zeal' to gather what survived before the tradition-bearers finally passed away. 'This story', she says, 'also reveals the thread of connection and circumstance which has kept the southeast Ulster song tradition alive in a fragile, but nonetheless continuous, unbroken, oral tradition.'[21]

Her collection of songs, singers, collectors, and mss. provides a context for Kavanagh's years in Monaghan. His poem 'Art McCooey' takes on a particular resonance when we remember that Art MacCumaigh was a popular poet in County Armagh and elsewhere in Oriel. At least nine of his poems survived in the songs of southeast Ulster. He wrote satires, praise poems, and vision poems, was regarded as a poet of the people, and lamented the loss of the O'Neills of Glassdrumman. His '*Úirchill a' Chreagáin*' is part of our consciousness. Kavanagh calls this poem 'whimsical' and criticises MacCumhaigh because he does not do what the true poet does, that is, 'name and name and name with love the obscure places, people or events'.[22]

Ag úirchill a' Chreagáin sea chodail mé aréir faoi bhrón
Is le héirí na maidne tháinig annir fá mo dhéin le póig,
Bhí gríosghruaidh ghartha aici agus loinnir ina céibh mar ór,
'S gurbh é íocshláinte an domhain a bheith ag amharc ar a' ríon óig.

By the graveyard of Creggan I slept last night in grief;
At day break a fair maid came towards me with a kiss;
Her rosy cheeks were glowing and her hair a golden sheen;
A healing balm for everyone to gaze on this young queen.[23]

MacCumaigh's poem follows the conventions of the *aisling*: the beautiful woman wants the poet to go with her to the land of honey where the stranger has no sway; he asks if she is Helen of Troy or why should she choose him; she replies that she is from the fairy world, she inspires poets, she lives with royalty – in Tara and Tyrone; he laments the passing of the O'Neills of the Fews; she grieves for the losses at Aughrim and the Boyne; he is reluctant to leave his friends and his young wife; she points out he is poor and distressed, it is better to go with her; he agrees but insists on being buried with the Gaels of Creggan.

A théagair 's a chuisle, más cinniúin duit mé mar stór;
Tabhair léigse is gealladh damh ar maidin sul má dtéim sa ród,
Má éagaim fán tSeanainn, i gcrích Mhanainn nó san Éiphte mhór,
Gurb ag a Gaeil chumhra an Chreagáin a leagas tú mé i gcré faoi fhód.

My beloved one, if destiny has fated me to be your own:
Guarantee and promise me before I take the road at dawn;
Should I die in Egypt, by the Shannon, or Manaan's Isle,
That with the Gaels of Creggan you will bury me in soil.[24]

Ironically, although he was duly buried in Creggan and the tomb was described sixty years later, it was then lost only to be rediscovered again in 1971 for the bicentennial of his death. A new headstone was erected in his memory, unveiled appropriately by Señorita Conchita O'Neill from Seville.

Kavanagh's 'Art McCooey' counters what he calls 'whimsicality' by ignoring the O'Neill connections and by naming local people and places. The aesthetics of mud and dung and the politics of the local and actual counter the mannered commemoration of lost leaders.

Down the lane-way of the popular banshees
By Paddy Bradley's; mud to the ankles;
A hare is grazing in Mat Rooney's meadow;
Maggie Byrne is prowling for dead branches.[25]

This refusal to celebrate the past is in keeping with his declaration that gods make their own importance and his dismissal of the commemorative habit in poets of the Irish Literary Revival: 'We sailed in puddles of the past / chasing the ghost of Brendan's mast.' Kavanagh's literal naming of places also counters Yeats's romantic evocation of place. It was part of his assertion of difference and independence.

In the McCooey poem he and another 'fiddle folly': 'We exchanged our fool advices back and forth', 'We played with the frilly edges of reality.' This is part of what it means to be a fool, to go beyond what is real to where poetry is 'shaped...Unlearnedly and unreasonably'. To be a fool, to be *idiōtes*, is to be released into a world where the imagination is supreme, where one can 'fiddle folly'. There one can be fool, saint, and poet. It is in this sense that Kavanagh identifies with Dostoevsky's Idiot, the seeming fool who becomes a model of Christian sanctity.

It is true that Kavanagh as a poet did not make much use of the historical and mythical associations of the place he grew up in. But Inniskeen is not without history. From there you can see The Hill of Slane, the plain of Muirthemne, the *Slighe Midluachra* (one of the four ancient roads), Ardee (The Ford of Ferdia). Sliabh Gullion is only ten miles away. The Kavanagh brothers made a point of climbing this mountain, which because of its mythical associations Kavanagh called the sacred mountain and a place of mystery.[26]

He makes the connection with the past in his own way, as here through the title of a poem and associations with a certain kind of poet. *The Green Fool* notes the presence of a vanishing Gaelic tradition: 'The ghost of a culture haunted the snub-nosed hills.' His place names are literal, but when he mentions the Fetearna Bush, Gortin, Glassdrumman, many are Irish names and many have associations in history and folk tradition. He notes 'the evocative poetry of place names': Fegevla, Shancobane, Oghil Cross, Baragroom.[27] He knows that the MacMahons, chiefs of Farney, are buried in Inniskeen. A poet may live beside a round tower or a monastic ruin or beside an ancient road and not make use of them in his poetry, but this not mean that they are not part of his consciousness or have no influence on how he sees the world. He is very aware of what has gone, of the diminishments, both cultural and spiritual, that have taken place. 'The hunger', he says, 'had killed our poetry.' This is Maguire country, place of the strangled impulse. Kavanagh laments that in his time, 'There was no love of beauty.' Underlying his poetic account is a regret that so much had been lost.

Nothing is stronger in Kavanagh's work than the instinct to counter that loss by a transformative love of nature, the fields and furrows, the whins, light striking on landscape. When he writes about Rocksavage in *The Green Fool*, it becomes a fine place for a dream-wanderer, that is, for someone like him. 'The whins on the Fort Hill', he says, 'grew ten feet high, and in between them were magical countries where cowslips and banshees' thimbles grew' (i.e. the wild foxglove). The world of Rocksavage, he declares, was boundless and uncharted as the broad places of the imagination: 'Time had no say in that place, a day could be as long as a dream. We were in the Beginning, before common men had driven the fairies underground.'[28]

It is as though Kavanagh goes beyond the *faeth fiada*, crossing to the Otherworld, as in old Irish stories where it was believed that there was an Otherworld, peopled by the Tuatha Dé Danann. There are many accounts throughout the early Irish and medieval period in which people crossed into this other place which was timeless, a land of the ever young, *Tír na nÓg*, The Land of Promise, where flowers are always in bloom and fruit always hangs from the boughs. In his lyrics Kavanagh recalls an edenic world, edenic not only because of its capacity to provide enjoyment, a sense of personal identity and fruitful connection, but because it has this subliminal and ancient presence.

The persona in several lyrics accords well with the sense of freedom and lightness associated with the fool. In fact the fool is untouchable. He is the *idiōtes* whose privacy is ultimately beyond reach. Nobody can pluck out the heart of his mystery. When Kavanagh maintains that being made a fool of is good for the soul, he expressed the paradox at the heart of his role as Fool and Poet, the mystical centre in which he eludes analysis and escapes definition. When he associates himself with Dostoevsky's Idiot, he is identifying with the figure of the poet as fool, with his openness to experience and the innocence which protects him.

In 'Verses from *Tarry Flynn*', released now from the cramped style of his early work, including those verses that resembled ones written by McEneaney, he has a buoyancy of mood and an independence of spirit that enable him to turn the place and the work about to be done into joyous experience. He walks 'Through fields that were part of no earthly estate'.[29] Father Mat stares through gaps at 'ancient Ireland sweeping / In again with all its unbaptized beauty.' The transformative impulse in 'A Christmas Childhood' permeates the natural setting; the child sees 'the transfigured face / Of a beauty that the world did not touch.' In 'The Long Garden' they dipped their fingers in the pockets of God, a case not so much of being touched by God as of touching God in an act of union and communion. This driving, passionate certainty is Kavanagh's strength. In it he makes the natural and the ordinary into the marvellous and the mystical. In 'Spraying the Potatoes' he praises the scene, the lazy veil of woven sun akin to the imagination in its animating transformations, and places himself happily in the picture: 'And I was there.' In walking through fields of no earthly estate he evokes an Otherworld of the imagination.

In his day Fairyland was not far away. In the folklore of the nineteenth and early twentieth centuries the experience of contact with the fairy world is recurrent. Kavanagh gives his experience in a chapter called 'Fairyland'. He drives his mother by donkey and cart to visit friends in Mullacrew. Going there is no trouble but the way back is difficult. They have great trouble in finding the right road. They ask directions but are given misleading advice. When they wander about country roads and cannot find the right way they know they are in Fairyland. 'Everything', Kavanagh says, 'seemed strange. The folk we saw were not ordinary mortals.'[30] They give the donkey his head; he brings them safely home. The neighbours understand.

> When old George heard the tale he felt like Saint Thomas when that Doubter who didn't doubt (Dostoyevsky was right, Saint Thomas believed all along) put his fingers into the wounds of Our Lord.
> 'Paddy', George stared at me, 'ye were with the Wee Fellas'.
> 'Only for the ass we'd never escape', I said.
> 'Indeed you would not', he supported, 'sure the ass is a blessed animal'.[31]

In Irish tradition the ass was associated with folk medicine, with cures for whooping cough, jaundice, and other illnesses. It was believed that he provided protection against the powers of the Otherworld; there was also the well-established belief that he got the cross on his back from the time he carried Christ into Jerusalem.

In Kavanagh's opinion the 'gods of poetry' pour their gifts of language, transcendent power, and the awareness of beauty on the young poet.[32] It is a natural gift, one not acquired through education or study. The poet is born, not made, he is touched by God and untouchable.

Notes

1   *Collected Stories of Benedict Kiely* (London: Methuen, 2001), p. 538.
2   (London: Faber and Faber, 1935), p. 237.
3   Frank Kermode, *Shakespeare's Language* (London: Allen Lane, 2000), p. 186.
4   Kermode, p. 186 and *passim*.
5   A. Willeford, *A Study in Clowns and Jesters and Their Audience* (London: Edward Arnold, 1969), p. 10.
6   Willeford, p. 13.
7   Willeford, pp. 27–9.
8   *The Idiot* (Penguin Books, 1975), p. 10.
9   *The Green Fool* (London: Michael Joseph, 1938; New York: Harper and Brothers, 1939), p. 10.
10 Faith Wigzell, 'Dostoevskii and Russian Folk Heritage', *The Cambridge Companion to Dostoevskii*. ed. W. J. Leatherbarrow (Cambridge: Cambridge University Press, 2000), p. 40.
11 *Collected Pruse* (London: MacGibbon and Kee, 1967), p. 65.
12 Peter Kavanagh, *Sacred Keeper* (The Curragh, Ireland: The Goldsmith Press, 1979), p. 28.
13 *Sacred Keeper*, pp. 29–30.
14 Antoinette Quinn, *Patrick Kavanagh: A Biography* (Dublin: Gill & Macmillan, 2001), p. 52.

15   Introduction to *Collected Pruse*, xiii.

16   Dáithí Ó hÓgáin, 'The Visionary Voice. A Survey of Popular Attitudes to Poetry in Irish Tradition', in *Image and Illusion: Anglo-Irish Literature and its Contexts: A Festschrift for Roger McHugh*, Maurice Harmon (Portmarnock: Wolfhound Press, 1979), pp. 44–61.

17   Séamus Mac Gabhann, 'Continuity and Tradition in the Poetry of James Tevlin [1798–1873]', *Ríocht na Midhe*, XVI (2005), pp. 83–104.

18   Interview with Chris McCarthy, Folklore Department, University College Dublin, 25 November 2004.

19   *The Green Fool*, p. 51.

20   *A Hidden Ulster: People, Songs and Traditions of Oriel* (Dublin: Four Courts Press. 2003), p. 16.

21   Ibid., p. 16.

22   'Patrick Kavanagh on Poetry', *The Journal of Irish Literature*, ed. John Nemo, VI, 1 (January 1977), p. 70.

23   *A Hidden Ulster*, pp. 250–51.

24   Ibid., pp. 250–2.

25   *Collected Poems*, ed. Antoinette Quinn (London: Allen Lane, 2004), p. 42.

26   Peter Kavanagh, *Patrick Kavanagh Country* (The Curragh, Ireland: The Goldsmith Press, 1978), p. 11.

27   *Collected Prose*, p. 39.

28   *The Green Fool*, pp. 64–5.

29   'Verses from *Tarry Flynn*', called 'Threshing Morning', *Collected Poems*, ed. Antoinette Quinn, pp. 112–13.

30   *The Green Fool*, p. 82.

31   Ibid., p. 200.

32   Ibid., p. 82.

11

JOHN MONTAGUE: 'RESTLESS SPIRIT'[1]

In examining John Montague's latest collections, this essay develops many of the thematic and individual characteristics first detailed in the selections included in Irish Poetry after Yeats, *and notes additional strengths in the poetry. Whether it explores a concern for the past in the region of his childhood, a sense of alienation, or the complex experience of love, the poetry is reflective.*

FROM the beginning John Montague's poetry has been concerned with a few basic issues – aesthetics, love, and Ireland. Although art as a subject is not the most prominent or most permanent issue in his poetry, it is central to his poetic life. The images in 'A Chosen Light' define an aesthetic that informs his work. Standing at the door of the *atelier*, the poet, sensitive to the processes of nature, smells the earth and interprets its activities: fresh green 'tendrils' 'plaited' across the 'humus', 'desperately frail' in their 'passage against / The dark, unredeemed parcels of earth'.[2] Purity of image and line is characteristic of his poetry.

Among the delights of the lines in this poem are their slow progress and the exactness with which the scene is depicted. It is not only pictured, but discloses the poet in relation to it. What he observes is enacted in the rhythm of the lines which by delaying the movement enable us also to focus on a sensual experience. The attribution inherent in words like 'frail', 'dark', 'unredeemed', and the carefully chosen 'desperately' ensures that the struggle and risk in nature suggest the human condition as well. The poem is particularly attentive to 'white light', 'silence', 'stillness', all preparatory for the central point:

> In that stillness – soft but luminously exact,
> A chosen light – I notice that
> The tips of the lately grafted cherry-tree
>
> Are a firm and lacquered black.

This delicately crafted lyric is an *ars poetica*. It stands for his kind of poetry, the ideals of his craft. The other two parts of the poem also focus on craft and endurance through the example of the exact and exacting art of Samuel

Beckett, the delicate synchronisation of the watch and the 'pale light' cast over unhappiness. Creativity and suffering intertwine.

In 'The Water Carrier', as he recalls a daily task, Montague acknowledges the source of his poetry in memory and landscape. It is a different kind of poem from 'A Chosen Light', being devoted more to the expression of insight than to the harmonies of vision, but it is also about the art of making poetry. He had, he says, hoped to stylise the scene. Instead, he is distracted, 'entranced by slight but memoried life'.

> I sometimes come to take the water there,
> Not as return or refuge, but some pure thing,
> Some living source, half-imagined and half-real,
>
> Pulses in the fictive water that I feel.

The images are clear, the description carefully shaped, the sensual connection evident all along the more-expanded line and in the flowing pace of the stanzas. But it is the concluding lines that carry the significant resonance: the self 'entranced', not by large vision, but by slight or frail things he remembers and by the half-mystical presence that emanates from this 'lively scene' which is created in part by actuality, in part through fiction, that is by the operation of the creative imagination. In poems like 'A Chosen Light' and 'The Water Carrier' the poet apprehends a scene in its particularity, recreating and repossessing it, discovering a personal truth in the exact focussing. The process moves beyond description.

In these poems there is often a genuine and slow repossession of that to which he belongs. Memory circles back to origins, the family farm in County Tyrone, the landscape, the Northern world, former loves, and moves away again. Poetry is created in the space between these two, out of their interaction. The universe of his imagination is extensive and layered; he inclines towards the extraction of insight from experience. There are times when he would make a myth of his own experience, there are times when he would place it within a larger, defining, and expanding context, such as the Troubles in Northern Ireland. But in particular he likes to retrieve and recreate experience by allowing language to have freedom and fluency. He is an image-maker who likes to name things rather than a narrative or philosophical poet and moves towards epiphany by indirection and intuition, rather than by argument or logic. The notion of frailty recurs – in the slightness of things that hold his attention; the fragility of old women; the sense of a rough world recurrently broken by warfare, sectarianism, progress, cultural losses; the perception of a personal world recurrently harmed by man's capacity for hurt.

'The Trout', a formal poem, is keenly attentive to what is happening; the rhythm of the run-on lines holds the occasion in suspension. The poet is once again in close communion with nature, indeed is able to catch the fish with his bare hands because he understands, is in tune with, the trout's habitat – 'where he lay, light as a leaf, / In his fluid sensual dream'. The poem moves calmly in slow motion, mimicking what it describes, able thereby to bring into existence the idea of being 'preternaturally close', 'bodiless', casting 'no shadow' – all this part of the revelation, the epiphany – and then broken by the 'terror' of the conclusion, the gripping of the alive creature.

> Bodiless lord of creation,
> I hung briefly above him
> Savouring my own absence,
> Senses expanding in the slow
> Motion, the photographic calm
> That grows before action.

Many of Montague's poems have this stylised exactness: 'Woodtown Manor' (with 'And all the menagerie of the living marvellous'), 'The Road's End' (with its 'Croziered / Fern, white scut of *ceannbhán*'), and 'Like Dolmens Round My Childhood The Old People', where the human figures are encysted on the landscape.

> Ancient Ireland, indeed! I was reared by her bedside,
> The rune and the chant, evil eye and averted head,
> Fomorian fierceness of family and local feud.
> Gaunt figures of fear and of friendliness,
> For years they trespassed on my dreams,
> Until once, in a standing circle of stones,
> I felt their shadows pass
>
> Into that dark permanence of ancient forms.

By giving them a presence in his poetry, he achieves a kind of exorcism; instead of haunting him in his dreams they become externalised in the durability of stone.

The delicate, tentative approach also characterises the love poems. Wary of excess, he shows restraint in tone and line, his lyric grace suited to the theme. At the same time, showing an indebtedness to Robert Graves's *The White Goddess*, to David Jones's *In Parenthesis*, and Carl Jung's *Archetypes of the Collective Unconscious*, his love poems sometimes convey a sense of a hinterland of archetypal reference and myth. 'All Legendary Obstacles' combines a credible portrait of separated lovers coming together. She has travelled across the American continent to where he waits in San Francisco.

The literal details of man and station, chilled hands meeting and emotion so strong it cannot be articulated are affected by the manner in which other images are presented – the 'long imaginary plain', the 'monstrous ruck of mountain', the 'hissing' of 'winter' rain, the compelling trains, the ominous black porter, a Charon figure, and the magic circle the old lady makes. Out of the ordinary human experience of separated lovers the poem adduces mythological accounts, the archetypal myths of separated lovers, such as Orpheus and Eurydice, the transcontinental crossing a journey to the Underworld, the trains a funereal cortège.

John Montague's lyric strength is evident in many of the love poems in *Tides*, 1971, where the line itself becomes short, pliant, and taut as though this rhythmic tension, the syllabic control, is the most appropriate means of expression for the many emotions present in the relationship between two people. Even the ampersand is brought into use as though the word 'and' were too slack a connector for the feelings involved. The clear and chastened language contributes to the curtailment of the space in which the poem moves. The tightness other poets might find restrictive is made part of the aesthetic.

>a pale radiance
>glossing the titles
>behind your head
>
>& the rectangle
>of the bed where,
>after long separation,
>
>we begin to make
>love quietly, bodies
>turning like fish
>
>in obedience to
>the pull & tug
>of your great tides.

That this entire section is made up of one sentence and that there are only four syllables in each line is part of the effective control.

That concluding section of 'Tides' offers lovemaking as a consummation in which he is attracted by her 'great tides'. Without the restraining scene setting of the preceding lines that final claim might be excessive. It is a characteristic of a Montague love poem that it does not shirk the harsher aspects of emotional relationships. Frequently, in this collection, in lyric and in prose poem, the sense of pain and threat is vividly asserted, images of violence being done to the naked body, nightmare scenes that the speaker cannot prevent. This is both a general perception of life and a context for the male–female relationship. Here the humans seem 'desperately frail' in a work where emotions cause anger and pain, where love itself is under strain. In the heat lovers crush insects on the wall, then quarrel like bats in an ugly choreography. Previously, in the opening section, a door is banging like a 'blow', pain bleeds in 'gouts / of accusation & / counter accusation'. Bitter speech is a 'heart's release'. The tides of sensuality in which the poem finally ends come after the waves of pain, bitter words, and bat movements. The poem moves from violence to peace, from anger to calm, the language of rage replaced not by words but by submission to her sensual power.

John Montague is a love poet of unusual tenderness, a feeling expressed all the more because of the constant awareness of loss and 'the monster / of unhappiness'. He appreciates love's 'intimacy of hand / and mind', gestures 'like court music', the transforming experience taking them out of themselves and out of the ordinary world to which they return. To him woman is complex. 'Life Class' is an extended tribute in the familiar short triple-lined stanza, to the female body as a sculpted figure, a maze of tempting recesses and textures, worthy of 'homage'. It is ironical that a poet so sensitive to the female shape experiences and causes so much pain in love or that the poet who admired the patient weathering of the master's face is so vulnerable to affliction. The sculpted figure is an inanimate object, the living reality is not so easily contained. In 'Special Delivery' the letter revives memories:

> . . . old sea-sick-
> ness of love, retch
>
> of sentiment, night
> & day devoured by
> the worm of delight
>
> which turns to
> feed upon itself; . . .

The Great Cloak, 1978, deals with a broken marriage, other loves and a new relationship, but the language is simple and direct. Once again he investigates the emotional complexities and upheaval in the relationship between men and women – the unhappiness, the letdowns, the nostalgia, the jealousy. Remarkably, he does not tire of these recreations of intimacy and pain. In *Smashing the Piano*, 1999,[3] love is still a recurrent theme, and with it the admission that to write is to find ease from the pain of love, his 'old-fashioned courtly poet's pilgrimage / towards the ideal, woman or windmill; / seething inside, but smiling like a sage'. He is a master of the love lyric and for him it is a sign of release and redemption from the inhibited and puritanical, even shameful response to sexuality he has known and recorded. One of the consequences of his prolonged and recurrent examination of his own experience, including adolescence, is that he has given evidence of what it was like to be young and Church-educated in the Ireland of his time. It is hardly accidental that as a young man he was drawn to the poetry of Austin Clarke whose extensive recording of repressive moral teaching showed the drama of conscience in the previous generation.

The title poem in *A Slow Dance*, 1975, is an invitation to strip away inhibitions, to be one with the earth. The prose section called 'A Dance' celebrates an abandonment to physical and sensual sensation: 'In wet and darkness you are reborn, the rain falling on your face as it would on a mossy tree trunk, wet hair clinging to your skull like bark, your breath mingling with the exhalations of the earth, that eternal smell of humus and mould.' The collection marks a return to sensuality. In 'For the Hillmother' the poet voices a litany of prayer to natural objects: 'Blue harebell / bend to us / Moist fern / unfold for us'. 'Small Secrets' has an unselfconscious artistry and an exactness of observation in its perception of a snail: 'and a fat / grass snail / who uncoils / to carry his / whorled house / over the top / of my table.' And in general he articulates an acceptance of experience, rather than protest. Moving away from socio-political concerns, he is in tune with his natural talent and the delicate perception of the natural world, although at times the language has recourse to an over-worked Montague style. In *The Great Cloak* he returns in the stylised and formal elegance of some earlier poems to observations of nature, the voice is mature and reflective.

> Then we were in the high
> ribbed dark of the trees
> where animals move stealth-
> ily, coupling & killing,
> while we talked nostalgically
> of our lives, bedevilled
> & betrayed by lost love –....

While the persona is cautiously self-observing, the poetry moves the reader in its shifting tones, its honest detail of love's complexity. The images come naturally, with freshness and fluency. *Mount Eagle*, 1988, revisits the theme of love, its grief and conflicts.

Montague also responds to old women, as in 'The Wild Dog Rose', a narrative poem in which he visits a hag-like creature of whom he had once been frightened. He wants to say goodbye to 'that terrible figure who haunted my childhood'. Landscape and figure reflect each other.

> The cottage,
> circled by trees, weathered to admonitory
> shapes of desolation by the mountain winds,
> struggles into view. The rank thistles
> and leathery bracken of untilled fields
> stretch behind with – a final outcrop –
> the hooped figure by the roadside,
> its retinue of dogs.

But the portentous images detract from the simplicity of the occasion. He is 'Obscurely honoured', hearing her 'rehearsing the small events of her life'. 'Memories', he says, 'have wrought reconciliation / between us, we talk in ease at last, / like old friends, lovers almost, / sharing secrets'. The secret shared is her account of an attempted rape; the poem concludes with the metaphor of the thornless dog rose that represents her meek nature.

When he writes lengthy accounts of old women who have lived their lives in humility, who are pious and frail, worn down by years of work, he reverts to the short line, although it is doubtful if the form suits the narrative method. 'The Leaping Fire' section of *The Rough Field* rehearses the ordinary lives of these women in a tribute to their devotion and simplicity. These are muted lines, exhaling sweetness, the women seen as repositories of virtues, the poetry scaled down to accommodate its frail theme.

Running throughout Montague's work is a delight in the natural world – birds and animals, water, grass, trees, smells: in *Mount Eagle* nature is a healing source.

> Let us also lay ourselves
> down in this silence
>
> let us also be healed
> wounds closed, senses cleansed
>
> as over our bowed heads
> the mad larks multiply....

And in *Smashing the Piano* again he is immersed in the natural world.

That deep, dark pool. To come upon it,
after driving across the Gap in midsummer,
the hedges freighted with fuchsia, hawthorn,
blood-red and white under shining veils of rain.

The question of how the lyric poet handles large subject matter is relevant to Montague's poetry. It is particularly so in relation to his treatment of the third area of his work: Ireland, a subject rendered most clearly and ambitiously in the long poem *The Rough Field*, 1972, in which he has drawn together poems written over many years and several new ones. The poem is about place, people, and time – an old culture disappearing, a family scattered, a language lost. It moves back and forth between poems about his own background and poems about historical events and figures. The poet is facing up to the problems of how to make connections between the two. It is a poem of return and of leave-taking in which the poet expresses his preoccupation with landscape, mythology, Gaelic culture, the lost heritage of Ulster, and the lost rhythms of rural life. Feeling that the present distress of Northern Ireland is best understood in terms of Elizabethan invasion, the driving out of Irish chieftains, plantation and consequent dispossession, he associates personal memories of place and event with historical accounts. He also introduces evidence of sectarian bigotry.

It comes close to being a unified work, even though the diversity of its ingredients and its method of juxtaposing personal subject matter with material drawn from historical and other sources – records, sectarian propaganda, family letters, fiction – puts a strain on the form. The poem spills over its drama of personal focus to peripheral notes and illustrations, which add dimensions of history and past experience, although not drawn into the language of the poem. By quoting directly and at some length from relevant documents, sometimes on the margins of the text, sometimes as part of the text, he challenges the reader to accommodate them to the poem's imaginative world. Where the poem enacts a personal drama within a public domain, the personal, autobiographical, and familial drama is central. The poet's feelings – love, anger, and nostalgia – flow through the poem and provide some of the best sections. There are key images – the old woman (mother, hag, maiden, source of the hearth-fire), the fire itself, the house, stories, wells, roads, music, fish, language, exile, and return – all implicated in the central theme of loss and change.

When in 'A Severed Head' section the political / sectarian material becomes central to the page, the heavily descriptive stanzas are less effective than the light lyric evocations, or the freer lines of 'The Road's End' in which Montague's ability to write a relaxed and fluent description, without the introduction of an editorialising voice, is pleasingly present.

> . . . As I take
> The mountain road, my former step
> Doubles mine, driving cattle
> To the upland fields. Between
> Shelving ditches of whitethorn
> They sway their burdensome
> Bodies, tempted at each turn
> By hollows of sweet grass,
> Pale clover, while memory,
>
> A restive sally-switch, flicks
> Across their backs.

Some of the strongest personal poems are those about his Republican father, forced to leave Northern Ireland because of political involvement and to live his life thereafter working in the Brooklyn underground. Montague approves that choice of the lesser of two evils, since he avoided 'a half-life' in a 'by-passed and dying place'. He traces his own bitter hatred of British possession of the six counties of Northern Ireland to his father.

> I assert
> a civilisation died here;
>   it trembles
> underfoot where I walk these
>   small, sad fields:
> it rears in my blood stream
>   when I hear
> a bleat of Saxon condescension,
>   Westminster
> to hell, it is less than these
>   strangely carved
> five thousand year resisting stones,
>   that lonely cross.

If we find unhappiness running through Montague's poetry, he finds it in his memory of that father 'the least happy / man I have known', exiled from the familiar fields and culture, as his son is. The deepest note in this long poem is sorrow for what has been lost – his childhood world, family unity, Ulster's heritage. In *The Dead Kingdom*, 1984, he returns yet again to incidents from his early years – the break-up of the family, the father's exile, the mother's brief sojourn in Brooklyn followed by her return to Tyrone, where she gave him to be brought up by another member of the family. That hurt has not eased: 'An unwanted child, a primal hurt.'

The riven nature of Montague's sensibility, the inherent sadness, the compassion makes his sympathy with the old women all the more understandable and the extended enumeration of their lives and virtues, meekness, unselfishness. But the most pervasive feeling in the poem is attachment to country; it emerges in many forms – in the litany of place names, in the laments for what has passed – the 'shards of a lost tradition', the 'Disappearance & death / of a world', the separation from a culture that was once unified and to which the individual could connect. Now the 'whole landscape' is 'a manuscript / We had lost the skill to read'. Progress in the shape of new roads cuts through local pockets of culture and beauty, 'All the sadness of a house in decay'; the turf fire in the hearth once a sign of permanence, blown alight each morning, is now quenched.

A mark of Montague's work is that he gives voice to personal hurt, becomes an honest witness to experience, whether in love relationships, in broken filial bonds, in political injustice, in mutilated heritage. He has not written a poetry of redemption or comfort, but his witnessing, including in this long poem the presentation of documents of exploitation and records of historical experience, is a singular achievement. In the concluding sections of *The Rough Field* – 'Patriotic Suite', 'A New Siege', and 'The Wild Dog Rose' – the note of melancholy exudes; the method becomes quietly lyrical and meditative, the speaker allowing the imagery to do the work.

> Sight of the Skelligs at sunset
> restores our Hy-Brasil:
> the Atlantic expands on the cliffs
> the herring gull claims the air

'A New Siege' telescopes images from the siege of Derry in 1689 with images from the more recent outbreak of violence in Northern Ireland. As it restates themes from earlier sections the poem is beautifully poised between past and present, the note of grieving for loss and the consequences of violence drawing the stanzas together in a fitting conclusion to what has been less a commemoration than a prolonged, hurt protest.

> Lines of leaving
>   lines of returning
> the long estuary
>   of Lough Foyle, a
> ship motionless
>   in wet darkness
> mournfully hooting
>   as a tender creeps
> to carry passengers
>   back to Ireland....

The poem concludes with 'The Wild Dog Rose' whose sweet melancholy provides a fitting final tone. In these concluding sections, the anger and bitterness, the supporting drama of documents are laid to rest.

In its recreation of old issues and techniques, *Drunken Sailor*, 2004,[4] reads like an affirmation. The poems have the same exactness of observation as before, the same loving control of line and rhythm, the same dedication to 'the snail progress of a poem'. The craftsmanship is evident in the handling of the short line and the coiled intensity of the longer line in compact stanzas. He is still the image-maker. 'The birds sing on summer evenings. / A cheeky robin balances on the buoyant bough / of its favourite lichened tree...'. As the poems alternate between elegy and commemoration in their investigation of violence, love, family hurt, death, history, mythology, and nature, the encompassing theme is 'endless death, ceaseless birth', both of which are accepted and recorded. Once again he testifies to the strength and comfort he draws from the place in which he was raised. Even in distant cities, he says,

> I am stopped suddenly by
> The sight of some distant hill
> Or curving twilight river, to see
> On a ghostly mound, my abiding
> Symbol, a weathered standing stone.

It is a measure of Montague's intelligence and integrity that he has not strayed from the source of his inspiration but, circling back, has continued to explore them to great effect in lyric poetry that is both lucid and accomplished.

Notes

1 Selections from Harmon's essay have been published in *Agenda Irish Issue John Montague – 75th Birthday Supplement*, 'John Montague: 'Restless Spirit', 40, 1–3 (2004), pp. 92–106.
2 John Montague, *Collected Poems* (Loughcrew, Oldcastle, Co. Meath, Ireland: The Gallery Press, 1995). Subsequent citations, unless otherwise indicated, are from this text.
3 (Loughcrew, Oldcastle, Co. Meath: The Gallery Press, 1999).
4 (Loughcrew, Oldcastle, Co. Meath: The Gallery Press, 2004).

12

SEAMUS HEANEY: VISION AND REVISION[1]

Harmon's first significant assessment of Seamus Heaney's poetry appeared in his anthology Irish Poetry after Yeats. *In the Introduction, he emphasised the importance of Heaney's 'auditory imagination' and recognised in* Death of a Naturalist, 1966, *a 'consciously different' use of 'concrete, sensuous imagery' from that of Yeats. In 1995 when Heaney was awarded the Nobel Prize for Literature, Harmon was commissioned to write the Introduction, 'Spaten und Wasserwaage: Seamus Heaney's Suche Nach Herkunft und Gleichgewicht' for* Seamus Heaney, Tod eines Naturforschers, 1995.[2]

SEAMUS Heaney has never lost touch with his rural origins. His early poetry, in *Death of a Naturalist*, 1966, and *Door into the Dark*, 1969, recovers a past animated by the crafts and skills of the farming community. He records with literal accuracy and mimetic skill: the belly of a cow in calf is 'slung like a hammock', in the 'musty dark' of the barn is 'hoarded an armoury' of implements, 'the spade sinks into gravelly ground', frogs are 'great slime kings'. Some poems evoke mystery at the heart of the craftsman's work: within the dark centre of the forge the blacksmith hammers out a 'fantail of sparks'; in the hands of the diviner the 'forked hazel stick' plunges unerringly towards the hidden source; his father's accuracy with a horse-drawn plough is exemplary. Admiring the work of thatchers, turf-cutters, sowers, and harvesters, and remarking their pride in work done well, he reveals what he values.

Death of a Naturalist concludes with 'Personal Helicon', a poem of the pleasures derived from exploring wells – 'I loved the dark drop, the trapped sky, the smells / Of waterweed, fungus and dank moss'; about musical echoes – and about why he writes – 'I rhyme / To see myself, to set the darkness echoing.'

The placing of 'Bogland' at the end of *Door into the Dark* not only confirms the imaginative depths of the poet's chosen world, but in its flowing definitions anticipates the style of poems in the next collection. Contrasting the American imagination that lifts to the far west with the Irish imagination that 'concedes to / Encroaching horizon', 'Bogland' accepts the limits within which the Irish artist works. But because the heritage is rich, such constriction is not defeating. The bogs of Ireland, once known as places of danger and decay, preserve and purify. The confident, fluid grace of this poem intensifies its declaration of faith in Irish sources. W. B. Yeats had memorably declared 'Things fall apart; the centre cannot hold.' Believing otherwise, Heaney affirms that the Irish psyche hoards experience; the heritage is not inferior; the history is layered. For him, 'The wet centre is bottomless', the imaginative possibilities unlimited.

In *Wintering Out*, 1972, his third collection, Seamus Heaney's mimetic ritualising imagination, his ability to reach out and identify with objects and people, become particularly evident as he explores the historical and cultural origins of his chosen ground and in the linguistics of its place-names reads evidence of sectarian conflict and colonial dispossession. He identifies with 'the long-seasoned rib / under the first thatch' in 'Bog Oak', with the hired boy in 'Servant Boy', with the young mother in 'Limbo' who drowns her baby, with the confined boy in 'Bye-Child', with the resentful, violent figure in 'The Last Mummer', with the lonely wife in 'Shore Woman', with the uprooted mer-maid in 'Maighdean Mara'. Unlike figures in the earlier poems, ploughman or thatcher, these are all outcasts. They suffer exposure, neglect or cruelty; they belong to the outback, they haunt the *pagus*. Heaney insinuates himself into their lives, making them masks for his sense of nationalist, Catholic isolation in a province governed by Unionists, Presbyterians, and Planters.

In 'Bog Oak' he reaches back through four hundred years of history, accomplishing the transition in an act of familiarity, in the force of 'tarry' and 'eavesdrop' in the lines 'I might tarry / with the moustached / dead' and 'eavesdrop on / their hopeless wisdom'. By such means he assumes proxim-ity and persuades us by his mimetic skill that his imaginative pilgrimage is credible, that he is one of these ancestors. It is a form of role-playing, with the self as a familiar of the past. All these poems are acts of empathetic imagining in which the poet enters the life and the situation of others, putting on the mask of other reactions and experiences.

Many poems are written in 'Bogland's' spirit of playful confidence. In 'Oracle', the speaker is the nameless one, inhabitant of natural objects, in the hollow trunk of a willow tree, its listening familiar. Heaney creates minuscule histories in the etymologies of place-names, in the identifying linguistic properties of townlands, in the telltale dialect words. By attending to the fidelities of spoken words he can touch upon history and culture in an intimate and unspectacular way. The auditory imagination delights in the music of its saying, the poems that grow from it are chords of attachment binding him to the landscape:

> He is hooped to where he planted
> and sky and ground
>
> are running naturally among his arms
> that grope the cropping land.

The poems are in effect mating calls by which the land rises to delight the poet, this 'hoarder of common ground', who hoards it like a miser in love with its riches, with the 'Soft voices of the dead … whispering by the shore', whose perception of that ground is of an archaeological hoard waiting to be revealed. 'Strangers' cannot 'manage' the sound of this personal world in which words such as 'Broagh', 'Anahorish', 'Moyola', 'Mossbawn', and 'Castledawson' form a literary landscape that like a Braille text has to be felt to be known.

In these poems the language of love, of intercourse, is sometimes the only adequate measure of the bonding closeness by which Heaney seeks to realise his sense of oneness with the land and its 'Traditions'. Or else, even more physically, the vocal organs themselves or the units of words, the vowels and the consonants, become the image and the metaphor for the idea heard like music in the sound of its saying: 'the soft gradient of consonant': 'Our guttural muse / was bulled long ago / by the alliterative tradition.' Or else, in a mirroring perspective, the processes of the natural world are linguistic codes: 'Broagh' is a 'low tattoo / among the windy boortrees / and rhubarb-blades'. 'Anahorish' is a 'vowel-meadow'; it evokes a way of life of 'mound-dwellers' who 'go waist-deep in mist'. Heaney comes close to the music of what happens; the ideal is music itself, pure idea. And in terms of realism and ceremony it is clear that such poems blend the actual and the ritual; what is verifiably real is drawn into metaphor, intimately mated in the act of poetic speech. His liberating breakthrough to a richly varied reading of landscape had been strengthened by his discovery in 1969 of the account by the Danish archaeologist P. V. Glob, in his book *The Bog People*, of the customs in early Iron Age Northern Europe by which young men were ritually sacrificed to Nerthus, goddess of the earth, to ensure good harvest. He was attracted by the similarities between what happened in Northern Europe and what had begun to happen again in Northern Ireland where endemic divisions now took more visible shape in bombings, murders, punishments, hunger-strikes, a cycle of killing and counter-killing that would persist and press in upon his work, demanding that he should voice nationalistic grievances and suffering.

'The Tollund Man' is a victim of cruelty. Nature embalms the body so that like the incorruptible flesh of Christian martyr saints it may transcend mortality, may bear witness to its own saintliness, and may comfortingly guarantee that death is a purposeful part of a larger design. The poem is reverently geared to create this design: the preserved body, so gently and lovingly described, is evidence of sanctity; the tone is reverent, as befits a pilgrim's promise. There, in Section II, in an act of apparent heresy, the Catholic poet can re-enact the vegetation ritual by which a human was sacrificed to Nerthus, the goddess of fertility. He can pray to the saint to bring germination not to crops or vegetation but to the dead of Northern Ireland, victims of ritual violence, whose flesh has been broadcast like seed upon the land. The final section too belongs to ceremony: it is a pilgrimage; the place-names are like numerous stations along the way; the pointing hands of the country people express in simple, unambiguous gesture that this is the way of salvation leading to the stunning moment of insight, of illumination, the final sign of the saint's power.

The metaphor of ceremony permeates *North*, 1975, a collection deeply concerned with the violence of Northern Ireland. The poems do not confront that violence. They do not speak of individual pain or individual outrage. Instead Heaney adopts a communal response. Whatever personal feelings he has about death and suffering are deflected into large ceremonial gestures. Faced with the horror of 'each neighbourly murder', Heaney declares 'we pine for ceremony / customary rhythms'. In 'Funeral Rites' every detail in the poem is appropriated to the ceremony. The boy achieves 'a kind of manhood' when he helps to carry the coffins of dead relations; the dead themselves are transfigured, even the coffins have a sombre beauty. Courtesy and unqualified admiration carry the description forward in a smooth syntactical momentum sustained by precise images of the dead, whose appearance belies the ravages of death:

> Their eye-lids glistening,
> Their dough-white hands
> Shackled in rosary beads.

The Northern violence disrupts such orderly initiation into the rites of manhood, in which the ugliness of death is mitigated by consoling ritual.

The remaining six stanzas of Section II provide supportive evidence for that statement, accumulating soothing images for a massive funeral composed of 'temperate footsteps', 'purring cars', 'somnambulant women' – a whole country tuned to the 'muffled drumming' of 'ten thousand engines'. The progress of the funeral is a 'slow triumph' towards the great megalithic burial chambers at the Boyne, its quiet shape linking the North of Ireland with the ancient tombs. What the community 'longs for' is this peaceful shape, this process that transmutes horror into peace, that binds people harmoniously together.

When, in Section III, the mourners return to the place of division and hatred, their grief has been assuaged. They are capable of responding to the beauty of Gunnar in his tomb. In the original saga, Gunnar's transfiguration in death is an arresting incident. We read that when two people were driving cattle past his burial mound 'it seemed to them that Gunnar was in good humour and chanting verses inside the mound'. When his son and some others stand outside the mound,

> Suddenly it seemed to them that the mound was open; Gunnar
> had turned round to face the moon. There seemed to be four
> lights burning inside the mound, illuminating the whole
> chamber. They could see that Gunnar was happy; his face was
> exultant. He chanted a verse so loudly that this could have been
> heard clearly from much further away.[3]

The introduction of the allusion to Gunnar is careful. In death Gunnar has
been liberated from vengeance. In art, in the saga and the poem, discord has
been transmuted. By transforming death, violence, and grief through the
beauty of language, the poet comforts his people and eases their suffering.
But he must retain his independence. The state of peace which the
mourners have achieved through their participation in the trance-like
ceremony of the extended, binding procession enables them to allay their
preoccupation with the past, to feel that the divisions that caused feuding
have been placated, and in this state of forgetting and of forgiving they
imagine that the victims of violence from their community whom they have
buried are 'disposed' like Gunnar 'though dead by violence' also and
similarly 'unavenged'. For the poet's comforting, assuaging purposes, the
image of Gunnar stands for peaceful coexistence, for the avoidance of
sectarian feuds, and for the liberation of a people from self-perpetuating
hatreds. When Gunnar turns a joyful face to the moon, his joy belongs to a
man who has transcended violence, responding instead to beauty and all
that the moon traditionally represents. The image is poised above the strife;
in its peace and triumphant joy the ceremonial elements of the poem reach
their highest point.

'North' is also a poem of visionary communication with the Viking dead.
First their voices warn the 'I' figure against the reality of their recurrent
violence, their thick-witted couplings, their revenges. Several stanzas
express alternative elements of the Norse sagas. But their voices warn him
of violence, of 'memory incubating the spilled blood'. It was the 'cud' of
such memory that 'Funeral Rites' sought to erase. When we realise that the
powerful destructive forces of the Vikings are paradigms for violent realities
in Heaney's own province, then the choices heard in the last three stanzas,
conveyed from the Viking dead, wiser in death than in life, prefigure the
issues that have dominated Heaney's work in the 1970s. The dead,
anticipating the advice that James Joyce offers at the end of 'Station Island',
1984, tell him to be true to himself, to work with language, to use his mind,
to compose in darkness, to expect only occasional illuminations, to be clear-
eyed, to rely on what he knows from his own experience. The advice comes
in a series of commands: 'Lie down / In the word-hoard, burrow ... / ...
Compose... / Expect... / Keep your eyes clear / ... trust the feel of what
nubbed treasure / your hands have known.' That advice counters Viking

hatred and internecine strife with the mysteries of poetic composition; the associations of hoard, barrow, and lengthy incursion are turned towards aesthetic creation. When we incline to the idea that Heaney's work seems to drift away from the issues that surround him, a poem such as 'North' reminds us of the complex, indirect, allusive, metaphorical way in which he handles many of them. The voices are also the means by which he declares his priorities as a poet.

'The Grauballe Man' again creates a portrait of the resurrected victim in images of beauty and repose; the anatomical details are represented in grave, natural images: 'the grain of his wrists / is like bog oak', 'the ball of his heel' is 'like a basalt egg'. The ennobling simile is a favourite mode of picturing the dead. Even the signs of violence have been altered: 'the slashed throat', for example, has 'tanned and toughened'; the 'cured wound / opens inwards to a dark / elderberry place'. Having thus created images through which violent death has been transmuted into beauty, Heaney can pose the rhetorical questions:

> Who will say 'corpse'
> to his vivid cast?
> Who will say 'body'
> to his opaque repose?

The figure, he declares, lies 'perfected' in his memory, imprinted from Glob's book, and goes on to create a perfect equation in which 'beauty' balances 'atrocity'. On the one hand is the classic figure of the Dying Gaul representing beauty, on the other, the hooded victim, 'slashed and dumped', representing atrocity. A static image poised at the end of the poem, like Gunnar, brings savagery under control. The Dying Gaul symmetrically disposed, is in Heaney's eyes too neatly placed within the rim of his shield; but, while he may be an aesthetic mask for a violent death, his image functions as a counter force to human disorder. Like the Grauballe man, he too has been perfected in the artist's memory. But the poem does not equate the Viking with the Gaul or with the hooded victims. He is shared equally with them; he hangs in the scales with them, encompassing the two forces that they represent. In these poised images Heaney's virtuoso kinetic art is replaced by a style in which an aesthetic image is distanced and stilled for our contemplation.

Heaney's empathetic imagination is fully engaged in the accounts of the processes by which the bog victims are made beautiful. He has not condemned violence, except indirectly, has identified with civilised outrage yet understands 'the exact / and tribal, intimate revenge'. By adopting the voice of the victim or by celebrating in itemized epiphanies the redeeming processes of the bogs, he avoids having to state directly how he feels. It is

the bog queen who narrates her story; it is the Viking dead from the early
Iron Age whose bodies become things of beauty. By analogy, present horror
is subsumed in the account of past atrocity and becomes an object of
beauty, aesthetically distanced. In 'Punishment' the method, intended to
clarify personal ambivalence, sweetens savagery; its soft intimacy is an
affront to the girl's dignity. 'Strange Fruit' atones for that lapse. Here the
beheaded girl outstares both atrocity and beauty, both 'axe / And
beautification', and escapes the poet's invasive 'reverence'. Seamus Heaney
draws the teeth of savagery, but that does not mean he either condones it or
is indifferent to the suffering it causes.

Other poems in *North* delight in linguistic and imaginative association.
The operation of the playful imagination is seen to best effect in 'Viking
Dublin: Trial Pieces', which deals with the art of dissembling. Beginning
with speculation about the reality of an object recovered from Viking
Dublin and put on display in the National Museum, it quickly moves away
from such relatively unimportant consideration with 'anyhow' and the
transition to the design cut in the object, 'a small outline', 'a cage / or trellis
to conjure in'. It is the act of conjuring that is important, the ability of the
craftsman to create a design that 'amazes itself', escapes as it were from 'the
hand / that fed it'. The pieces on display are *trial pieces*, and the poem, in
a complex, free-wheeling associative linking, interprets the lines in a variety
of ways: 'foliage, bestiaries', lines of 'ancestors and trade', the poet's script.
Magnified, the imagined 'nostril' of the design becomes the prow of a
Viking ship entering the Liffey, 'dissembling itself' in the various artefacts
recovered by archaeologists.

Section III tells of the ship's becoming stuck in the mud, the repository
now, in another act of recovery, of artefacts, including the particular trial
piece on which the poem expands. Section IV adopts this object, this trellis
made for conjuring and proceeds by a serious of imaginative leaps, via Saxo
Grammaticus and Shakespeare, to a histrionic performance:

> I am Hamlet the Dane,
> skull-handler, parablist,
> smeller of rot
>
> in the state, infused
> with its poisons,
> pinioned by ghosts
> and affections...

In this uninhibited exploitation of the artefact, Heaney identifies with
Hamlet: like him he interprets the dead, speaks in parables, knows there is
corruption in the state, is 'pinioned' by the dead and by his own affections

for his country. Like Hamlet he is 'coming to consciousness / by jumping in graves / dithering, blathering'. To put on such an antic disposition is to be a mummer and a moralist, a realist and a romantic visionary; the artist who sees and the artist who feels but who retains his freedom. His ability to execute his dance of the imagination within the circumstances of his place is an expression of awareness and an admission of an inability to act decisively to rectify what is wrong.

Section V invites participation in this play of identifications – 'Come fly with me / come sniff the wind' – become a Viking, enter his way of life, understand his behaviour. The lines recall the Vikings' murderous, mercenary ways, even their tribal mutilation of defeated rivals in which the rib cage was torn apart from the spine and made to resemble the spread-eagle saturated in gore:[4]

> With a butcher's aplomb
> they spread out your lungs
> and made you warm wings
> for your shoulders.

Such behaviour is outrageous but not more so than atrocities closer to home. Heaney's apostrophe, 'Old fathers, be with us', may remind us of Joyce and Yeats, but the point is to remind us that these 'old, cunning assessors' are like us. The poem concludes in milder movement by way of another theatrical connection, Synge's *The Playboy of the Western World*, in which Jimmy Farrell gives a confused but self-delighting account of Viking skills in Dublin. It ends with Heaney's quiet acknowledgement of his own fascination with that city's 'skull-capped ground', a fascination that the poem ably demonstrates in its imaginative playfulness.

The combination of reality and ritual in the poetry of Seamus Heaney during this ten-year period, 1966–76, gives way in Part II of *North* to a realistic portrayal of the social self. 'Exposure' uses a mask but creates a drama of internal irresolution in which much is revealed and little is resolved. It has depth and elusiveness. Its imagery and allusions are both literal and symbolic; it is explicitly personal, yet its meanings live and recede within the lines. We sense more than we can account for. Instead of certainties, unanswered questions are exposed: 'How did I end up like this?' The voices that reply lack the reassurance of the Viking dead; they speak with forked tongues of 'let-downs and erosions' but also of 'diamond absolutes'. Instead of solutions they echo internal divisions. The imagined hero stands for a simplified ideal of action that is inapplicable. Heaney's defensive 'I am neither internee nor informer' distances him from the nationalist perspective; but the alternatives – the one acceptable, the other contemptible – cancel each other out. The mask of the wood-kern, neither historical validation nor comforting metaphor, simply explains his need for space and time in which to decide how best to live. He is an 'inner émigré', one, like Osip Mandelstam, who is within the state yet removed from it, and one who lives, as in this poem, within himself. Heaney's withdrawal may seem to be an opting-out, but is not. Paradoxically, by hiding he is exposed to 'Every wind that blows'. The ending to these, and other, complexities lacks the affirmation of 'Bogland' and the playfulness of 'Viking Dublin: Trial Pieces', but has a quieter strength. Regrettably, he has missed 'The once-in-a-lifetime portent, / The comet's pulsing rose'. But he is about the proper business of the poet: he attends the fire of the imagination, modestly and sensibly imagined here not even as Aurora borealis but as 'sparks' that give but 'a meagre heat'.

In *Field Work*, 1979, poems interrogate the poet's role in the midst of continuing violence. 'What will become of us?' 'Our island is full of comfortless voices.' What is the value of poetry? What is its function? The answer is conveyed more by image and metaphor than by the expression of hope. In 'The Toome Road' the poet meets the armoured convoys of British soldiers; they are on *his* road. In the elegies for dead friends Heaney looks more directly at sectarian murder, without the mythologising procedures of *North*. When he describes the assassination of his cousin, in 'The Strand at Lough Beg', he concludes with words of comfort and blessing:

> Then kneel in front of you in brimming grass
> And gather up cold handfuls of the dew
> To wash you, cousin. I dab you clean with moss
> Fine as the drizzle out of a low cloud.
> I lift you under the arms and lay you flat.
> With rushes that shoot green again, I plait
> Green scapulars to wear over your shroud.

In a similar gesture Virgil wiped Dante's face at the beginning of the *Purgatorio* and the figure of the Italian poet is present throughout *Station Island*, 1984, the next collection in which there are many encounters with those killed by violence in Northern Ireland.

The troubled voice in *Field Work* is heard more directly in *Station Island*, which begins with poems that question the value of poetry itself. In the title poem, an account of the poet's pilgrimage to Lough Derg, through a series of encounters with figures and incidents from the past, the poet is challenged. The murdered cousin, for example, accuses Heaney of confusing evasion and artistic tact.

> 'The Protestant who shot me through the head
> I accuse directly, but indirectly, you

> who now atone perhaps upon this bed
> for the way you whitewashed ugliness and drew
> the lovely blinds of the *Purgatorio*
> and saccharined my death with morning dew.'

Another victim vividly relives his assassination and thereby confronts the poet's 'circumspect involvement'. Heaney replies: 'forgive the way I have lived indifferent'.

> 'I hate how quick I was to know my place.
> I hate where I was born, hate everything
> That made me biddable and unforthcoming.'

He wants to atone, to reveal in the poem's drama how he has been touched by events. But he also wants to assert his rights as a poet. By doing the pilgrimage he hopes to clear his conscience and earn the right to be free. James Joyce, whom he encounters at the end of the pilgrimage, advises him:

> 'Keep at a tangent.
> When they make the circle wide, it's time to swim
>
> out on your own and fill the element
> with signatures of your own frequency,
> echo soundings, searches, probes, allurements,
>
> elver-gleams in the dark of the whole sea'. . . .

And provides the answer the pilgrim-poet seeks.

Poems about Sweeney in the final section of the collection illumine the truth of that admonition. Through the figure of this Irish king who fled to the forest and made poetry out of his isolation and separateness, Heaney celebrates poetic freedom. *Sweeney Astray*, 1983, a version of the Irish story *Buile Suibhne*, may be read, he has said, 'as an aspect of the quarrel between the free creative imagination and the constraints of religious, political and domestic obligation'. Sweeney runs free of the crowd, bound neither by state or church. He represents Heaney's understanding that poetry should be 'rare and strange and other', not dutiful and communal. In these lyrics Heaney takes an old story and draws from it images, metaphors, tones, and situations within which he can express personal views and reactions.

In the *Haw Lantern*, 1987, and *Seeing Things*, 1991, he lives even more strongly and securely in the republic of his own conscience. He is not tied to the quotidian. 'Invisibles' shimmer, appear, disappear. The spirit world, in all its meanings and manifestations, is the secret, shifting, luminous, sometimes fearful, apprehended subject. In a poem in 'Squarings' the 'visible sea' seems empty when scanned, but once you turn your back on it 'Was suddenly all eyes like Argus's'. And when you looked again it felt 'Untrespassed still, and yet somehow vacated'. The speaker turns his attention to what is there: 'Perfect vision' – when things are observed in exact, luminous vision. The language deals with reality, but also with absent reality, or a reality that existed in the past, like the chestnut tree that was:

> Its heft and hush became a bright nowhere,
> A soul ramifying and forever
> Silent, beyond silence listened for.

Beyond silence, beyond the visible, but not beyond retrieval and not inferior to what is within the immediate compass of the poet's senses, 'Who ever saw / The limit in the given anyhow?' The marvellous also lives within the ordinary – in a spinning wheel, in slides, in rides on a swing, in lying on cut logs, in letting go and coming back, as Aeneas did, enriched and strengthened: 'whatever is given / Can always be reimagined'. This, too, is a pilgrimage 'Beyond our usual hold upon ourselves'.

Contrasting views of reality are placed side by side within poems, and from one poem to its companion. The balancing and pairing, the steadying equations are a measure of the poet's own equilibrium. He stands at the still centre where the carpenter's spirit level comes to a halt, poised between competing attractions: 'In apposition with / Omnipresence, equilibrium, brim'. In seeing things, he may cross from one state of being to another, may see clearly what is there, may also imagine what is not there or what has been there. It is his re-creation that is important. The vision of reality that poetry offers should, Heaney declares, be transformative, not just a mirroring of actualities:

> The truly creative writer, by interposing his or her perception
> and expression, will transfigure the conditions and effect thereby
> what I have called 'the redress of poetry'.

But the poetry of *The Tree Clock*, 1990, published by the Linen Hall Library in a limited edition of 870 copies, emphasises the power of actualities and has no trace of the questioning present in these two, as well as the earlier, collections. There is none of the agonising over issues of poetic responsibility, the conflict between the demands of public and politics on the one hand and the requirements of art on the other. Now Heaney's poetry takes us into 'the heartland of the ordinary', but we must not underestimate or misunderstand what this means. Take the first stanza of 'The Butter-print'.

> Who carved on the butter-print's round open face,
> A cross-hatched head of rye, all jags and bristles?
> Why should soft butter bear that sharp device
> As if its breast were scored with slivered glass?

The lines are dense with concrete, specific terms, but the softer, more open elements work within and against the sharper, jagged ones: 'round, open face' and 'jags and bristles'; 'soft butter' and 'sharp device'; 'breast' and 'slivered glass'. The questions challenge. The issue is not unimportant. The small narrative that follows in two quatrains gives answers, describing how the child swallowed a bead of rye, the sharp sensation, the fright, the coughing, then the contrasting, heartfelt relief, like a blessing – 'inhaling airs from heaven'. A tiny parable.

At one time Heaney thought of Yeats's ability to speak to his time, from within history, imparting wisdom on the grounds of lived experience. The poet had stature and authority. Heaney seems to have moved away from that concern. He speaks in these poems with conviction, in a sturdy style, and with fewer chameleon conceits. He is less the antic dissembler than the confident spokesman for what he knows to be true. The consolatory urge is more controlled and arises from within the poem. 'The Butter-print' illustrates a truth, and gives answers to age-old questions: it makes the pat of butter a mythic sign, a truth-telling object. The force of the answer is conveyed in the natural evolution of the lines. 'The Skylight' is also about opening, as is 'The Pitchfork' – it is about the willingness to try, to explore, to change, to shift attitudes, and to transform.

The importance of that transformative power is present throughout Heaney's *The Redress of Poetry. Oxford Lectures*, 1995, and *The Spirit Level*, 1996, a collection which returns to an issue that has been present in his work from the beginning: the value of poetry, or to put that in the context in which he has had to consider it, how should the poet conduct himself at a time of serious political upheaval? How can he be true to his responsibility towards poetry and at the same time respond with intelligence and compassion to social and political realities?

Poetry's transformative power is manifest in *The Spirit Level*. 'A Sofa in the Forties' joyfully recreates a childhood game, when the children knelt on the sofa and imagined they were in a train. 'First we shunted, then we whistled, then /… Moved faster, *chooka-chook*, the sofa legs / Went giddy and the unreachable ones / Far out on the kitchen floor began to wave.' In the transformative power of the children's imaginations what is ordinary and real becomes what is extraordinary and unreal and in the process the imagined seems more real. In tune with this spirit of lift and movement, the poem has a rich freight of sound and rhythm. It credits marvels and makes them creditable. Through the power of the poetic imagination and skill our spirits, too, are moved and lifted: 'Where does spirit live? Inside or outside / Things remembered, made things, things unmade?' We participate in the childhood game, happily acknowledging its truth to remembered experience. The child's invention also transcends shortcomings – 'the insufficient toys' – and that, for Heaney, is another of poetry's values: the redressal of disappointments. The 'imaginative transformation of human life', he says, 'is the means by which we can most truly grasp and comprehend it'.

Man's capacity for play that both releases and sustains runs through these poems; so, too, does the sense of poetry's stabilising power. It can restore equality, enable us to readjust, to regain our composure, and maintain our emotional level. All the meanings of 'redress' are relevant. In 'Keeping Going', Heaney's brother performs as a piper; for sporran a whitewash brush, for bagpipe a kitchen chair upside down on his shoulder. But it is his ability to pretend, to enact, and to revel in so doing that is supreme: 'Your pop–eyes and big cheeks nearly bursting / With laughter, but keeping the drone going on / Interminably, between catches of breath.' The performance is primary. And it is that capacity that the poem affirms in comparing the early memory of fun and frolic with the contemporary bomb and bullet. The whitewash brush now cleans away the marks of an assassination.

> Grey matter like gravel flecked with blood
> In spatters on the whitewash. A clean spot
> Where his head had been,

Finally, Heaney addresses his brother – 'you have good stamina. / You stay on where it happens.' He keeps up appearances, laughing and waving; it is another, redemptive performance. In the past he was the Pied Piper in the kitchen, but now 'you cannot make the dead walk; or right wrong'; but he is able to endure.

Heaney faces the dark, writing specifically and with a more earthy voice about evil and ugliness. The boyhood home had its fear and dread, its brimstone threat. There were few moments when 'the soul was let alone'. The violence that happened later made real what had been intuited. The reckoning is level–headed and sobering. 'Good tidings' amount to no more than this principle:

> This principle of bearing, bearing up
> And bearing out, just having to
> Balance the intolerable in others
> Against our own, having to abide
> Whatever we settle for and settled into
>
> Against our better judgement.

Finding the right balance, being equal to what happens, is important. When the saint, in 'St. Kevin and the Blackbird' is kneeling with his arms outstretched and one arm out through the window of his narrow cell, a blackbird nests and lays eggs in his palm. He is moved to pity, 'finding himself linked / Into the network of eternal life', he has to hold his hand out until the young are hatched, fledged, and flown. Heaney's interest comes in the questions: What was it like? How did it feel? Is he self-forgetful or in agony all the time?

> Alone and mirrored clear in love's deep river
> 'To labour and not to seek reward', he prays.

It is another balancing. The poems in *The Spirit Level* are rich with Heaney's unmistakable language, truly imagined, vibrant in rhythm, with an exuberant strength and playful delicacy of tone. In 'The Swing' there is another metaphor for balance and equation, for letting go and coming back, for seeing 'Light over fields and hedges, . . . like a nativity / Foreground and background'; the swing itself is 'A lure letdown to tempt the soul to rise'. His language contains the observed realistic detail and the revealed beauty in the altered perspective, 'the bright rim of the extreme'.

Seamus Heaney writes about poetry with persuasive force, in a prose style that is figurative and supple. In addition to accounts of his early years in Northern Ireland, other essays in *Preoccupations: Selected Prose*, 1980, deal with poets who have influenced him – Gerard Manley Hopkins, whose accentual, consonantal music he once imitated; Patrick Kavanagh, who confirmed the validity of rural life as subject matter; Wordsworth in whom he noted the relationship between 'the almost physiological operations of a poet composing and the music of the finished poem'.

Just as *Preoccupations* responds to subjects that are found within the early poetry, so *The Government of the Tongue*, 1988, takes up issues, which have permeated *North*, *Field Work*, and *Station Island*. Here, too, he is troubled by the question of poetry's right to exist. Does it not betray suffering? Should one write lyric poetry at a time of grief? His considerations of literary figures who have responded to suffering answer these questions: Anton Chekhov's drinking cognac within sounds of the convicts at work represents the poet's right to his gift; Osip Mandelstam's metaphor for *The Divine Comedy* as a vast beehive makes the point that poetry is determined not by ecclesiastical or philosophical ideas, but by the intuitive swarming within the poet's subconscious. In poets who have resisted political repression, Mandelstam, Zbigniew Herbert, Czeslaw Milosz, Heaney presents those whose espousal of poetry before politics ratifies what he himself has expressed. Their ideal of plain, anti-lyrical poetry, responsive to reality, using parable to outsmart censorship and oppression, comes close to what he does in *Field Work*. He argues for the self-validating singularity of poetry. 'Station Island' resembles Chekhov's journey to Sakhalin. Both are rituals of exorcism; both achieve psychic and artistic freedom. Both writers face the horror, show themselves deeply moved, but with equal firmness, unflinchingly show themselves obedient to their consciences as writers. Lyric utterance, in other words, is a form of radical witness. The ungoverned tongue is its freed tongue. There is a point of balance in the result: when the poem is completed something occurs, 'which is equidistant from self-justification and self-obliteration'. A plane, he says, is fleetingly established where the poet is intensified in his being and freed from his predicament. Released from social obligation, his tongue is also freed. In that image, already figured in the balancing of beauty and atrocity in *North*, Heaney anticipates the theme of his next book of essays.

The Redress of Poetry. Oxford Lectures, 1995, studies a variety of poets – W. B. Yeats, Philip Larkin, Elizabeth Bishop, John Clare, Oscar Wilde, Dylan Thomas – and believes that the imaginative transformation of human life is the means by which we can most truly grasp and comprehend it. The idea of redress encompasses the idea of counter-weighting – 'tilting the scales of reality towards some transcendent equilibrium'. Heaney works with an authority gained through his experience of writing and makes what he has discovered through writing the subject matter of his imaginative insight. He has always been attentive to the mystery of creativity, the intimate, hidden processes by which poems rise to the surface of the consciousness, the connection between a given, instinctive language and the language acquired by reading and education, and the actuality of composition in which, he says, a personal force is moved through an aesthetic distance.

Notes

1   Sections of this essay have appeared in the following: '"We pine for ceremony": Ritual and Reality in the Poetry of Seamus Heaney (1965–1975)', *Studies in Seamus Heaney*, ed. J. Genet (1987), reprinted in *Seamus Heaney: A Collection of Critical Essays*, ed. F. Andrews (1992).

2   Maurice Harmon, 'Spaten und Wasserwaage: Seamus Heaney's Suche Nach Herkunft Und Gleichgewicht', *Seamus Heaney Tod Eines Naturforschers* (Lachen am Zürichsee: Coron Verlag, 1995).

3   *Njal's Saga*, trans. Magnus Magnusson and Hermann Pásson (Harmondsworth: Penguin, 1960).

4   A. P. Smyth, *Scandinavian Kings in the British Isles, 850–880* (London: Oxford University Press, 1977).

13
THOMAS KINSELLA: POET OF MANY VOICES

The sombre cast of Thomas Kinsella's mind appeared early in work that was concerned with the issues of decay and death, forces which could, he believed, be countered by those of love and creativity. His interest in the creative process has been constant, as found in 'Finistère', which as well as being an account of a journey of early people to Ireland is an allegory of creation. Harmon has written The Poetry of Thomas Kinsella, *1974, and numerous articles and lectures on the poet's work. The present essay, given as a talk at the annual Yeats International Summer School in Sligo, 2003, and published in the* Journal of Irish Studies, *2003, has additional material, which brings the discussion up to 2006.*

> Sick of the piercing company of women,
> I swung the gate shut with a furious sigh,
> Rammed trembling hands in pockets and drew in
> A breath of river air.[1]

THESE opening lines of Thomas Kinsella's 'A Country Walk' create a vivid portrait of the poet self. From the bluntly assertive 'Sick of' and through a succession of active verbs – 'swung', 'Rammed', 'drew in' – all in dominant positions – and strong adjectives – 'piercing', 'furious', 'trembling' – we are left in no doubt as to his emotional state. We hear a personal voice and recognise the language of the everyday self. It is the first example of Kinsella's creating an extended, objective portrait of the self, which is brought onto the page in a charged emotional state.

The persona, emotional, and responsive to the natural world, is defined in these opening lines. He is also an active presence – 'I clapped my gloves...I knelt, baring my hand, and scooped and drank'. Active verbs bring him alive. The direction is not towards descriptions of nature, although these are exact and evocative, but towards the graph of emotional change in the walker. He is a particular kind of walker. The violence of the past goes with him. He speaks bluntly, identifying place and event. Things happened at 'that shallow ford', 'There' and 'there' and 'twice more' and on the day 'Christ hung dying' brothers fought. The 'day darkened', there was 'a full eclipse'. Irish saga and biblical narrative fuse. He also connects the Norman massacre of his 'fathers' and Oliver Cromwell's butcheries to the place.

In the references to the Anglo-Irish War and the Civil War the tone changes. In Kinsella's sarcastic account we hear one of the voices that will emerge in the later poem *Nightwalker*, 1968. 'Our watchful elders', he tells us, 'have exchanged / A trenchcoat playground for a gombeen jungle'; the word 'gombeen' is a reference to a middle-class Ireland in which commercial values are more prevalent than idealistic ones.

These references to Irish revolution and commerce are reminiscent of Yeats's observations on the Paudeens at their greasy tills. But Kinsella keeps his distance. His voice will not be lost in the language of the Celtic Revival or in the attitudes of romantic nationalism. The way he describes the countryside is also different from the imprecise and delicate depiction of landscape in Yeats's early poetry. Unlike Yeats, Kinsella deals with an actual landscape. The difference from Yeats is more sharply marked in the tone he uses to recall nationalistic figures. Yeats celebrated those who had brought about the terrible beauty of the 1916 Rising.

> I write it out in a verse –
> MacDonagh and MacBride
> And Connolly and Pearse
> Now and in time to be,
> Wherever green is worn,
> Are changed, changed utterly:
> A terrible beauty is born.[2]

Kinsella's voice is deflating.

> I came upon the sombre monuments
> That bear their names: MacDonagh and McBride,
> Merchants; Connolly's Commercial Arms....

Yeats raises his nationalists to heroic status, Kinsella lowers them to a mercenary reality. Yeats's energy and passion are countered by Kinsella's levelling speech in which there is no tolerance for violence and no trace of admiration.

The first person narrator in 'Downstream', the second long poem in the collection *Downstream*, 1962, has a more muted voice, interacting at a diminished rate with the natural world into which he brings a narrower and more burdened sense of historical violence. The connection between the two poems is that Kinsella's voice is again literary and historical and that the issue of violence is central, a matter of terrifying reality, not of romantic glorification. To an even greater degree than 'A Country Walk', 'Downstream' affirms a sense of historical catastrophe not within the comforting cycle of Yeats's *A Vision*, but within a disturbing evolutionary progression. The 'I' figure is not as vividly present as the figure in 'A Country Walk'. He and his companion are literary travellers who talk of poetry as they set out. The narrator reads out a page from Ezra Pound's *Cantos* and then as he takes the oars names 'old signs' above the Central Plain. As in Dante's *Inferno* this, too, is a journey into the abyss; the voyagers resemble Dante and Virgil, the *terza rima* in which much of the poem is written being a further attempt to relate this journey to *The Divine Comedy*.

Those self-conscious literary allusions, however, give way to a sense of dread: the 'black cage' closes in; 'furred night-brutes' stop and listen. At once the narrator remembers the frightening story of the man who died among these bushes, the shell of his body half-eaten before it was found. That revived memory has an instant effect: the 'cold of hell', 'a terror in the glands' stops his blood. He associates that 'terror' with the massive evil of the Second World War in which 'swinish men' replicated what 'furred night brutes' did in the woods.

> ... Each day a spit
>
> That, turning, sweated war. Each night a fall
> Back to the evil dream where rodents ply,
> Man-rumped, sow-headed, busy with whip and maul
>
> Among nude herds of the damned.

This perception of evil men is all the more traumatic because he had been innocent, 'impervious to calamity', before he heard as a child the story of the dead man in the woods.

> Imagining a formal drift of the dead
> Stretched calm as effigies...

But the story of the dead man thrust

> Pungent horror and an actual mess
> Into my very face, and taste I must.

That shocked confrontation with the facts of evil and of death is one discovery he wants us to know about. By the end of the poem, a more positive one will replace it.

Now, as he journeys into the 'alleys of the wood', he remembers the body 'Spreadeagled on leaves'. Now, however, the horror is transmuted to a calm encounter between the dead man and the stars. At the heart of the journey as the boat trembles across the 'abyss', the poet has a radiant insight, signalled by the movement of the swan, 'A soul of white with darkness for a nest'. In the heart of darkness this creature 'bore the night so tranquilly' the narrator raises his eye to see the pattern of order in which the stars descend to the starlit eye of the dead man.

> The slow, downstreaming dead, it seemed, were blended
> One with those silver hordes, and briefly shared
> Their order, glittering.

The slow-moving stream carries a slow moving poem that is freighted with significance, past and present joined, all the memories determining the consciousness of the speaker. He is burdened by the past, by the experience of evil, by the shock of its discovery, but the plot of that past is summarised, its mystery plucked from the stream of existence and vividly realised. The voice is earnest and purposeful, a witness to a truth arising from blackness. What is new is the perception of order, the countering of brutish evil with the swan's serenity. The movement is internal as well as external, from dread to tranquillity.

'Old Harry' is also preoccupied with the evil that men do. The speaker finds American President Harry Truman's attack on Hiroshima and Nagasaki so horrific that he speaks in surreal images of massive transformation – convulsive wreckage, physical distortion conveyed in ironic images of sexual response, fiery immolation, and a devastation so extreme that mythic creatures, part animal, part human, abandon the world. The two chosen cities of the plain, he tells us, in biblical echoes,

> Lost their flesh and blood – tiles, underwear, wild cries
> Stripped away in gales of light. Lascivious streets
> Heightened their rouge and welcomed baths of pure flame.
>
> In broad daylight delicate creatures of love
> Opened their thighs. Their breasts melted shyly
> And bared the white bone. At that sight
>
> Men blushed fiercely and became shades.

In place of the two 'cities of wickedness', as he calls them with withering irony, are two sightless ducts; and the twittering animals, in the vicinity of the man who unleashed this abominable terror, draw blood as they stroke one another.

If Kinsella's voice in these three poems is serious in manner, the persona in *Wormwood*, 1966, is even more earnest. The tone of solemnity pervades the prose introduction.

It is certain that maturity and peace are to be sought through ordeal after ordeal, and it seems that the search continues until we fail. We reach out after each new beginning, penetrating our context to know ourselves, and our knowledge increases until we recognise again (more profoundly each time) our pain, indignity and triviality. This bitter cup is offered, heaped with curses, and we must drink or die....

The speaker is serious and forthright, a measured voice assessing personal experience. Like a scientist he lays out evidence in a logical manner in the knowledge that his conclusions are both valid and incontrovertible. Through a process of discovery made through successive trials, he has worked out a philosophy of survival. He believes that the ability to absorb and transmute bitterness is the only way to handle the ordeals of life successfully. That belief is predicated on the sustaining force of love. It is an ethic of suffering similar to that found in Christian teaching whose images of cup, ordeal, communion, and purification through suffering it adapts.

This sequence of seven marriage poems matches images and vignettes of suffering and endurance against those of love and support. The emblematic tree, obsessively undergoing self-punishment, stripping itself of leaves, invites us to see the state of the marriage partners. The riddle 'What cannot rest till it is bare, / Though branches crack and fibres tear?' has only one answer. The allegory of intertwined trees in the title poem dramatises the self as victim of nightmare and suffering. Yeats used the image to represent the continuance of love after death; Kinsella uses it to represent death-in-life – life itself, love itself, marriage being a form of death that must be endured.

I have dreamt it again: standing suddenly still
In a thicket, among wet trees, stunned, minutely
Shuddering, hearing a wooden echo escape.

A mossy floor, almost colourless, disappears
In depths of rain among the tree shapes.
I am straining, tasting that echo a second longer.

If I can hold it ... familiar if I can hold it.
A black tree with a double trunk – two trees
Grown into one – throws up its blurred branches.

The two trunks in their infinitesimal dance of growth
Have turned completely about one another, their join
A slowly twisted scar, that I recognise...

>A quick arc flashes sidewise in the air,
>A heavy blade in flight. A wooden stroke:
>Iron sinks in the gasping core.
>>I will dream it again.

The speaker is caught in nightmare, straining to hold onto the 'echo', possessed and in agony: 'I have dreamt it again'. . . 'I am straining'. . . 'I recognise'. . . 'I will dream it again.'

In 'Mask of Love' the partners jointly suffer 'stress', are wearied by the struggle, face each other across an abyss. The speaker warns us repeatedly not to turn to them for peace. The final stanza offers a tableau of a bizarre relationship, their

>>nocturnal
>Suicidal dance:
>She, bent on some tiny mote;
>I, doubled in laughter,
>Clasping my paunch in grief
>For the world in a speck of dust; . . .

'The Secret Garden' provides a more balanced picture of the relationship. Here destruction and beauty coexist – bramble and dewdrop, father and child, death and birth, the 'sour encounter' and procreation. In a tentative and tender voice the 'I' figure accepts the conditions of life, appreciates beauty, of nature, of childhood, even as he knows both are subject to the all-encompassing withering. He is more human and more likeable in this poignant elegy, gentler in tone than 'Mask of Love' or 'Wormwood'.

>A child stands an instant at my knee.
>His mouth smells of energy, light as light.
>I touch my hand to his pearl flesh, taking strength.
>He stands still, absorbing in return
>The first taint. Immaculate, the waiting
>Kernel of his brain.
>How set him free, a son, toward the sour encounter?

In this sequence Kinsella reduces the complexity of the individual and the variety of human nature to an essential bleakness, closer in this *reductio ad absurdum* to Samuel Beckett than to W. B. Yeats. The plenitude and beauty of the natural and social worlds are excluded. Through reduction and simplification he achieves intensity and starkness. The figure clutching his paunch is close to Job on the dung heap or Lear on the heath, hauntingly stripped down, more clearly seen as a bare, forked animal.

Nightwalker is a poem in many voices and various tones. In this poetry of the first voice, to use T. S. Eliot's distinction, descriptions of place reflect the consciousness of the walker-narrator. The Dublin suburb of Sandycove is a city of the dead. He is the worn commuter who has to endure the daily journey from the dull and depressing surroundings of Sandycove to the dispiriting routines of the Civil Service. He is the Civil Servant who reacts with scorn and anger to the First Economic Programme, his disappointment interfaced with the noble inscription on New York's Statue of Liberty. Kathleen Ní Houlihan has become a debased figure identified as Productive Investment. The tone is unctuous, filled with the clichés of the business world, the seductions of the new programme.

> Robed in spattered iron she stands
> At the harbour mouth, Productive Investment,
> And beckons the nations through our gold half-door:
> Lend me your wealth, your cunning and your drive,
> Your arrogant refuse. Let my people serve them
> Holy water in our new hotels,
> While native businessmen and managers
> Drift with them chatting over to the window
> To show them our growing city, give them a feeling
> Of what is possible; our labour pool,
> The tax concessions to foreign capital,
> How to get a nice estate though German.
> Even collect some of our better young artists.

There is no mistaking the bitter sarcasm of these lines. Violence has been done to his country's values. He sees violence in the birth of the Moon, which was a sundering from the earth. He sees it in the shift in values by which commercial interests take priority over cultural and moral values, in the debasement of education, in the cynical misuse of the Irish language, in the reduction of religion to pious platitudes, in the educational failure to prepare the young for the realities of the modern world. If the traveller in 'Downstream' lived in a dream, the walker here has been shocked wide awake and the many topics in the poem are a catalogue of events and issues that have jolted him into honest assessment and into the fundamental conviction that it is essential to be clear-eyed.

The narrator's tale bristles at times with detail, as in the political fable of the Wedding Group that tells of a friendship that turned to enmity. The Groom, Best Man, the Fox, and their three ladies from the Wedding Group. Their sundering into violence and slaughter summarises what happened when former friends – Kevin O'Higgins, Rory O'Connor, and Eamon de Valera, who had been at the wedding of Kevin O'Higgins – took opposing sides in the Civil War, and the first two were killed.

> Look! The Wedding Group...
> The Groom, the Best Man, the Fox, and their three ladies.
> A tragic tale. Soon, the story tells,
> Enmity sprang up between them, and the Fox
> Took to the wilds. Then, to the Groom's sorrow,
> His dear friend left him also, vowing hatred.
> So they began destroying the Groom's substance
> And he sent out to hunt the Fox, but trapped
> His friend instead; mourning he slaughtered him.
> Shortly, in his turn, the Groom was savaged
> No one knows by whom. Though it's known the Fox
> Is a friend of Death, and rues nothing.

The section continues its parable to take in the State's execution of '77' Republicans, de Valera's appointment of Ernest Blythe to the board of the Abbey Theatre. Blythe, The Weasel of the poem, dances under the Player King, that is, William Butler Yeats, while de Valera, the Fox, looks on. The tone becomes elegiac.

In reference to Yeats's role as Player King, however, in the collection *Responsibilities*, 1914, he stepped out of the shadows of the Celtic Revival to publicly condemn the people of his time, the Paudeens at their greasy tills, the pious and demoralised people who would be unable to recognise a Robert Emmet or a Wolf Tone if they came back to life. Kinsella's political attack is equally unexpected. His poetry had not been political, but in *Nightwalker* he directs his gaze with withering honesty on his own time, place, and generation. The fable form distances the account, but the relevance is clear, deliberate, and highly charged.

It is significant that as the walker approaches the Martello tower in Sandycove he appeals to the prose master James Joyce rather than the master poet W. B. Yeats, the Martello tower at Sandycove rather than the Norman tower at Thoor Ballylee. He is signalling the stance he has taken. On the one hand some sections of the poem resemble the stream of consciousness technique used in certain parts of *Ulysses*. The same fluidity of movement through incidents, memories, ideas, images, appears here. On the other hand, in invoking James Joyce, Kinsella declares an allegiance to a writer who made his work out of the gritty and often unattractive reality of life in twentieth-century Dublin rather than to a writer who preferred to commemorate the fallen majesty of the Ascendancy.

If the *Wormwood* sequence is realised in a strait-jacket, the voice of the persona in *Nightwalker* is at once freer and more complex. Here the Tiresian consciousness in a sea of transient and changing circumstances seeks for structure and in the end finds it within. In its shifting scenes and changing voices the poet's anger at what has been done to a generation is palpable – the debasement of cultural values, the nationalistic pleading, all adumbrated in the phrases 'a dish of scalding tears... The food of dragons / And my own dragon self.' Juxtaposed with this ironical and angry summary is the elegiac voice of Amergin, the Old Irish poet, as a seamew lamenting what has happened to the country. Then in a dramatic change of mood and rhythm the self makes an imaginary flight to the Moon, whose barren surface gives an unrestricted view of the depressive conditions the walker has seen. The poem concludes:

> I think this is the Sea of Disappointment.
> If I stoop down, and touch the edge, it has
> A human taste, of massed human wills.

'Disappointment' is the appropriate word for a generation that was fed on the pap of false nationalism, for whom growing up meant being thrust into a reality for which they had not been prepared. It is central to this poem that Kinsella projects himself as a product and victim of this Ireland. He may detest many of its features, he may deeply regret and resent what has been done to Irish culture and life, but as a writer he will not turn away from them. From this position he will transmute its negative aspects into something positive in the life of the poem.

The psychological directions taken by the narrator in *Nightwalker* are deepened in [*Notes*] *From the Land of the Dead*, 1972. If *Nightwalker* is politically challenging, the poems in the new collection mark a change – in the portrayal of the self, in the explicit autobiographical material, in the style that enables him to use language that is at one and the same time positive and negative.

Kinsella now dramatises himself as a Faustian adventurer prepared to face abnormal states, one who has 'turned to things not right nor reasonable', as Faust did when he made his compact with the devil.

> Dear God, if I had known how far and deep,
> how long and cruel, I think my being
> would have blanched: appalled.

In an exclamatory style the 'appalled' self remembers and recreates the extreme experience. The method involves us, bears witness for us, acts out what was private and traumatic, as it had done in the *Wormwood* poems. Now we have the self as magician with his implements, preparing to go out of his mind into the depths of the unconscious, to fall out of this world into the abyss; 'So far from the world and earth'. He falls where there is –

> No bliss, no pain; dullness after pain.
> A cistern hiss... A thick tunnel stench
> rose to meet me. Frightful. Dark nutrient waves.
> And I knew no more.

The loss of consciousness is followed by an embryonic state in which he drifts, seeking an empty shell in which to grow. The narrator remembers the ordeal, the fall, and the search for a way back to the upper world. This emblematic account prefigures what happens elsewhere in the collection, in particular in several poems that concentrate on the significance of a child's encounter with his grandmother.

Kinsella's initial impulse to write a poem about one of his grandmothers becomes an exploration of the significance implicit in that encounter, the one setting out on the road of life, innocent, and untested, the other at the end of that road, aged, dying, shrivelling into death; the images associated with her are blackness, decay, smells, and fear. To the little boy she is a figure of dread, witchlike, predatory, mysterious, someone he is urged to visit, to encounter, to kiss. The meeting is allegorical, a terrifying conjunction of youth and age, innocence and experience, the pristine consciousness and the consciousness burdened with life's ordeals.

In these poems the 'I' narrator is a witness. In 'Hen Woman' the tone is one of serious attention – alert, detailed, perceptive, reading the small event, the trivial scene, packing it with significance. He gives the details of place, time, and the atmosphere surrounding the event. The older self looks back at the earlier self. The objectivity of his narrative freezes the moment, the figures, and the event into a diagram – the woman hurries out, the egg falls and breaks but in slow motion. 'Nothing moved', 'time stood still' – bird, woman, and child 'locked there... gaping'. Then the dung beetle, bearer of life, advances; the egg falls, thunder sounds. This witnessing, this exact recording, this brooding searching into the substance for significance is presented as part of the way in which the imagination seizes experience and takes it in to be processed. 'I feed upon it still,' he tells us.

> there is no end to that which, not understood,
> may yet be hoarded in the imagination,
> in the yolk of one's being, so to speak,
> there to undergo its (quite animal) growth,
>
> dividing blindly, twitching, packed with will,
> searching in its own tissue
> for the structure in which it may wake.
> Something that had – clenched in its cave –
> not been now was: an egg of being.

Throughout the Peppercanister publications, 1972–2006, and ongoing, Thomas Kinsella's handling of voice and persona is complex and varied, but on the whole it is objective and rational, as though the recovery from the descent into the underworld of the self and into classical and celtic myth has been restorative. Instead of the diagrammatical tension of 'Hen Woman' we have the separate but interactive portrayals of *The Good Fight*, 1973 – John F. Kennedy, Lee Harvey Oswald, Robert Frost, Plato. It is the interaction of these figures, their individual wills and values, and their interpretations of human psychology that gives the poem its particular force. Similarly, in other poems in the Peppercanister series, such as *Her Vertical Smile*, 1985, and *Out of Ireland*, 1987, the presence of contrasting figures is significant. The poem's meaning is revealed through distinct voices, each enunciating a particular point of view, no individual voice articulating the entire meaning.

In *The Good Fight* John F. Kennedy evokes the promise of New Frontier politics by his vigour and idealism, his ability to imbue a people with a vision of what is possible. His point of view is based on the idea that 'All reasonable things are possible.' Kennedy's voice in its positive rhythms and choice of words embodies the forward-looking drive of the political leader – 'we will march along', 'bend their wills together', 'admit no limit...'. The call is to urgent 'adventuring', 'aspiring to the sublime', 'to greatness'. 'Let us make ourselves vessels of decision.' 'The old order changes!' These passages pulse with the dynamism of Kennedy's language and are interspersed with Kinsella's voice as he reflects on this language and the limits within which Kennedy framed his appeal. Side by side with the heightened, motivational, political rhetoric is the calm analysis of the poet. Kennedy's final speech is measured against Plato's observations on the dangers and pitfalls of leadership.

The portrait of Lee Harvey Oswald begins with objective third-person narration as Kinsella describes him settling into the room from which he will shoot at the President, but this changes to the first person voice of the alienated being. It is a moving threnody for what it feels like to be a nobody and how that feeling motivates him to counter the negative state.

> I have seen very few
> cut so dull and driven a figure,
> masked in scorn or abrupt
> impulse, knowing content
> nowhere.

Oswald is broodingly self-aware and at the centre of his own drama of changing response. He can decide to end this state through suicide or through reaching out and touching. The question then becomes 'Who was that? / What decision was this?' Again, as in the earlier section dealing with Kennedy, Kinsella recalls Plato's remarks on feelings that afflict the individual – passion, greed, reason submerged. He counters Oswald's mood with Plato's observations on man's brutish propensity for evil.

The final voice is that of Robert Frost, who has been stunned by the calamity of the assassination, concluding.

> That all *un*reasonable things
> are possible. *Everything*
> that can happen will happen.

His conclusion challenges Plato's philosophy of harmony, a balance between Body and Mind. The twentieth-century post-Freudian intellectual knows what man is capable of, the evil that men do. The artist can cope with that.

> it is we, letting things *be*,
> who might come at understanding.
> That is the source of our patience.

The Good Fight works through a number of voices that are characterised at some length. In *Out of Ireland* the presentation of voices is more complex and more concise. The setting is St Gobnait's cemetery in Ballyvourney, where the composer Seán O'Riada is buried. The voices are several: a crow, the Black Robber, which is a human head over the chancel of the church, a Síle na Gig on the south wall, and an open grave. As Irish scholars on the continent used to advertise their skills in the streets, so each figure here declares its particular values: the crow offers knowledge of flesh and blood, the Black Robber counters that deathly invitation with the fact that he is native born in our 'foul deeds', one with us in committing evil; Síle na Gig offers her vaginal orifice, source of life, superior to the other two; the grave offers redemption after death. Like instruments in an orchestra these conflicting appeals, sequential and contrapuntal, sound their values with accumulating force.

The poem shifts to selective appropriation of the philosopher Eriugena's metaphor of instrumental harmony, the dance and fiery immolation, to express his philosophy of the return of all mankind to God. In the next section Kinsella uses the image of the dance to memorialise the dancing figure of O'Riada, his shifting rhythms, throaty piping, and dry taps on the drum skin. In the real world, however, drawing again from Eriugena, Kinsella says in his own voice:

> and it grows dark and we stumble
> in gathering ignorance
> in a land of loss
> and unfulfillable desire.

In the final section, called 'Exit', as they leave the cemetery, Kinsella comments in his own voice about man's 'suspended understanding' as he waits for the end, the evidence in the cemetery of death; but he says, 'The dance is at our own feet': it is up to us to dance, putting the cemetery behind us. It is up to the poet to write: 'reach me my weapon / in the goat-grey light'. The conclusion suggests a dedication to art before everything else, but in the context of all that the poem has expressed.

The undefined 'us' in this poem connects with Kinsella's habit in several poems of moving from the 'I' persona to the general 'we'. It is particularly effective in the collection *One*, 1974, where much of the material is drawn from *The Book of Invasions*, that work of pseudo-history that relates the coming of successive groups of people to Ireland in pre-historic times. In 'Finistère', for example, Kinsella celebrates the voyage of people from continental Europe to Ireland. The 'I' speaker is both Amergin, the first Old Irish poet, and the male principle, the undivided one. It is he who responds creatively to the idea of voyaging into the Atlantic, he who observes a 'point of light' on the horizon; it is in him that

> A maggot of the possible
> wriggled out of the spine
> into the brain.

The poem moves with rhythmic intensity and persistence changing at once from 'I' to 'we' as the people set out: 'our heads sang with purpose / and predatory peace'. They respond more to an excitement in the blood than to an idea in the head, but as they advance they carry with them the megalithic civilisation they have created in Finistère and will build again in Ireland. The poem bears witness to the mystery that motivates them, asking unanswered questions about the source of their excitement and the origin of this 'ghostly hunger' that causes them to leave what they have and voyage into the unknown. The rhythms in this celebration of the human instinct for reaching forward carry the poem forward, mimicking the motions of the ocean. It becomes a womb journey as they move 'as one' through 'salt chaos', praying for peace to the moon, source of their 'unrest', whose power they have tried to depict on 'great uprights':

> ... whose goggle gaze
> and holy howl we have scraped
> speechless on slabs of stone
> poolspirals opening on
> closing spiralpools
> and dances drilled in the rock
> in coil zigzag angle and curl....

The 'I' speaker fuses naturally with the 'we' and 'us' of the poem. As they step ashore the speaker/narrator recites Amergins's famous 'Hymn to Creation', an affirmation of beginnings.

Several other poems in the collection *One* speak with this inclusive 'we' voice. 'The Oldest Place' recreates the processes that affected the early people, a settling in, a taking possession, persistence, endurance, the land responding to their care. The poem in its various sections sketches things that happened to them. The speaker changes from 'we' to the 'I' who survives in the land of the dead, the barren plain with a standing stone. A similar transition takes place in some of the autobiographical poems, such as '38 Phoenix Street', where the 'I' becomes 'we', the individual child and the collective children. The fluid interaction of 'I' and 'we' is perfectly adapted to the pervasive thrust of these poems, these explorations of Kinsella's past in the immediate past as percolating through recent generations, and the distant sources of beginnings. At the heart of this backward turning is the concept of process, the ways in which things develop, a country's past, language, and culture, the creative process itself both in evolutionary terms and in terms of the hidden ways in which works of art are processed – experience absorbed, acted upon within the psyche, brought forth as a work of art. It is appropriate that the speaker should be both the single voice of the artist/poet and the collective voice of the family or the people. To be fully alive is to be creatively engaged. The imagination reaches out.

A similar method of varied dramatisation is found in its companion collection *Songs of the Psyche*, 1985, in which Kinsella moves towards the unconscious by autobiographical markers, many of which have a Jungian implication. Not a fall into the unconscious by the appalled self as in [*Notes*] *From the Land of the Dead*, the poem is a deliberate descent into the dark, nutrient waters of the unconscious. In a 'reverie' of submission, invoking the number nine as a guarantee of safety and return, Kinsella begins his Dantesque journey to Middle Earth, to his encounter with the grin of the goddess from which he returns with a clearer sense of how the psychological and creative process works: 'a matter of / negative release'. The suggestive, allegorical method releases a familiar philosophical concept of the interlocking forces of the creative and the destructive; the metaphorical figures are joined once again in a mutually wounding relationship, both 'tender' and 'brutal', consumed in the flame imagery of 'Phoenix Park' and of Eriugena, and meditative. They have a compulsive need to absorb: 'they have eaten / and must eat'. Similarly, in using again the metaphor of the intertwined trees, Kinsella restates his philosophy of the centrality of love and persistence.

The high point of Kinsella's dramatic interplay of voices comes in *Her Vertical Smile*, 1985, which has an Overture, two movements divided by an

Intermezzo, and a Coda. Many of the issues that permeate Kinsella's collections from 1985 to 2006 – the nature of existence, the relevance of the divine, the role of the artist – are encapsulated in a superbly orchestrated work. Set in Vienna at the time of the collapse of the Austrian Empire, the beautifully poignant Overture responds to the Earth Mother's song in Gustav Mahler's *Das Lied von der Erde*. In a delicate evocation of the ending of *Der Abschied*, it mimics the voice of a sorrowing woman, as she slowly repeats the single word '*ewig*' (eternal) nine times. She grieves for her son but also for the end of the world. As in Mahler's music, where splendour and energy oppose desolation, *Her Vertical Smile* plays out incidents, metaphors, and occasions of hope and promise against those of disappointment and destruction. Kinsella evaluates man's capacity for creation and destruction. Moving between commentary and evaluation, he sees in Mahler's counterpoint of creation and destruction an accurate reflection of the reality of existence.

Mahler is the exemplary artist – committed to his work, and constantly searching for new ways in which to embody his complex vision. His vision of a happy outcome to the conflict between creation and destruction, expressed through a matriarchal litany in the symphony's celebration of Faust's ascent to an affirmative vision, is juxtaposed with Michelangelo's depiction of the Creation. Neither of these, in Kinsella's view, is fully satisfactory. Considering Mahler's and Michelangelo's depictions – old Vienna destroyed, the collapse of the Empire, and the outbreak of war – he asks the rhetorical question: what is the value of empire and civilisation when everything turns to mud and gore, when we ourselves produce this 'curse'. Mahler dissolves grief and death in transcendent music. Kinsella relies on the defusing corrective of ironic counterpoint.

But he does not repeat the scale of this poem. He has other things on his mind: more immediate signs of moral evil. *Her Vertical Smile* presented its panorama of good and evil. Subsequent collections, such as *Poems from Centre City*, 1990, and *Personal Places*, 1990, deal with more contemporary examples. Dublin is defined as a place of the damned, stalked by evil in the figure of a mysterious Stranger and marked by the presence of destruction, waste, and the absence of spiritual authority. Poems about these matters, some satirical, lead to Aogán O Rathaille's vision of absolute meaninglessness in 'At the Western Ocean's Edge'. In the face of such negative, destructive reality, how should the poet behave?

In the first place, keeping a 'local watchfulness', he should condemn when condemnation is required. Kinsella is fiercely critical of greedy speculators who destroy parts of the city, Corporation officials, who erect offices for themselves on a Viking site, who build but do not maintain apartment blocks for the poor – 'concrete piss-towers for the under-privileged' – and clerics who, instead of upholding a moral code, connive with the speculators. Raised on high, the god of commerce has replaced the Christian God; and man, once the measure in the Vitruvian ideal, is debased and violated. Man is 'lifted', 'enlarged', 'cruciforked', 'jacked up', 'splayed like a target'. Society is sick, Dublin a Dantean underworld, Kinsella its outspoken judge.

The artist's task is not only to call a spade a spade, but above all not to be deflected from his pursuit of beauty. Using the classical image of a 'lovely beaker/with the slim amphibian handle', Kinsella provides an abstract equation of an ideal work of art, difficult in execution yet 'the most rewarding':

> – in fact a web of order,
> each mark accommodating
>
> the shapes of all the others
> with none at fault, or false;
>
> a system of live images
> making increased response
> to each increased demand
> in the eye of the beholder,
>
> with a final full response
> over the whole surface
> a total theme – presented
> to a full intense regard; . . .

In the second place, when times are particularly bad he can do his best to record. In *The Pen Shop*, 1997, Kinsella is the reflective maker, the voice of the exact recorder of his walk through the city, with his personal memories and associations. The poem is grounded in the reality of streets, shops, and directions. It draws in places with an autobiographical significance. In a reflective trope the pen shop to which the poet goes for refills for his pen becomes the source of his work, which the poem subsumes in innumerable echoes and allusions. The poem becomes an archetypal descent into the underworld, with Joycean parallels and echoes of Aeneas's meeting with his father in Hades.

Other poems at this time deepen the significance of past events, in particular his meeting with Eleanor, who becomes his wife and who is present in a number of poems – 'The Familiar' (*The Familiar*, 1999), 'Glenmacnass' (*Littlebody*, 2000), 'First Night' (*Marginal Economy*, 2006).[3] These poems increase the significance of her arrival in his life; they vary from the allegorical to the explicitly sexual to the ritualistic and ordinary.

The voice and the characters, mainly himself and Eleanor, are both the social selves and their metaphorical extensions; she is both Eleanor and Proserpina, he is both himself and Hephaestus; their union is both physical and mystical. Their breakfast together becomes a ceremony, which is described in a lightly mocking manner, he in his dressing gown extending his arms in a priestlike gesture, she remarking, 'You always make it nice.' Nevertheless, it is ceremony, it endures, satisfies, and takes place in the real world. In a characteristic reprise in 'Glenmacnass', the couple sit at the breakfast table and hear the voices of the companionable crows flying 'to their places'. In 'First Night' she is a footstep about to enter his life just at the moment when he has left home and started a new phase.

These are serious matters. Kinsella's latest work engages with basic issues, including the role of Divinity. *Godhead*, 1999, scrutinises the Divine at a time when religion has lost much of its authority. Its contemplation of the Trinity is austere. The Father is passive; what He has done is not enough. He knows 'how it is possible to grasp completely / while remaining partly incapable'. The Divine and the human are alike in that both understand the impossibility of achieving perfection. In response to the poet's prayer, the Father insists that he write about mortality. Kinsella uses this dialogue to authenticate a lifelong preoccupation with death. In His insistence on the fact of waste, God verifies the menace of the waiting Stranger. At a higher level that menace is dramatised in Mary's loveless union with the Stranger. Drained of Divinity, the baby that results wails like any human child. The absolute stillness, the sealed feelings of the Godhead contrast with the 'unrest' of the ocean, its capacity for disorder and disarray.

Poetry and the natural world are expressions of God's work, when religion fails. Framing poems celebrate the 'unearthly power' of the ocean. 'High Tide, Amagansett' is richly descriptive of waves coming in and breaking noisily along the shore, one wave withdrawing and meeting the next as it advances. 'Midnight, San Clemente: a gloss' deals with the same 'unearthly power', which is earthed and deified in the Irish tradition. The thunder of the waves is a metaphor for the Holy Spirit, whose 'black breath' it is.

> *All metre and mystery*
> *touch on the Lord at last.*
> *The tide thunders ashore*
> *in praise of the High King.*

The natural world manifests God's creation.

Kinsella also believes that we are not communicating with one another, but looking into our hearts, finding the inadequacy there and seeing it all about us. We are talking as clearly as we can to a projection of ourselves. This bleak outlook permeates the later collections: *The Familiar* and

Godhead, 1999; *Littlebody* and *Citizen of the World*, 2000. The poems help to explain some of the directions found in them: the voice speaking to itself, the searching reappraisal of past incidents, the use of exemplary figures – Valetin Iremonger, Aogán O Rathaille, Oliver Goldsmith, St Augustine, Marcus Aurelius. In Valetin Iremonger he praises the good man who suffered and endured. In Aogán O Rathaille he depicts a man who faces the ultimate meaninglessness. Yeats fought the middle classes, O Rathaille fights the force inside his head, using the turmoil of the ocean as its appropriate metaphor.

> the energy of chaos and a shaping
> counter-energy in throes of balance;
> the gale wailing inland off the water
> arousing a voice responding in his head.
> storming back at the waves with their own force
> in a posture of refusal, . . .

O Rathaille stares into the wholly unknown, the totally negative milieu.

The question of how the poet conducts himself comes up again and again – in the Joycean definition of beauty in 'A Portrait of the Artist', in the poet moving from the 'long workroom', place of artistic effort in 'The Black Lane' into the world of raw material, 'waste', 'ruin', and death. In *Citizen of the World* the voices of Oliver Goldsmith and James Boswell reflect what it feels like to be ignored and unappreciated. Unable to enjoy life – 'I was quite sunk. / I looked with a degree of horror upon death!' – and afraid of death, Boswell thinks of hiding from the world, but realises sensibly that people are too busy with their own affairs to notice what he does. Therefore he will behave with dignity and rely on his own good common sense. The ideal of independence may be ironical in the light of Goldsmith's actual life, but clearly has value. Like a number of Kinsella's projections he suffers from feelings of inadequacy, faltering between optimism and disappointment. Marcus Aurelius was also a divided man, required to defend the Empire in arms but preferring to work on his *Meditations*.

Developing the attractions of the natural world, 'Glenmacnass', the key poem in *Littlebody*, moves simply and naturally from one set of associated images to another; in each section natural images serve as emblems of beauty, freedom, fidelity, and orderliness. The stiff and abstract language of 'God-head' is replaced by fluency and grace. The dwarf musician, Littlebody, appears in a context of black turf, white cottonheads, an old stone marker, the prow of rock: 'the music of pipes, distant and clear'. It is a moment of vision: a pagan shape in the air, a guttural dance, then the figure hugging his *uileann* pipes, playing in the open air, away from the hissing assemblies and the huckstering.

Kinsella's voice has become more neutral, the language simple and unadorned, only inflated at times as a means of qualifying content. In 'Marginal Economy', people have a bleak existence. They work towards the edge but find little, their search requires more and more care, their reward diminishes steadily until they have to move on again. It is a life characterised by bleakness, persistence, and stoic acceptance.

> We accepted things as they were,
> with no thought of change.
> The only change was in ourselves
> moving onward, leaving
> something behind each time.

It is a modest achievement, but it is achievement and in its own way defines a point of view that Kinsella has always held. The 'We' make no great claims for what they do, but they do it. Under no illusions, they do not wait for the Word to change their lot. The key words in the adjoining poem, 'Songs of Understanding', are 'waste', 'process', and 'inadequacy'. The speaker is resigned to their presence. Through them he finds an ongoing, dynamic, positive effect. The moral insight is similar to what Kinsella has imagined in 'Landscape and Figure' and through the ethic of suffering in *New Poems*. The difference lies in the subdued style, the less insistent tone, so that the philosophy of acceptance, endurance, and discovery is filtered through a linguistic minimalism. There may be little reason to celebrate, but every reason to create the well-wrought cup, to value ceremony, to enjoy the grace and fluidity of the natural world.

Notes

1   All quoted selections, unless otherwise indicated, are from Thomas Kinsella, *Collected Poems* (Oxford: Oxford University Press, 1996); *Collected Poems 1956–2001* (Manchester: Carcanet Press, 2001) is a slightly revised edition.

2   W. B. Yeats, *The Poems: A New Edition*, ed. Richard J. Finneran (Dublin: Gill and Macmillan, 1983).

3   Peppercanister 24 (Dublin: The Dedalus Press, 2006).

14

IRISH POETS: FRESH PERSPECTIVES, DIFFERENT VOICES

In July 2002 Harmon directed a poetry seminar at the IASIL[1] Conference at São Paulo, Brazil, which resulted in this written account. Its contents were determined in part by the choice of material and lively exchange of views of the participants during seminar meetings in which more attention was paid to the work of some poets than the work of others. This concluding essay is, therefore, neither a comprehensive outline of Irish poetry since the time of Yeats nor a complete interpretation of the work of any one poet. It is a general assessment of contemporary Irish poetry among international readers, and a recapitulation.

IN considering Irish poetry after W. B. Yeats and before the arrival of Seamus Heaney, we are dealing with two generations of poets that include Austin Clarke, Patrick Kavanagh, Louis MacNeice in the first, John Montague, Richard Murphy, and Thomas Kinsella in the second.

The publication of Seamus Heaney's 'Bogland', *Door into the Dark*, 1969, was a landmark in the history of Irish poetry after Yeats. Almost everything about it – the acceptance and transmuting of restriction, the declarative manner, the fluid movement of lines and stanzas, the tone of confidence – gave it authority and sense of liberation. Accepting encroachment and limitation in the Irish landscape, it went on to transform them with glowing evidence of depth and richness – the Great Irish Elk set up as 'An astounding crate full of air',[2] butter preserved in the bog, the bogland made into a limitless source. The poem laid claim to heritage, to the possibilities of Irish tradition, to the Irish psyche – layered, infinitely nourishing. Positive, affirmative, celebrating what it claimed in a rich forward movement, the poem came at the right time, when Irish poetry was undergoing another Renaissance.

Poets in the generation of Austin Clarke, Patrick Kavanagh, and Louis MacNeice had struggled to find their individual voice and conscious of the achievement of W. B. Yeats were in danger of imitating his sounds and echoing his music. By 1969 the line of Irish poetry had been extended from Austin Clarke's generation through that of Montague, Murphy, and Kinsella. As that line of succession extended further with the emergence of Seamus Heaney, Michael Longley, Derek Mahon, Paul Muldoon, and with the arrival of women poets – Eavan Boland, Eiléan Ní Chuilleanáin, Nuala Ní Dhomhnaill, Medbh McGuckian, and Paula Meehan, who opened up new areas of experience and developed their own voices – Irish poetry has been enriched and strengthened.

If Seamus Heaney can write a manifesto on behalf of Irish writers, he can do so because of what has been accomplished by his predecessors, Yeats, of course, but also Patrick Kavanagh, who has been a particular focus of his attention. When Heaney began to write, Kavanagh's example was significant. Here was a poet who wrote from a rural background, gave expression to the life of the small farm, its activities and speech, created for the first time a gritty sense of rural culture. But Kavanagh is a curious case. For one who has had such a big influence on Heaney and other poets, he has in fact written only a handful of memorable lyrics and one long poem, *The Great Hunger*, 1942, which in the manner of Liam O'Flaherty's *Famine*, 1937, or John McGahern's *That They May Face the Rising Sun*, 2002, gives an indelible and accurate portrait of rural life at a particular period. *The Great Hunger* is a social, psychological, and spiritual panorama that rings true. From its opening lines we have the feeling that this is a meditation on life and death as seen in the experience of one man, Patrick Maguire. The lines move at once to the idea of loss and missed opportunity: 'Is there some light of imagination in these wet clods?'[3] At the centre of the poem is the complex, bewildered man who takes pleasure in the peasant wisdom of self-preservation and caution, and deceives himself with the notion that he can find satisfaction in the land to the exclusion of a wife and children. The tension between illusion and reality persists. 'O God if I had been wiser!'

> But now a crumpled leaf from the whitethorn bushes
> Darts like a frightened robin, and the fence
> Shows the green of after-grass through a little window,
> And he knows that his own heart is calling his mother a liar,
> God's truth is life – even the grotesque shapes of its foulest fire.

Maguire is capable of an occasional refinement of feeling.

> Yet sometimes when the sun comes through a gap
> These men know God the Father in a tree:
> The Holy Spirit is the rising sap,
> And Christ will be the green leaves that will come
> At Easter from the sealed and guarded tomb.

It is sometimes said that Kavanagh's short poems are also realistic portraits of rural life. That is true up to a point. In them he looks back at the world of his youth and transforms it in the light of his imagination. A poem like 'Spraying the Potatoes' appeals as an account of a familiar activity, but is not merely a realistic portrait.

> The barrels of blue potato-spray
> Stood on a headland of July
> Beside an orchard wall where roses
> Were young girls hanging from the sky.
>
> The flocks of green potato-stalks
> Were blossom spread for sudden flight,
> The Kerr's Pinks in a frivelled blue,
> The Arran Banners wearing white.
>
> And over that potato-field
> A lazy veil of woven sun.
> Dandelions growing on headlands, showing
> Their unloved hearts to everyone.
>
> And I was there....

There is a deceptive simplicity to lines that begin with a declarative statement about real things in a real place – barrels, headland, July, orchard wall – as though fixing the scene. But by the fourth line, the style slips into metaphor and we are called upon to imagine the relationship between roses and girls. The language becomes sophisticated in its use of images of flight and colour. The imaginative associations of flocks and flight anticipate the lift-up sustained to the very end of the second line and is followed by the delicate touch of 'frivelled' in conjunction with the colours in the names of potatoes. In the third stanza that lazy veil might stand for the way in which the imagination casts a spell across an ordinary scene. Even the dandelions, normally ignored, will show their beauty, as much part of the animation as the girl-roses in stanza one. As so often in these lyrics Kavanagh places an alert consciousness at the centre: 'And I was there with the knapsack sprayer / On the barrel's edge poised', poised and ready to participate in the quickened scene. At the end Kavanagh makes the claim:

> And poet lost to potato-fields
> Remembering the lime and copper smell
> Of the spraying barrels he is not lost
> Or till blossomed stalks cannot weave a spell.

In the return to the terms of its opening the poem achieves completion; this declaration is an act of faith in the world of his boyhood here reclaimed and redeemed: 'On the barrel's edge poised'. In its implications that go beyond its contexts, this is one of the most significant moments in Irish poetry. Not only does it associate itself with those other moments in Kavanagh's lyrics of the countryside but with the unlikely figure of Patrick Maguire who can 'sometimes' see the 'Holy Spirit in the rising sap'. As long as the poet can weave that imaginative veil, he is secure in his repossession of the world he has left.

Poetry in some of its most rewarding occasions creates these intimations of spirituality, moments when we have an awareness of the supernatural, as when Thomas Kinsella, with his understanding of the ways in which music can render these intimations, records a visitation by the ghost of Seán Ó Riada when he plays *Das Lied von der Erde,* the song that excited them as young men.

> With a contraction
> Of the flesh... A year exactly since you died!
> I arrested the needle. The room filled
> with a great sigh. In terror and memory
> I lowered the point toward our youth
> – into those bright cascades![4]

Although Kavanagh's output is small and although Heaney has in many ways replaced him as the poet of rural Ireland, Kavanagh's place seems secure. He showed the way for poets such as John Montague, Derek Mahon, and Heaney; and his decision, made in the face of the weighty presence of the poets of the Irish Literary Revival and their linking with a vast cultural heritage of myth and saga, to rely on what he knew, to be a poet of the parish, has been of immense importance to virtually all subsequent Irish poets. With Kavanagh as an example anyone can have the confidence to write out of his or her particular experience, no matter how limited it may seem to be. Smallness is not the decisive factor, but the significance one can bring to it.

Kavanagh chose to exclude the literary heritage that Yeats, Lady Gregory, Douglas Hyde, and others had created and made part of the Irish consciousness. The need to reach across the linguistic and cultural divide from English language and culture to the distinctive Gaelic world runs through Irish literature. Many of the poets in the nineteenth century, including those Yeats specifically mentioned – Thomas Davis, James Clarence Mangan, Samuel Ferguson – seeing that culture being eroded and in danger of disappearance, made connections with it, wrote versions of Irish sagas and poems and tried to give their work a distinctive Irish dimension through the use of place names and events. Their scholarly contemporaries undertook a vast amount of editing, translating, and collecting. The impulse – and the need – has permeated the literature, seen nowhere so distinctively as in Thomas Kinsella's translation of the Old Irish epic *The Cattleraid of Cooley* (*The Táin,* 1970) and his translations from Irish poetry from the beginning down to the twentieth century. It could be argued that the awareness of cultural and linguistic erosion drove poets to underpin and enrich their work by grafting it onto the Irish heritage. Heaney could in 'Bogland' speak with confidence from within a tradition that by then had proven itself, but his immediate predecessors had no such certainty. When they searched into the past for literary models and exemplars, they could see Yeats, but beyond him only the weaker poets of the nineteenth century. If they wished to go back further, they had to cross over into the Gaelic world. Kavanagh's choice of the limited horizons of Monaghan, while understandable, cut off what might have fed his imagination. His successors set aside such limitations.

If Patrick Kavanagh wrote his major poem about the deprived life of the countryman, Louis MacNeice, his contemporary, in *Autumn Journal* wrote a long account of London on the brink of the Second World War. His aim was to express the mood of a generation in the persona of one individual registering the feelings and events of the time. Just as Austin Clarke realised that the plight of the individual may represent the state of many, so MacNeice recognised that his own case was symptomatic. He is a social observer. Throughout the 1930s he registered the society, of the time, its politics and values, the consumer society and his own spiritual despair. *Autumn Journal* captures an era, illustrating its glittering surfaces and moral vacuities.

> But now it seems futility, imbecility,
>   To be building shops when nobody can tell
> What will happen next. What will happen
>   We ask and waste the question on the air.
> Nelson is stone and Johnnie Walker moves his
>   Legs like a cretin over Trafalgar Square.
> And in the Corner House the carpet-sweepers
>   Advance between the tables after crumbs
> Inexorably, like a tank battalion
>   In answer to the drums.
> In Tottenham Court Road the tarts and negroes
>   Loiter beneath the lights
> And the breeze gets colder as on so many other
>   September nights.[5]

Another issue in his poetry is his relationship with Ireland, analysed sharply in Canto XVl of *Autumn Journal*. He will not accept sentimental, sham images of Irishness, or cheap nationalism. In 'Valediction' he writes, 'I can say Ireland is hooey, Ireland is / A gallery of fake tapestries', but he admits... 'I cannot deny my past to which myself is wed, / The woven figure cannot undo its thread'.

Lacking a set of supportive beliefs, MacNeice puts his faith in the life of the senses, saluting what he values – liveliness, sensation, variety, things being incorrigibly plural. 'The Sunlight on the Garden' is a haunting expression of tears in the nature of things, beauty in the midst of transience, love that will inevitably undergo alteration and death. The poem brings a wonderful play of rhymes to its theme of change and impermanence.

> The sunlight on the garden
> Hardens and grows cold,
> We cannot cage the minute
> Within its nets of gold,
> When all is told
> We cannot beg for pardon.
>
>   II
> Our freedom as free lances
> Advances towards its end;
> The earth compels, upon it
> Sonnets and birds descend;
> And soon, my friend,
> We shall have no time for dances.

Unlike Patrick Kavanagh, Austin Clarke accepted the heritage of the Irish Literary Revival, initially writing long narrative poems drawing upon the same sources in Irish myth and legend as those used by the Revival writers such as W. B. Yeats. But it was his discovery of the Christian medieval period that best suited his emotional and spiritual needs. Focusing on that era, he could comment indirectly on the puritanical Church of his own time and its inhibiting society. Clarke's most original collection, *Night and Morning*, 1938, matches Patrick Kavanagh's *The Great Hunger* in so far as the rural poet's extended account of the spiritual impoverishment resembles the urban poet's compressed dramatisation of moral conflict. Many of the poems in this collection use Christian images and allusions as metaphors for spiritual crisis, and project the anguished self in a convincing manner.

> I hammer on that common door,
> Too frantic in my superstition,
> Transfix with nails that I have broken,
> The angry notice of the mind.[6]

Clarke's concern for those who suffered at the hands of an authoritarian Church or an uncaring State manifested itself in social satire, in condemnations of cruelty to children, unmarried mothers, and those socially disadvantaged. Told from the point of view of a man whose freedom of movement has been diminished by illness, 'The Loss of Strength', one of several long autobiographical poems, uses the metaphor of curtailment to represent restrictions on the national, cultural, and spiritual levels.

In the next generation John Montague wrote of the world he knew in County Tyrone, but read the landscape in relation to its historical and mythical associations. If Kavanagh casts an imaginative veil across the landscape of Monaghan, Montague casts a different kind of spell through suggestions of a former world.

> Rough Field in the Gaelic and rightly named
> As setting for a mode of life that passes on:
> Harsh landscape that haunts me,
> Well and stone, in the bleak moors of dream,
> With all my circling a failure to return.[7]

Montague's attempts to connect with a confirming heritage are of course mingled with an autobiographical strain that runs throughout Irish poetry. He speaks of circling back to Tyrone, of his father's return from New York, his own return as a child to be reared by aunts, and the sense of separation and rejection that resulted. The effects of English invasion, of sixteenth-century wars in Northern Ireland, of endemic Republican violence are extensions of that wound he experienced in being torn from his parent's home. While some of his poems, in particular *The Rough Field*, 1972, are historical meditations that require the scope and inclusiveness of the long poem, Montague is a lyric poet of unusual skill. He is also a love poet who writes with tenderness of the power of love and of the pain of loss and separation. Here, too, myth is a subliminal presence, as in 'All Legendary Obstacles':

> All legendary obstacles lay between
> Us, the long imaginary plain,
> The monstrous ruck of mountains
> And, swinging across the night,
> Flooding the Sacramento, San Joaquin,
> The hissing drift of winter rain.

While the event at the centre of this poem is a man waiting for his beloved who travels towards him across America, the manner in which it is presented gives it, as the title suggests, a legendary association with lovers in myth and legend.

If poets feel drawn to the past, they tend to feel the need for more space than is provided by the lyric. The need for the long poem is recurrent and it brings its inherent problems of scale, organisation, and coherence. Historical meditation is a way of examining the past in order to see present directions and to define one's own situation. Since the Irish imagination retains and exploits a sense of myth and history, it is understandable that memory and its associations require more scope than the lyric form provides. Historical meditations by Austin Clarke ('The Loss of Strength'), John Montague (*The Rough Field*), Richard Murphy (*The Battle of Aughrim*), Thomas Kinsella (*Nightwalker*), and Seamus Heaney ('Station Island') clearly demonstrate this. But it is difficult to control the material. Montague and Murphy work through a series of vignettes in a kind of mosaic effect, sometimes by contrasts of various kinds. They also make direct use of documentary material, such as extracts from letters, historical documents, narratives of one kind or another. Kinsella and Heaney seek unity through the device of an observing consciousness, a single walker who conjures up a variety of scenes or a central pilgrim-figure who is confronted by a succession of voices.

Richard Murphy's sense of land and land ownership is also strong. Since his ancestors were given large tracts of land as rewards for their support of English settlement, thereby dispossessing the native Irish, he investigates this division, knowing that many of the subsequent tensions in Irish society come from it. *The Battle of Aughrim*, 1968, explores the complexities of the past to find out what happened. It balances the experiences of Protestant and Catholic, Ascendancy and peasantry, myth and reality, past and present. Its finest sections are those in a lyrical rather than a narrative mode, such as this account of a hound refusing to leave the body of his master who has been killed in the fighting.

> Nights she lopes to the scrub
> And trails back at dawn to guard a skeleton.
>
> Wind shears the berries from the rowan tree,
> The wild geese have flown.
>
> She lifts her head to cry
> As a woman keens in a famine for her son.[8]

Murphy's need to locate his imagination in a space between Big House and peasant cottage leads him to write poems about landscape and seascape in the west of Ireland. The long poem called 'The Cleggan Disaster' recreates the skill and courage with which a boatman was able to keep his boat and its crew alive through a storm that drowned many others.

> Down in the deep where the storm could not go
> The ebb–tide, massive and slow, was drawing
> Windwards the ninety-six fathom of nets
> With hundreds of mackerel thickly meshed,
> Safely tugging the boat off the mainland shore.
> The moon couldn't shine, the clouds shut her out,
> But she came unseen to sway on his side
> All the waters gathered from the great spring tide.

He also wrote poems about the creatures of the west, seabirds or seals, as in 'The Seals at High Island'.

> Swayed by the thrust and backfall of the tide,
> A dappled grey bull and a brindled cow
> Copulate in the green water of a cove.
> I watch from a cliff-top, trying not to move.
> Sometimes they sink and merge into black shoals;
> Then rise for air, his muzzle on her neck,
> Their winged feet intertwined as a fishtail.

Murphy is interested in the values by which a man may live honestly, or the attachments that may destroy him. The moral cost of amassing money is a recurrent theme in *The Price of Stone*, 1985. The price paid is the expenditure of human resources in selfish, greedy pursuit and the erosion of humane feeling. By contrast the concluding sonnet, 'Natural Son', is a celebration of birth and feeling.

> No worse pain could be borne, to bear the joy
> Of seeing you come in a slow dive from the womb,
> Pushed from your fluid home, pronounced 'a boy'.
> You'll never find so well equipped a room.
>
> No house we build could hope to satisfy
> Every small need, now that you've made this move
> To share our loneliness, much as we try
> Our vocal skill to wall you round with love.

The internationalisation of Irish poetry has become more pronounced in recent decades as Irish poets, no longer insular, range freely from one culture to another. The terms of Patrick Kavanagh's choice between trust in the parish and anxiety about being provincial are outdated. Michael Longley, with Seamus Heaney and Derek Mahon, was part of the revival of poetry in Northern Ireland. His work lacks the glamorous texture and subject matter of Heaney and the witty elegance of Mahon, but he has built up a rooted connection with the recent troubles in Northern Ireland. He has a particular affinity with classical literature, seen in his economical use of language, clear diction, fondness for lists, and controlled syntax across several lines. Longley's parallels between incidents in classical texts and events in Northern Ireland have been fruitful. With the publication of *The Echo Gate*, 1979, and *Poems 1963–1983*, 1985, his true stature as a poet became more visible. His dispassionate voice characterises a poetry that is objective and detached with a marked fidelity to the actual. He delights in exact observation of minute animations in nature, as in 'Botany' or 'Fishing for Sand Eels':

> They are hungry enough to fish for sand eels,
> Except that it's hardly fishing
> To parade so closely between the tides,
>
> To be one of the moonlit multitude,
> To slice sand and sea with a blunt sickle
> Lest the harvest bleed when it is cut.

Longley is a botanist of the imagination; he takes pleasure in the myriad, complex structures of nature whose healing power grows stronger for him in a violent age. Notes of forgiveness and healing together with a more relaxed manner suggest that his relationship with Northern Ireland, its landscape, people, and events is increasingly fertile. 'Ceasefire', 1994, published on the occasion of one of the cessations to violence in Northern Ireland, makes moving use of the account in Homer's *Iliad* when Priam goes to the Greek camp to beg for his son Hector's body so that it may receive honourable burial.

> Taking Hector's corpse into his own hands Achilles
> Made sure it was washed and, for the old king's sake,
> Laid out in uniform, ready for Priam to carry
> Wrapped like a present home to Troy at daybreak.
>
> When they had eaten together, it pleased them both
> To stare at each other's beauty as lovers might,
> Achilles built like a god, Priam good-looking still
> And full of conversation, who earlier had sighed:
>
> 'I get down on my knees and do what must be done
> And kiss Achilles' hand, the killer of my son.'[10]

Seamus Heaney, whose international connections are extensive, has made many comparisons between the barbaric rituals of early Iron Age Europe and the cruelties in the Northern Ireland conflict, particularly in *North*, 1975. In 'Tollund Man' the central figure is Christlike in that he has been sacrificed to the goddess of the earth so that life may be renewed. In the poem, Heaney adopts the persona of the pilgrim who will journey to Denmark to the shrine of this martyr-victim. Affirming the familiarity of the savage ritual that caused his death, the poet as pilgrim will pray that the saintlike figure may bring peace to Northern Ireland and, remembering what is happening in the land he comes from, declares

> Out there in Jutland
> In the old man-killing parishes
>
> I will feel lost,
> Unhappy and at home.

By drawing upon material outside the Irish context, poets can achieve a distancing effect, enabled to filter their perception of native experience through the lens of comparable events elsewhere. The examples are numerous: Derek Mahon's use of Samuel Beckett's sense of reality, or his use of Japanese decorum and formality to highlight European sectarian violence. Paul Muldoon's *Madoc: A Mystery*, 1990, with its American settings and material is about colonisation, a subject of particular relevance to Ireland. It is not a question of setting poems in foreign parts – poets recognise the danger of writing 'tourist' poems – but of illuminating Irish experience through references to what has happened elsewhere.

The strength and variety found in Irish poetry today, the accomplishment in technique are part of that confidence heard in Heaney's 'Bogland' and declared in this challenging manner in 'Station Island'. Irish poets operate in a sophisticated relationship with their Irish legacy in both languages. They have as well a relationship to literatures abroad that includes modern European languages, Eastern European poetry, classical and medieval sources, particularly Dante, and writers in North America. Although complex in terms of subject matter, their work is inventive and accomplished.

That confidence is also heard in the voices of women poets whose number has grown in the last twenty years: Eavan Boland, Paula Meehan, Eiléan Ní Chuilleanáin, Medbh McGuckian. Eavan Boland, in particular, has been a strong advocate of the need for the voices of women to be heard. Just as Kavanagh depicted men within the unsung confines of the small farm and Clarke expressed the pain of moral conflict, Boland has made the condition of being a woman poet within a male defined and male dominated tradition the subject of much of her poetry. When she began to write, she did so under the influence of predecessors such as W. B. Yeats and Thomas Kinsella, but became increasingly uneasy in that role. Their definitions of women became less and less satisfactory, less relevant to her experience, and, as she developed the mythic and emblematic portrayal of women in Irish poetry, seemed increasingly inadequate. She began therefore to examine her life for herself, to place it at the forefront of her work and in the process to counter the male legacy. Sometimes she made that heritage the central issue as in the poem 'Bright-Cut Irish Silver' where male domination is brought into exacting focus.

> I take it down
> from time to time, to feel
> the smooth path of silver meet the cicatrice of skill.
>
> These scars, I tell myself, are learned.
>
> This gift for wounding an artery of rock
> was passed on from father to son, to the father
> of the next son;
>
> is an aptitude
> for injuring earth while inferring it in curves and surfaces;
>
> is this cold potency which has come
> by time and chance,
>
> into my hands.[11]

Recurrently she looks at the product of male intelligence and skill in order to remind herself of what she must do. She has entered this succession and must be equal to its 'cold potency', its 'aptitude', its 'gift for wounding'.

Such honesty works also in Boland's depiction of woman in the house as in 'Woman in Kitchen' where the nameless woman is trapped. The white surfaces of machines and crockery are like a mortuary. 'The silence is death.' She is deprived of colour.

> White surfaces retract. White
> sideboards light the white of walls.
> Cups wink white in their saucers.
> The light of day bleaches as it falls
> on cups and sideboards. She could use
> the room to tap with if she lost her sight.

It is a new world for her as a poet, colourless, dispiriting, engulfing in its trivial round of activities, unless she can give it significance, unless she can rescue it from the oblivion in which it has been cast. In 'The New Pastoral' she seeks to define herself as a housewife and poet. She and women like her everywhere are outside history. She is a pioneer, an explorer and discoverer of a territory that has not been absorbed into the literary consciousness. Within this world she must find the themes and images that will satisfy her imagination. The poems in the collection *Night Feed*, 1982, focusing on and re-creating domestic activities, are warm and attractive. The title poem celebrates the relationship of mother and child, and in its touches of humour and relaxed pace adds to the feeling of fulfilment.

> This is dawn.
> Believe me
> This is your season, little daughter.
> The moment daisies open,
> The hour mercurial rainwater
> Makes a mirror for sparrows.
> It's time we drowned our sorrows.

She knows, of course, and it adds to the moment's enjoyment, that process affects this scene as every other; growth, change, the 'long fall from grace'.

Paula Meehan also writes of women's experience – of love and loss, sexual union, miscarriage, pregnancy, marriage under strain, longing and passion. Although her poetry often reflects the poverty of Dublin's inner city, the tenement world of O'Casey's Dublin trilogy, her response is warm and positive. In 'Buying Winkles' her imagination transforms the urban setting when as a child she jumps over cracks in the pavement, waves to women in doorways, sees pubs as warm places.[12] 'The Pattern' begins with a memory of conflict between mother and daughter and then develops warm portraits of the mother, as she waxes and polishes the floor, or remakes an old dress. When the mother knitted, the daughter held the skein. 'One of these days I must / teach you to follow a pattern.' The pattern the poem makes in its piecing together of changing scenes is the handing on of that talent.

'Laburnum' exposes the pain in love lost. It may be laburnum time, but the speaker's sense of abandonment fills the poem not only with dejection and grief but also with the determination to face this loss.

> You will live breath
> by breath. The beat of your own heart
> will scourge you. You'll wait

in vain, for he's gone from you.
And every night is a long
slide to the dawn you
wake to, terrified in your ordinary room
on an ordinary morning, say
mid May, say the time of laburnum.

Fifty years ago, except for W. B. Yeats, Irish poets lacked models within their own country. The poetic tradition was thinly defined and had a short history. At the end of his life Yeats had words of advice for those who would come after him.

Irish poets, learn your trade,
Sing whatever is well made,
Scorn the sort now growing up
All out of shape from toe to top, ...[13]

Now, since Yeats's time Irish poetry has extended its range of subject matter, sources, and associations. Poets have responded to an Ireland that is less nationalistic and more cosmopolitan, where the influence of the Catholic Church has waned, where the farming community has decreased, while cities have grown, where the feminist movement has secured greater equality for women in the market place and the professions, if not in politics. The period from 1970 to the present has deepened the sense of renewal that was announced in 1962 in *The Dolmen Miscellany of Irish Writing*,[14] whose contents identified a new generation of writers and reflected a moment in the history of Modern Irish Literature that began with the publication of first collections by John Montague, Richard Murphy, and Thomas Kinsella. In a society increasingly at the mercy of spin doctors and the debased currency of political and business speak, poets have realised the importance of saying what they have to say in words as accurate and true as possible, and they have been faithful to imaginative truth. They have learnt their trade.

Notes

1   The International Association for the Study of Irish Literatures.
2   Seamus Heaney, *Selected Poems 1966–1987* (New York: Farrar, Straus and Giroux, 1990). All subsequent quoted selections are from this text.
3   Patrick Kavanagh, *Collected Poems*, ed. Antoinette Quinn (London: Allen Lane, 2004). All subsequent quoted selections are from this text.
4   Thomas Kinsella, 'Vertical Man', *Collected Poems* (Oxford: Oxford University Press, 1996).
5   Louis MacNeice, *Collected Poems* (London: Faber & Faber, 1966). All subsequent quoted selections are from this text.

6 Austin Clarke, *Collected Poems* (Dublin: The Dolmen Press, 1974). All subsequent quoted selections are from this text.

7 John Montague, *Collected Poems* (Loughcrew, Oldcastle, Co. Meath, Ireland: The Gallery Press, 2000). All subsequent quoted selections are from this text.

8 Richard Murphy, *Collected Poems* (Loughcrew, Oldcastle, Co. Meath, Ireland: The Gallery Press, 2000). All subsequent quoted selections are from this text.

10 Michael Longley, *The Ghost Orchid* (London: Jonathan Cape, 1995). All subsequent quoted selections are from this text.

11 Eavan Boland, *Collected Poems* (Manchester: Carcanet, 1995). All subsequent quoted selections are from this text.

12 Paula Meehan, *Mysteries of the Home* (Newcastle upon Tyne: Bloodaxe Books, 1996). All subsequent quoted selections are from this text.

13 W. B. Yeats, *The Poems: A New Edition*, ed. Richard J. Finneran (Dublin: Gill & Macmillan, 1983).

14 See *The Dolmen Press: A Celebration* (Dublin: The Lilliput Press, 2001) for Harmon's Introduction and his essay, '*The Dolmen Miscellany*', with other essays in the collection narrating the history and development of the Press.

AFTERWORD: DEAR EDITOR

In 2001–02 Harmon edited four issues of Poetry Ireland Review*: 69-72. As editor, reading hundreds of poems and letters from aspiring poets, he was moved to write the 'Reply to a Poet', for poets who had asked for help. His editorials, each under a thousand words, are witty, thoughtful, full of sound advice for writers and readers alike. As he completed his year as editor, he wrote the poem 'Dear Editor'.*

Reply to a Poet

OVER a year ago, after spending most of my life as a university teacher and a writer, I was invited to become editor of *Poetry Ireland Review*, which is the country's main poetry periodical. I had always known that many people in Ireland want to write poetry, but nothing prepared me for the amount of work that awaited me when I first made my way into the tower of Dublin Castle, once the centre of British power in Ireland, where the magazine was published.

Realising I couldn't possibly read all the poems that afternoon, I bundled them into a large plastic bag, and left. I had arranged to meet an American friend in a pub. Terrified of losing the bag, I kept a tight grip on it as we drank our pints of Guinness. Then as we were leaving I tucked it firmly under my arm. Only then did my friend make a comment.

'What do you have there?' she asked.

'Two or three hundred mute inglorious Miltons', I replied.

'What?' she asked, frowning slightly, clearly not understanding what I had said.

'Two or three hundred mute inglorious Miltons', I replied, more clearly.

She made no response, but I could see her thinking to herself, 'I always felt this guy was a bit daft. Now I'm sure of it.'

At home, I went through the poems methodically, choosing those I might publish and putting aside those I would have to return. Deciding to reject poems never became easy, since I knew the disappointments that followed. Everybody, I felt, wanted to be published in this periodical, and rightly so. For emerging poets, it was a mark of recognition, a form of initiation. For established poets, it was a means of communicating with their primary audience and with fellow poets.

In the weeks that followed, reading the letters of explanation and the appeals for guidance that often accompanied the submissions, I began to work out a set of guidelines. Because so many poems came in each week, I couldn't write to each poet individually, although that would have been the kindest and most helpful thing to do. My 'advice to a poet', expressed somewhat bluntly at times so that the message would sink in, did turn out to be useful. Poets took from it what they found helpful or relevant to their state of development.

*

I can't answer all your questions. Learning to be a poet takes time, years.

First of all there's the matter of submissions. When you finish a poem do you send it off to an editor at once? You shouldn't. Allow the excitement to subside. Put the poem aside. Give yourself time to become detached. This may seem like an unnecessary piece of advice, but in fact most poets succumb to impetuosity from time to time. They like the poem, are exhilarated by it, pop it into an envelope, and bung it off to an editor. Invariably they live to regret this haste. No matter how perfect a poem may seem on first completion, it will benefit from an objective reassessment at a later stage.

Do you proofread carefully before sending a poem off? For typos? For consistency in punctuation? Do you expect or half-expect someone else to catch and correct errors? You shouldn't. This is sloppy. It suggests lack of discipline. It is unprofessional. Editors find it irritating.

I mention punctuation because poets are supposed to be concerned with small matters – line length, rhythm, spacing, precise usage, and punctuation. The first doubt raised in an editor's mind may come from signs of inconsistency in punctuation. Typos quickly add to that doubt. And when in doubt, an editor may simply reject. That is the easier option. Do you want a poem of yours to be turned down because you didn't take sufficient care with the preparation of the manuscript? Another reason for not rushing is to find the objectivity to look closely for grammatical or syntactical faults.

Do you think of the reader? How do you see him? A bit doddery, you feel? Needs to be told everything more than once? Not so. Don't feed him pap – repetitive clauses, repeated words, helpful adjectives and adverbs, a rhythm so slack it would put a monkey to sleep. Forget Dopey at your shoulder. Stop helping lame dogs over stiles.

Be rigorous: select, cut, reduce. Don't be bland. Test for excess. In the process you may find a poem inside the poem you are trying to write. Usually it is better. In the process your imagination will become more fully engaged. Your poetic intelligence will certainly be more alert.

Trust the reader. Give him a chance to use his mind, to discover meaning, to be alert to language and to rhythm, to see implications, to make connections, to hear the music, to use his imagination. Otherwise reading poetry is no fun, there's no challenge, no stimulation.

The worst fault is looseness of language, hackneyed speech, the old phrase, the available image. I'm not talking just about clichés. I'm talking about a lazy attitude that puts up with the familiar expression, the easy phrase, the available word. All forms of laziness are fatal in poetry. Think of other ways of saying, find words you did not think of at once. Check the dictionary for meanings. Look in the thesaurus for words with the meaning you want. See if you can find a fresher idiom. If you do, then reading the poem becomes a more arresting experience. It holds the attention better.

Laziness affects how we write. Sometimes one has the feeling, reading a poem in a periodical, that the author has an idea how the poem should look, thinks that lines must be broken up as though nothing else is required, no rhythm, no cadence, no freshness.

Sometimes one has the feeling that the author thinks a mood must be suggested and left at that. These are forms of posturing, of adopting attitudes, of fitting into some notion of what a poem is.

Poems must have something to say, either directly or by implication. Arranging lines on a page to give the appearance of poetry is not enough. Robert Frost made a remark that is worth keeping in mind. Like a piece of ice on a hot stove, he said, a poem should ride on its own melting. What is laid down at the beginning should continue and evolve to the end. All the elements should flow in one direction. This is good advice, a corrective to keep us in check, advice we can apply to our own work.

You can test your poem against it, not only for flabbiness of language, not only for awkward rhythm, not only for collapsed line endings, but for overall effectiveness. Is everything working? Do things earn their place? Is each element contributing?

Anything that doesn't fit should be excluded. Frank O'Connor used to say that the hardest thing for a young writer to learn is that even good writing has to be jettisoned, if it doesn't fit.

Knowing when to start and when to end is important. Have you moved into the subject too slowly? Did you begin too far back? Very often you find you can discard a number of opening lines, as you realise where the poem really begins, at what point the ice begins to ease downward. There is a point at which the poem starts to be itself, to discover its direction, that inner vein of feeling, rhythm, or thought that gives it its individual character.

Sometimes you can remove endings that are unnecessary, which make the point already made, or are implicit in the poem. There is a natural tendency to want to summarise, to round off, even to sound off, with an eye-catching line, with a striking rhyme. Dopey at your shoulder may find that helpful, but your alert reader will not. He doesn't need it.

A poem has to hold our attention. It has to do something with language that is attractive. How often do you read a poem without the slightest twinge of interest?

We are inclined to think that the fault lies in us, that we are not bright enough, or not sensitive enough to understand or to appreciate. In truth, it is more often the case that the poem is simply not interesting. Another bland statement. Another fanciful mood.

It leaves us unmoved and indifferent.

A poem should hold your interest from the first line; it should evolve down the page still holding your interest, controlled all the way, every line, every image, every nuance, every allusion having a function. We are makers, craftsmen, we learn our trade. There is much to learn and it cannot all be learned at once. The reward comes in the doing, in the occasional successes, in the gradual feeling that we know what we are doing, not in appearances in periodicals, although these are encouraging at first. One way to test a poem is to see if it will pass successfully under the eyes of an editor.

There are poems that repeat or imitate what has been said or done by hundreds of other poems. At any time hundreds of poets write the same kind of poem, in the same kind of rhythm, in the same kind of language. It is easy for the young poet to fall into the pattern, to imitate what others are doing. Student poets reflect current fashions. At one time everyone wrote in the manner of the early T. S. Eliot, then everyone wrote like W. H. Auden or Dylan Thomas or Philip Larkin. The only way to learn is from current writing, and by reading critically in the past.

But you must break away. You must, and will in time, find your own way of saying. You will discover your particular subject or subjects. Don't strike attitudes. Poetry is above all a way of telling the truth, your truth, in your words. It requires exactness in how we handle language. We learn as we go.

Many poets attend writing workshops and there is nothing wrong with that. But I have the impression that poets sometimes imitate one another within a group. This can be limiting. As well as creative writing there is creative reading. Read poetry. Think about it. It is essential to read the work of other poets and to do this constantly and critically, to see how others write, not what they write but how they write, how they handle language, how they structure a poem, how they make connections within it. Poetic intelligence includes the ability to make effective linkages within a poem. There is much to learn. Be patient. You cannot learn everything at once. Be observant. Go outside your immediate circle.

Incidentally, rejection need not be much of a setback. It may mean that the poem does not work, that you need to revise it. It may be rejected because the editor has too much material and wants to clear his desk. It may be that he doesn't respond well to your kind of poem. For you it is part of the learning process. If you sit an examination, you may not do as well as you'd like, but that would be no reason to stop studying. Having a poem turned down is no reason to stop writing. You keep working.

Along the way a poem may surprise; it may move into magic, to that region of beauty, or mystery that lies beyond the actual, above the merely documentary where many poems have heavy feet. By writing in a disciplined way, learning your trade, you may move to that other level. Poetry aspires to this. Again, be your own best critic. While you can show poems to friends, it is really up to you, to your judgment, your sense of what is right. And that only comes in time, over time. When you discover this power in yourself, you will have arrived as a poet.

Ultimately, there is something mysterious and inexplicable about the way poems are conceived and born. It is difficult to explain the sources, or why some subjects come to us rather than to someone else, what kind of psychic response takes place. We do not know how poems arrive. Most of us do not even know when they are on their way. We seem to enter a state of reverie, of inattention to the things around us. The wife of one senior poet says she knows when it is happening because his mouth falls open!

Some writers have private rituals, ways of pleasing the Muse or gods. Some must have a set of sharpened pencils ready; others must have a cup of coffee by their side; some read other people's collections to get in the mood; some write at night, some in the morning.

I suspect writers have a time that suits them, when ideas come, when the house is quiet, or the children in bed. I prefer the morning, early morning, and I know from experience that if I wake during the night or towards morning with a poem in my head, or certain images or an idea that want to be put on paper, it is essential that I either put them down on a pad kept by the bedside, or go directly to my desk and write them down. This first version may be rudimentary and I will revise it later, but the essential thing is that I get it down. If I put it off, or tell myself if will still be in my mind when I finally wake up, it is certain it will be lost, or so diminished or muddled that I will not be able to recover it.

The poem we write never has the perfection of its initial imagining; we can only try to get as close to that as we can, usually through successive drafts. Most poems have to be worked through; they undergo many drafts. This may seem onerous, but you get to like it. This is where you learn about writing, where your skills are sharpened, where your command of language improves, where you feel the inner strength that drives you through draft after draft until the moment arrives when you know the poem is finished. There is a kind of calm, as after a long journey or a spell of hard work. You feel you have done all that needs to be done or all that you can do.

Some poems arrive virtually complete, requiring but a minimum of tinkering. That is a welcome gift; enjoy it. Anything more, you feel, will spoil the poem. Put it aside. Don't rush it off to an editor. Let the hare sit.

Certain poems are indispensable as we measure what has been achieved. It would be a great achievement to write even one indispensable poem.

Editorials

Poetry Ireland Review, Summer 2001, Editorial 69

Poetry Ireland Review welcomes the work of established poets and encourages beginners. It has an extensive network of readers throughout the country – in schools, in writers' groups and among individual poets. Readers in Ireland and abroad, poets here and elsewhere, students and teachers, those in centres for Irish studies, look to this magazine to see what is happening in Irish poetry. The network stretches far and wide in the world – to universities, libraries, embassies.

PIR is an important magazine, a platform for the best in Irish poetry, but we can sustain and develop it only if we attract the interest and support of all poets. While I know poets find it necessary to publish in magazines abroad, I would like to see more of them publishing here where those interested in Irish poetry expect to find them. In this issue we have work by several well-known poets such as Robert Greacen, Gerald Dawe, and Bernard O'Donoghue. Back issues are an important repository in the history of Irish poetry, the best evidence of what has been happening.

The magazine needs the creative energy of all poets and wants to reflect the changing styles, issues, and influences that affect an individual poet's work over the years, and the variety of emphases, directions, and techniques that occur in a country's imaginative growth. Poetry reflects a country's spiritual state but *PIR* cannot do that unless we have ongoing connections with the poetic imagination of the country.

In a fundamental way this is your magazine. It is only as good, as exciting, as satisfying, as profound, as innovative, as challenging as its contributors.

It is not only Irish poets or poets living in Ireland who contribute. One of my discoveries as editor is the number of Irish poets living abroad who send work in. This is a natural consequence of the increased internationalism in Irish culture. And it is a strength. Themes and issues are likely to be broader, the influences more varied. In addition, many poets who send in work from New Zealand, Australia, Canada, and the United States have Irish roots. The magazine reflects this wider constituency.

In any country it would be difficult to produce a poetry magazine of over a hundred pages four times a year in which every poem would be a major contribution. Without the support of all poets we cannot even begin to do it. But we have the potential.

PIR is generous towards emerging poets. It includes unknown or little-known poets, encourages newcomers, spots and fosters talent. It is sometimes difficult, however, to decide what to include and what to leave out. Many of the poems sent in need more work, are too general in their handling of language, do not strive enough for the most appropriate word or phrase, are vaguely lyrical, or loosely descriptive. To those poets who have asked for advice the best response I can make is to suggest that they read 'Reply to a Poet' in the December 2000 issue. I directed remarks there to the younger poet and hope they are helpful.

The area of book reviews is also to be developed. *PIR* should be the place where poets receive a fair, intelligent, and perceptive response. The emphasis will be on the text, not on literary theory or colonial theory or post-modernism, or any other ism. I want lively and perceptive engagement with the poem on the page.

The cover photograph of the statue of Justice over the gateway leading into the Upper Castle Yard, not far from this office, draws attention to Austin Clarke as a political satirist. Although we hear more and more about the injustices of the past, I wonder if we will ever fully appreciate the effects of bullying and beating, sarcasm, authoritarianism, and repression on the mind and hearts of young people? Conditions have changed but as they do we see all the more clearly how the previous generations suffered and how those who might have helped or who had responsibility hid behind a mask of silence. Children were terrorised, unmarried mothers were ostracised, the poor were treated abominably. It is as though past evil has been magnified in our time and of all the poets Austin Clarke was the one who spoke out and who bore the marks of suffering in his life and work.

Not all poets want to be satirists or indeed can be satirists, but there is a sense in which all poetry is political. Almost every day we see language abused by politicians, spin doctors, and others. Poets counter that abuse in the precision and clarity with which they write. Poetry refreshes, purifies, and strengthens the language. It is one of its vital functions.

That is why we work hard. That is why we are not content with the second-rate. That is why we pursue clarity and accuracy; that is why we try to move a poem beyond the ordinary.

Send in your best work. Surprise and delight us. This is your magazine.

Poetry Ireland Review, Autumn 2001, Editorial 70

Send in your best work. Surprise and delight us. This is your magazine.

The response to that request has been good. The editor's postbag has increased. The quality of the work has improved. There is a sense that poets are availing of the opportunity to have their work read where it reaches a wide audience at home and abroad, in the magazine where those most interested expect to find their latest work.

In this issue we have work of outstanding merit and of varied achievement. John F. Deane's dialogue and Rita Kelly's reflections, so different in style, subject matter, and approach, are deeply imagined and engaged with their subjects in a significant way. They compel us to attend seriously to what they say and how they say it.

It is important that poets write when they can in a major key, as Patrick Kavanagh did in 'The Great Hunger', Austin Clarke in *Mnemosyne Lay in Dust*, Brian Coffey in 'Missouri Sequence', or Seamus Heaney in 'Station Island'. We need to engage in an extended manner with issues that cannot be adequately managed in a short poem. But the consequences can be dismaying.

For a number of reasons the long poem has become difficult to write, but also difficult to publish. Periodicals cannot find space for them. Publication in a collection puts them in the public arena, but there is an immediacy to publication in a magazine that cannot be matched elsewhere.

Publishing these long poems in *PIR* means that they become part of our common currency, contributing to and stimulating discussion and response. Other poets and serious readers of poetry see them. This kind of serious exchange is something *PIR* can facilitate.

Not that we wish to ignore the short poem. I point with gratitude to lyrics by Tony Curtis, to the presence of Pearse Hutchinson and John Ennis, and welcome work by Michael Hamburger and John Kinsella.

We begin to see what *PIR* can do, the kind of serious contribution it can make, the kind of discussion it can generate. With this issue we bring many Irish poets together – more established figures such as Deane and Kelly, and emerging poets like Sean Lysaght, Sheila O'Hagan, Greg Delanty, and Eugene O'Connell.

Our cover picture of Jim Larkin and the quotation from Thomas Kinsella's *The Pen Shop* remind us of that poet's critical engagement with corruption in Irish political and social life. We live at an interesting time in which successive tribunals have exposed unseemly behaviour, in which the influential and the wealthy have been shown to be dishonest and corrupt. More generally, we see vast changes in society, a deterioration in personal standards, and a culture of greed and selfishness. Some of Kinsella's poetry responds with shock and anger to the evidence of corruption. His stature as a poet gives him the right to be critical. His sustained dedication to his craft, examined in the current issue of the *Irish University Review* (Spring/Summer 2001), counters the betrayal we have suffered at the hands of those we should be able to trust.

Not all poets respond as satirists. Many will want to distance themselves.

There are few poets who write political poetry. But it will be interesting to see how such a profound revelation of wrongdoing may be reflected in poetry, how it may seep into the psyche and affect the language.

The invitation from the previous editorial still stands. Send us your best work. We are open to all kinds of poetry. We began with the notion of not publishing work by the same poet without a lapse of time, but it is difficult to stick to this. Several poets, encouraged by publication, submitted more work. Some, challenged by the invitation, withdrew work in order to send in better. Some revised poems and sent them in again. Others whom we had criticised came back again, with better work.

Something exciting and heartening is happening. We have a sense of communication, of energy, of interaction, of forces gathering. The reactions are encouraging. Already much material has come in for the next issue. Pressure on space increases. Regrettably, reviews have to be curtailed.

This is your magazine. Ensure that we reflect the best. Make every page count.

Poetry Ireland Review, Winter 2001, Editorial 71

Poetry, we say, answers our need. I realised this yet again when my copy of the last issue arrived on 14 September. In it I found elegies that answered our grief for what had happened to the Twin Towers in America: Tony Curtis's notes of loss in 'What Darkness Covers', Sheila O'Hagan's expression of sorrow in 'Asphodel', the pain in Eugene O'Connell's poems.

I had the satisfaction of finding work that was fully realised, thinking that we are right to produce the best that is in us, knowing that the creation of fine work is its own reward and serves its own purpose. I read at random – John F. Deane, Sean Lysaght, Susan Connolly, Gabriel Fitzmaurice, Michael Hamburger, and many others – admiringly, grateful that work of such a high standard passed through my hands and now resides where others can find it.

I've returned to that last issue as one returns to a book of poetry enjoyed in the past knowing that time will not have lessened the enjoyment. There are examples in it, by established and emerging poets, of what I talk about below: discipline, an achieved form, the grace of the good poem. One could write at length about it – its variety, its subject matter, the different techniques, the intelligence at work, the purity of language, the care with rhythm and tone.

There is a danger that we may forget the richness of the heritage. There is the danger that we write the same kind of poetry, learning from one another over a narrow range. We need to read widely, to go beyond this country to see what is being written elsewhere, to read back in tradition, as well as being aware of the great variety and depth within Irish culture in both languages. We have to educate ourselves all the time, examining what other poets do at home and abroad. I wonder if writing groups do this, or are they merely content to read each other's work. As well as creative writing there is creative reading.

In a recent letter an American poet remarked that he keeps poems for two years before publication, taking them out and changing a word or two from time to time, and this after he has submitted them to the intense process of rewriting in the early stages. This is where poetic intelligence comes into play, where we seek the best combination of words and images, the most appropriate form and structure, where we test the poem along its entire range to ensure that all the parts are working effectively.

It cannot be completed quickly. It requires time, it requires detachment and distance, it requires cold intelligence. What we have written must be allowed to sink away so that we are able return to it dispassionately.

I don't know why I still receive so much work that would benefit from rewriting, so much that has to be turned down because of a careless use of language, and little attention to form, where five words do the work of one, where three lines could be expressed in one, where beginnings could be removed, where there is no controlling voice, where there is no interaction, no harking back as one reads forward.

Many things arise from Beckett's 'vision' which he associated with the anemometer on Dun Laoghaire pier, photographed on the cover. I want to mention two in particular: first the importance of discovering our real selves and of writing in the light of that knowledge; second, keeping on with the task until we get it right. This requires the poetic intelligence mentioned above, but there is also the informed intelligence that brings ideas into the poem, directly or indirectly, where the poet has views he wants to express, values he feels are important.

With this kind of intelligence we can position a poem in relation to other poems, or other poets. A poem can resonate in a literary context, as well as in a mythic context. It takes understanding to do this, not only the knowledge of what has been written, and how it has been written, but the ability to place our poem in a creative relationship with other poems. Few poems show familiarity with work that has gone before.

The combination of long poems with short poems in the last issue excited some comment, some discussion of the problems of writing the long poem. It is a daunting undertaking. But how about the discontinuous narrative or the mosaic poem in which poems, even different kinds of poems, have connections and echoes of various kinds over an extended work? Might be worth trying.

There seems to be a preference at present for poetry in which the pressure of ideas is not a factor. There is nothing wrong with this in itself, but it seems a pity that so much is being left out. The thoughtful poem is hard to find these days.

Poetry Ireland Review, Spring 2002, Editorial 72

> Who will go drive with Fergus now,
> And pierce the deep wood's woven shade,
> And dance upon the level shore?
>   W. B. Yeats, 'Who Goes With Fergus?'

'Poetry', Thomas Kinsella once wrote, 'is an investigation by concerned beings of the vital processes of their lives in youth, in maturity, in happiness, in misery, in old age... poetry can be, for poet and reader, the most serious, intimate and useful thing in the world.' That investigation, as Tom Halpin's review of the *Collected Poems* makes clear, has continued throughout Kinsella's career, as has that view of poetry as a serious, rewarding, and necessary activity.

In its own way *Poetry Ireland Review* participates in this activity, making itself available to poets who examine and give imaginative expression to experience. In this issue we have poems that focus on a variety of experience at different stages of individual lives and do so in a serious manner. The editor tries to find some balance among the various topics and styles. But central to what we do is the shared conviction that it is important.

After four issues we see it can be done. It is possible to provide poetry of a high order consistently. Poets continue to send in material on the understanding that the aim is to publish the best and to ensure that we can be proud of the result. *PIR*, as I said initially, is only as good or as challenging, as profound, or as innovative as the poets make it.

There is also the sharing. There is a core of poetry-readers, many of them subscribers, who attend to what is going on, who delight in a new publication by Eiléan Ní Chuilleanáin, or a first collection by Tom French or Mark Granier, to name just three who have recently appeared, or who notice when Geraldine Mills brings out a booklet of promising poems.

There is always room for play – Iggy McGovern and Vincent Woods in the last issue, Michael Coady and Tony Curtis in this. Coady's poem is an example of the imagination transcending pain, running freely, 'taking on' the Vatican along the way, and at the same time commemorating those who attended him in hospital. The Curtis poem begins light-heartedly in the metaphor of poets taking part in a race, portraying each of the contestants, then turns into a magical evocation of the poetic imagination and concludes with an elegiac reflection on how the race may end.

PIR provides standards and models. In the last issue it seemed to me we had work as good as any being written. It was a delight to discover Eric Ormsby whom I had known for his scholarship, not for his poetry. And there were other significant figures, other examples of fine poetry.

It may also note when a poet changes style, as Aidan Mathews and John Ennis did in the last issue, as Mary O'Donnell and Eamon Grennan do in this issue. In the case of John Ennis I decided not to use poems I had intended to publish so that we could focus on the elegy, 'Miriam'. In this issue we mark the transition in the work of Gréagóir Ó Dúill to writing in English; he moves without loss of quality from one language to the other. Appropriately, Angela Bourke provides a critical comment on his *Rogha Dánta*.

We learn from one another. Eamon Grennan, who has already caused us to think in his collection of essays, *Facing the Music*, calls attention to what he is doing as a poet. He wants 'to step out of shelter to see what I see in the free air, and say it'. The poem, he says, 'though not all things to all men, should have many things in it' and then proceeds to chisel images into our minds. It is a declaration of intent, bravely made and backed up with evidence. And this, I suggest, is the right place to say it.

Our photograph on the cover suggests Spring, the flight of the imagination, the connections we make with myth, and the lasting fruitfulness of tradition:

> Where wings have memory wings, and all
> That comes of the best knit to the best.

> W. B. Yeats, 'Upon a House Shaken by the Land Agitation'

Dear Editor

Dear Editor,

I've been writing poetry since I was 12.
I'm a founder member of the Balscaddan Writers Association
and have received numerous prizes for my poetry.

I won the Stamullen Best Writer of the Year award
and was runner-up in the Gormanstown Annual Festival of New
Writing.

I have been given honourable mention in the Painestown Creative Arts
Competition.

My poems have been published in the *Little Magazine*, the *Mullingar
Starling*, *The Glass Case*, the *Statue*, the *Mind Sweeper* and many other
prestigious journals, at home and abroad.

Three of my poems have been published on the Internet.
Seamus McDall, a judge in the Gormanstown Festival, said my poems
'have the ring of true sincerity'.

I would be thrilled to have my poems in your prestigious periodical and
chosen by you of all people.

I enclose just 16 but I have loads more if you'd like to read them.
I am preparing my first collection which will have about 140 poems.
Do you think is that enough?
I enclose a SAE in case you want to send some back.
I'm going to send them to another prestigious magazine.
Thanking you for your attention.
My mother says she went to the Arcadia with your father.
Isn't that a kick?
My husband says he marked you when you played top of the left for
Lough. He says you were a 'dirty hoor'.

With best wishes,
Yours sincerely,
Jasmine,
P.S. That's the name of a flower.

[Editor's Note: 'Dear Editor', by the editor of *Poetry Ireland Review*, 2001–02, is published here for the first time.]

Appendix
Conversations with Mary Lavin

During the preparation of the Mary Lavin Special Issue of the Irish University Review *(Spring 1979), Maurice Harmon talked with her many times. What follows is an edited record of their conversations.*

MH: When did you know that you wanted to write?

ML: I am very interested in why people write. Being an only child had something to do with it. There was the need to fill a vacuum with imaginary people. I remember at a very early age being tantalised by the longing to get inside the body of someone else to see if it felt the same as being me. This was almost an obsession.

    Words, too, have always meant much to me. An ever-growing love of words has something to do with why I am a short story writer. I read Pears *Dictionary* with fascination. I love the power of words, the power of implication, of association, of detonation. One weighs words, for exactitude, for sensory quality, for atmosphere. Later it was the philosophical ideas and the attitudes to life that I wanted to express, but love of words preceded that.

MH: Did you find the adjustment difficult when you left America to live in Ireland?

ML: I was only a child when I left America. I was conscious only of leaving my father behind. When the boat pulled out I could see him for a long time driving back in what we used to call a banana wagon. Later I felt nostalgia for the lawn around the house, woods at the back, flowers like white violets and yellow violets, little harebells, and the lake where I used to skate with him on the ice. Years later, in Connecticut, the incredible feeling of familiarity made me realise how great a shock it must have been to the eyes and ears of a child to leave that small town in Massachusetts and in a few days arrive in a small town in the west of Ireland. For all I know it was the shock to eye and ear that made me a writer. An abrupt change of continent, such as I had when I came to Ireland from America, could awaken one's awareness. The first eight or nine months in Athenry made a profound visual impression on me. For many years I almost always placed my characters in Athenry. When I thought of a human situation, I seemed to see it enacted in the streets of that little town and often in my grandmother's house, where I had lived. Many of the characters in my stories were suggested by the people I met at that time, and I sometimes used the same character in different stories, or gave him or her a different name. Naida in 'The Convert' turns up again in 'Limbo' and is Leila in 'The Mouse', but all three were suggested by the one person in Athenry long ago.

The kind of person who writes is born.

I never wanted to be a writer, never, never, never.

MH: You've written novels, of course, but your chosen genre has been the short story. Why is that?

ML: Early in my career I felt I had too much to say to be a novelist. The novel, it seems to me, is too ambitious. I write short stories because I believe in the form as a powerful medium for the discovery of truth; the short story aims at a particle of truth. I hope to convey something of what I have learned. I like its discipline, its combination of experience, imagination, and technique. It combines them, compresses them, telescopes them, working towards a solution. The short story should not be spoken of as a miniature. At its greatest it magnifies life in much the same way that a snowflake under a microscope or a smear under a slide is seen to have an immensely complex design.

There are two kinds of stories. One is the plot story, which does not really satisfy me, although I have written a number of them with pleasure, such as 'The Small Bequest', 'Posy', and even 'The Great Wave'. The other is one in which life is put on the page. It can almost stand without plot and without a resolution, but life is absolutely caught, as in 'A Cup of Tea', 'The Will', 'In a Café'. It requires an ingenuity by which you get a line of development, such as psychological growth, which has much the same graph of the plot type of story. There are many short stories, such as Hemingway's 'Hills Like White Elephants', in which you get moments of absolute truth. These moments also occur in the novel, but because of the novel's scale, have to be cemented here and there to other fully imagined moments of truth by the kind of cement that is merely inventive. In the short story such cementing is cut to a minimum by the ingenuity of the writer.

MH: How did you prepare to write those 'fully imagined moments of truth'?

ML: The greatest stimulation is to read the work of a writer one reveres. I have found that because it creates an urge to do better it is sometimes the less than perfect work that stimulates. I enjoyed Willa Cather's 'A Wagner Matinee' but felt a great urge to rewrite it, thinking there was a psychological flaw in it.

I like novels short enough in concept, if not in length, such as *Ethan Frome* or even *Madame Bovary*, to have a unity equal to the unity of a short story. I think that the long short story and the novella are one. I even think of the novel and the short story as being the same at times and that the novel is coming nearer to the short story. Think of the distance that *The Mayor of Casterbridge* has travelled to become *To the Lighthouse*. And is *To the Lighthouse* so very different from Katherine Mansfield's 'Prelude'? After all Edith Wharton's *Ethan Frome* is a short story, isn't it? And Wharton's *Summer* and Willa Cather's *My Mortal Enemy* and *The Death of Ivan Ilyich* by Tolstoy, even Turgenev's *Torrents of Spring*?

Virginia Woolf had a great impact on me. *Jacob's Room* was the first thing I read by her. It was like a painting, seen at one glance, tremendously new. Other favourites are Racine, George Sand's pastoral novels, Sarah Orne Jewett, and I like the stories by Katherine Mansfield in which she is homesick for New Zealand.

MH: Would you say something about your own method of writing?

ML: I seem to have evolved a cumbersome way of writing. First of all I don't write a story until it has been in my mind for years; this can be anything from ten to twenty years. An incident, or more likely an idea, catches my interest, but after that it remains in my mind. What moves me deeply is rarely transmuted into a work of the imagination for a long period. From time to time echoes of it are awakened by something I see, or hear, or even read, until suddenly, like a drop of rain on a windowpane to which one final accretion is added and it starts to flow, a story is ready to be written. Each new experience gives a little more insight into the human heart, but the artist must wait until it has been absorbed into the main stream of such wisdom as he has managed to accumulate over his whole lifetime. As well as growth there must be a certain continuity or stability of that philosophy he formed early in life by reason of some precociousness in him that is slightly different from that of his fellows.

The real short story is possibly an idea, buried deep in the writer's consciousness. I carry round a question in my mind, a question that teases and torments me, and then one day I think I see an answer in a person or an incident. Some detail would strike me as an echo of similar things that had been happening throughout my whole life and that might touch off writing a story that I have been thinking of writing on other occasions. You accumulate ideas and emotions; something is forming in your mind, a concept of life perhaps, and then outside yourself you see an exemplification of it. You then use that outside or objective incident to convey what was originally a subjective thing.

MH: You find your materials in many places then?

ML: Yes, in the compost heap there are hard twigs as well as leaves and all are recycled. Materials are absorbed by the imagination, then reproduced. All the original components are present, but changed in the process. I am always interested in tracing a story back to its origins. The germ may go back many years, even to a time before I began writing. The idea for 'The Lost Child', for example, was in my mind when I was a young woman. I was obsessed with the idea of Limbo, which seemed repellent. I realised later that my instinctive rejection of that idea was part of other things that I could not accept in the doctrine of my church, while feeling at the same time that I had every right to consider myself a member of that church. Then I was ready to write the story.

'The Lost Child' came to me in a flash. Sometimes a whole story flashes into the mind like a landscape lit by lightning. But when the flash has gone, you have to recover it. You may know the landscape before the lightning lit it up, but you never really saw it before. After the experience you not only do not see what it illumined, but are almost blind and have to work back. You work entirely in the dark and often wrongly place elements of the original vision. After several revisions there is a strange feeling of recognition. You feel you have really got it. The whole plant is in the seed.

MH: You suggest that you have several drafts, many revisions.

ML: Yes, but I have first of all to get the whole story down as fast as I can. This has to be done at breakneck pace. It is a terrible job to get even a very short story – and mine are mostly long – down on paper with all the details, or notes about them. I often omit bits that I feel certain I won't forget and put little shorthand signs to indicate where they should be inserted later. When the whole story is safely dragged out of the deeper recesses of my mind, and secured or tied down in some sort of words, I begin the work which others see as the hardest but to me is often very pleasurable. Every story goes through draft after draft, sometimes twenty, even thirty, before it is anything like what I think it ought to be.

At one time I thought drafts were a sign of affectation, or pernicketyness, but have learned that to understand a character fully and to understand how he may behave, I have to create all the necessary background information. I even have to place him in situations other than the situation which may become the vital one in the story. I frequently place characters in relationships with characters other than those who will be the sole protagonists in the final version.

MH: Many of your stories seem to me to have deeply moral themes. Am I correct?

ML: Religion almost seems to be a place one is born in. As a child I was not allowed to judge my actions by my own private conscience. I remember resenting that anybody would think or decide for me. We ought to be able to know what is right and wrong more easily than the churches allow. Churches and educational systems and above all parents have attached all kinds of complications to right and wrong. It is almost impossible for people to know what is right and what is wrong.

Certain principles I stood for as a young woman have remained and been carried forward in my work, yet life changed my attitude to many things and this has shown in the stories through the years. When I came to Ireland the religious thing bowled me over. Catholicism was much different from what I had known. I saw a whole new concept of sin in my aunts who were scrupulous and harrowed. My mother's family were at the mercy of what we now call superstition. They did not think for themselves, they accepted everything they were told, and I am sure often misinterpreted it. In America there were transgressions, but no sins and people did not go burrowing into your conscience.

MH: I was thinking in particular of your story 'The Will' and wondering if its plot and theme were based on a real incident.

ML: I was very young when I wrote 'The Will', but I had a firm belief in the right of private conscience. I drew upon the experience of an aunt of mine. She made a runaway marriage and she was very unhappy. The glamour went and she ended up with really nothing. She didn't have the romance. She didn't have what she ran away from and she didn't have what she ran towards. I thought her life very, very sad, but my grandmother left her out of her will. In the story she is the only one who really loved her mother. She thinks her mother's soul can only be saved through her having the Masses said for her mother's soul. It was very complicated, something I felt very strongly, but could only tell through this love story.

In another early story, 'A Wet Day', I was groping towards the idea of pastoral renewal which I handled with more confidence later in 'A Pure Accident'. 'Happiness' shows a preoccupation with religion and in particular with private conscience, and possibly with the problems of pastoral renewal. But those interests are not new: the convictions out of which they grew were as strong in the past as they are now. 'The Lost Child' may seem to be more emphatic, but that may be the result of greater technical control or expertise.

MH: In your writing there is certainly a recognisable thematic progression.

ML: I believe there is a certain continuity in the artist and in his work. Time and new experience only give him more insight. Since 'The Will' and 'The Lost Child' my convictions have deepened, but the techniques have not changed.

I see priests and nuns as just the same as the rest of us, victims of curial despotism. Sometimes I have portrayed clergymen as less than they ought to be or as downright destructive, but that is not anti-clericalism. It only means that when a man acts according to his nature, he sometimes behaves in a way that is contrary to the accepted purpose of his calling. I've written of similar failings in doctors and mothers.

MH: We haven't yet talked about the sexual themes in your stories.

ML: 'One Evening' puzzled some editors. They thought it leaned towards an interest in sex, but they couldn't see what it was. A woman editor said she thought it had strong sexual connotations. 'Was this sex?' she asked. I said yes.

MH: What stories are your favourites, if that's a fair question.

ML: There are some stories written in a way that nothing would ever induce me to write again, even such praised stories as 'The Small Bequest' and 'The Pastor of Six Miles Bush'. I like 'The Convert', 'The Cuckoo-Spit', 'The Will', 'A Tragedy', and 'The Living'. I hate the framework of 'Posy', but I like the real story.

Every framework becomes obsolete. George Moore's *The Lake* has a structure that we can't now understand, because his theme is not celibacy, but the bondage which was intolerable. We are used today to priests leaving the church. Moore's theme is the man's discovery that he has made a mistake in dealing with another human being; he then questions his own authority.

MH: Do you believe your writing to be more negative or affirmative?

ML: It's not often conceded that there is an affirmation of life in my stories. Rather I am spoken of as one who writes about death and the shortness of life. I think 'The New Gardener' has the quality of affirmation. There is an indirect emphasis on hands in 'The New Gardener' – the winding of the reel, the picking of the seeds, the breaking of the branches, the fingering of the hooks, the ironic fact that he has a green hand but that this brings death, not life.

And there is the other stupid notion that I write about the middle class.

A short story writer has to be judged ultimately by the whole body of the work. The most anthologised stories are often the least important in the body of the work.

Out of a happy life I wrote sad stories.

MH: What is your idea of the role of the artist?

ML: The artist is a kind of Christ figure giving his life for others. This may sound arrogant, but is not. The artist himself seldom knows what he is doing, seldom knows his motives, is often abashed by his own egotism, his self-interest, and this abasement speeds him on his sacrificial self-destruction.

Women's minds have a flexibility and subtlety not in men's minds, especially in emotional matters.

MH: To what degree would you say your writing is autobiographical?

ML: I have always said that it is the way you write that is you, that it is the technique not the material that is subjective. It is what you do with your material and how you shape it that is the autobiographical element. We talk about an impeccable style, but what one seeks is faultless construction. The inner shape of the short story reminds me of lightning in which the zigzagging flash seems to gather force when it goes back in order to go forward with even more deadly intent. Its course is ordained, and the line of development from the beginning to its destination is a true line.

SELECT BIBLIOGRAPHY

Allingham, W., *William Allingham: A Diary*, eds H. Allingham and D. Radford (London: Macmillan, 1907).

Boland, E., *Collected Poems* (Manchester: Carcanet Press, 1995).

— *Outside History: Selected Poems, 1980–1990* (Manchester: Carcanet Press, 1990).

Carleton, W., *Valentine M'Clutchy*, 3 vols (Dublin: James Duffy, 1845–1847; New York: D. & J. Sadlier & Co., 1868).

— *Traits and Stories of the Irish Peasantry, 1830–33* (London: William Tegg and Co., 1876).

— *The Emigrants of Ahadarra* (London: George Routledge & Sons, 1875).

— *The Works of William Carleton* (New York: P. F. Collier, 1881).

— *Autobiography*, Vol. I, *William Carleton*, ed. D. J. O'Donoghue, 2 vols (London: Downey and Co., 1896).

— *The Black Prophet: A Tale of Irish Famine*, Intro. D. J. O'Donoghue, illus. J. B. Yeats (London: Lawrence & Bullen, 1899).

Clarke, A., *The Vengeance of Fionn* (Dublin: Maunsel, 1917).

— *The Fires of Baál* (Dublin: Maunsel & Roberts, 1921).

— *The Sword of the West* (Dublin: Maunsel & Roberts, 1921).

— *The Cattledrive in Connaught* (London: George Allen & Unwin, 1925).

— *Pilgrimage* (London: George Allen & Unwin, 1929).

— *The Bright Temptation* (London: George Allen & Unwin, 1932).

— *The Singing Men at Cashel* (London: George Allen & Unwin, 1936).

— *Collected Poems* (New York: MacMillan Co., 1936).

— *Night and Morning* (Dublin: Orwell Press, 1938).

— *Ancient Lights* (Dublin: The Bridge Press, 1955).

— *Too Great a Vine* (Dublin: The Bridge Press, 1957).

— *The Horse-eaters: Poems and Satires* (Dublin: The Bridge Press, 1960).

— *Later Poems* (Dublin: The Dolmen Press, 1961).

— *Twice Round the Black Church* (London: Routledge and Kegan Paul, 1962).

— *Collected Plays* (Dublin: The Dolmen Press, 1963).

— *Mnemosyne Lay in Dust* (Dublin: The Dolmen Press – Editions III, 1966).

— *A Penny in the Clouds* (London: Routledge and Kegan Paul, 1968).

— *Collected Poems*, ed. Liam Miller (Dublin: The Dolmen Press, 1974).

Colum, P., *The Fiddler's House* (Dublin: Maunsel, 1907).

— *Three Plays* (Dublin: Maunsel, 1917; New York: Macmillan, 1925).

Cooney, J., *John Charles McQuaid: Ruler of Catholic Ireland* (Syracuse, NY: Syracuse University Press, 2000).

Dostoevsky, F., *The Idiot* (London: Penguin, 1975).

Ferguson, S., *Poems of Sir Samuel Ferguson*, ed. and Intro. Alfred Perceval Graves (Dublin: Phoenix Publishing Co., n.d.).

— *Congal: A Poem in Five Books* (Dublin: Edward Ponsonby; London: Bell and Daldy, 1872).

— *Poems* (Dublin: William McGee, and London: George Bell and Sons, 1880).

— *Hibernian Nights' Entertainments: First Series: The Death of the Children of Usnach; The Return of Claneboy; The Captive of Killeshin* (Dublin: Sealy, Bryers & Walker; London: George Bell and Sons, 1887).

— *Hibernian Nights' Entertainments: Second Series: An Adventure of Shane O'Neill's; Corby Mac Gillmore* (Dublin: Sealy, Bryers & Walker; London: George Bell and Sons, 1887).

— *Hibernian Nights' Entertainments: Third Series: The Rebellion of Silken Thomas* (Dublin: Sealy, Bryers & Walker; London: George Bell and Sons, 1887).

— *'Lays of the Western Gael' and Other Poems* (Dublin: Sealy, Bryers & Walker; London: George Bell and Sons, 1888).

Ferguson, Lady Mary C., *Sir Samuel Ferguson in the Ireland of His Day*, 2 vols (Edinburgh: Blackwell, 1896).

Glob, P. V., *The Bog People*, trans. Rupert Bruce-Mitford (London: Faber and Faber, 1969).

Hardiman, J., *Irish Minstrelsy or Bardic Remains of Ireland*, 2 vols, Intro. Máire Mhac an tSaoi (Shannon: Irish University Press, 1971).

Harmon, M., *Seán O'Faoláin: A Critical Introduction* (Notre Dame: Notre Dame Press, 1967; rev. 1985).

— *Modern Irish Literature, 1800–1967: A Reader's Guide* (Dublin: The Dolmen Press, 1967).

— *The Poetry of Thomas Kinsella* (Dublin: Wolfhound Press, 1974).

— *Select Bibliography for the Study of Anglo-Irish Literature and its Backgrounds* (Dublin: Wolfhound Press, 1977).

— 'Cobwebs before the Wind', Daniel J. Casey and Robert E. Rhodes (eds), *Views of the Irish Peasantry 1800-1916* (Hamden, CT: Archon Books, 1977).

— *A Literary Map of Ireland* (Dublin: Wolfhound Press, 1977).

— (ed. and Intro.), *Richard Murphy: Poet of Two Traditions* (Dublin: Wolfhound Press, 1978).

— (ed.), *Mary Lavin Special Issue. Irish University Review* (Spring 1979).

— *Irish Poetry after Yeats: Seven Poets* (Dublin: Wolfhound Press, 1979).

— (ed.), *Images and Illusion: Anglo-Irish Literature and its Contexts. A Festschrift for Roger McHugh* (Dublin: Wolfhound Press, 1979).

— '"We pine for ceremony": Ritual and Reality in the Poetry of Seamus Heaney (1965–1975)', J. Genet (ed.), *Studies in Seamus Heaney* (Caen: Centre de Publications de l'Université de Caen, 1987; rptd, E. Andrews (ed.), *Seamus Heaney: A Collection of Critical Essays* (London: Macmillan, 1992).

— *Irish Writers and Politics*, Okifumi Komesu and Masaru Sekine (eds), *The Irish Literary Series*, 36 (Gerrards Cross: Colin Smythe, 1989).

— *Austin Clarke: A Critical Introduction* (Dublin: Wolfhound Press, 1989).

— 'Seamus Heaney, 'The Tree Clock', *Linen Hall Review*, 7, 3/4 (Winter 1990).

— *Seán O'Faoláin. A Life* (London: Constable, 1994).

— *The Book of Precedence* (Cork: Three Spires Press, 1994).

— 'Spaten und Wasserwaage, *Seamus Heaney* Suche Nach Herkunft und Gleichgewicht', *Seamus Heaney, Tod eines Naturforschers* (Lachen am Zürichsee: Coron Verlag, 1995).

— *A Stillness at Kiawah* (Cork: Three Spires Press, 1996).

— (ed. and Intro.), *No Author Better Served: The Correspondence between Samuel Beckett and Alan Schneider* (Cambridge, MA: Harvard University Press, 1998).

— *The Last Regatta* (Cliffs of Moher, Co. Clare: Salmon Publishing, 2000).

— (ed. and Intro.), *The Dolmen Press: A Celebration* (Dublin: The Lilliput Press, 2001).

— '*The Dolmen Miscellany*', in M. Harmon (ed. and Intro.), *The Dolmen Press: A Celebration* (Dublin: The Lilliput Press, 2001).

— 'Seán O'Faoláin: Man of Ideas', in Donatella A. Badin (ed.), *Seán O'Faoláin: A Centenary Celebration* (Turin: Trauben, 2001).

— *Tales of Death* (Belfast: Lapwing, 2001).

— 'John Montague: "Restless Spirit"', *Agenda Irish Issue John Montague – 75th Birthday Supplement*, 40, 1–3 (2004).

— *The Doll with Two Backs and other poems* (Cliffs of Moher, Co. Clare: Salmon Publishing, 2004).

Harmon, M., and R. McHugh, *A Short History of Anglo-Irish Literature from its Origins to the Present Day* (Dublin: Wolfhound Press, 1982).

Heaney, S., *Death of a Naturalist* (London: Faber and Faber, 1966).

— *Door into the Dark* (London: Faber and Faber, 1969).

— *Wintering Out* (London: Faber and Faber, 1972).

— *North* (London: Faber and Faber, 1975).

— *Field Work* (London: Faber and Faber, 1979).

— *Preoccupations: Selected Prose 1968–1978* (London: Faber and Faber, 1980).

— *Sweeney Astray: A Version from the Irish* (London: Faber & Faber; Derry: Field Day Production, 1983).

— *Station Island* (London: Faber and Faber, 1984).

— *The Haw Lantern* (London: Faber and Faber, 1987).

— *The Government of the Tongue: The 1986 T. S. Eliot Memorial Lectures and Other Critical Writing* (London, Boston: Faber and Faber, 1988).

— *The Tree Clock* (Belfast: The Linen Hall Library, 1990).

— *Seeing Things* (London: Faber and Faber, 1991).

— *The Redress of Poetry* (London: Faber and Faber, 1995).

— *The Spirit Level* (London: Faber and Faber, 1996).

— *Opened Ground: Poems 1966–1996* (London: Faber and Faber, 1998).

Hyde, D., 'Preface', *Love Songs of Connacht* (Dublin: Gill and Son, 1905).

Kavanagh, P., *The Green Fool* (London: Michael Joseph, 1938; New York: Harper and Brothers, 1939).

— *The Great Hunger* (Dublin: The Cuala Press, 1942).

— *Tarry Flynn* (London: The Pilot Press, 1948).

— *Collected Pruse* (London: Martin Brian and O'Keefe, 1967).

— *Collected Poems*, Antoinette Quinn (ed.) (London: Allen Lane, 2004).

— 'Patrick Kavanagh on Poetry', *Journal of Irish Literature*, John Nemo (ed.), VI, 1 (January 1977).

— *Patrick Kavanagh Country* (The Curragh, Ireland: The Goldsmith Press, 1978).

Kavanagh, P., *Sacred Keeper: A Biography of Patrick Kavanagh* (The Curragh, Ireland: The Goldsmith Press, 1979).

Kermode, F., *Shakespeare's Language* (London: Allen Lane, Penguin Press, 2000).

Kiely, B., *The Collected Stories of Benedict Kiely*, Intro. Colum McCann (London: Methuen, 2001).

Kinsella, T., *Collected Poems* (Oxford: Oxford University press, 1996).

— *Collected Poems* (Manchester: Carcanet Press, 2001).

— *Marginal Economy* (Dublin: Dedalus Press, 2006)

Lavin, M., *The Stories of Mary Lavin*, 2 vols (London: Constable, 1964, 1974).

— *In the Middle of the Fields* (London: Constable, 1967).

— *A Memory* (London: Constable, 1972).

Longley, M., *The Echo Gate: Poems 1975–1979* (London: Secker & Warburg, 1979).

— *Poems, 1963–1983* (Dublin: The Gallery Press,1985).

— *The Ghost Orchid* (London: Jonathan Cape, 1995).

McCarthy, C., Interview, Folklore Department, University College Dublin, 25 November 2004.

McGahern, J., *That They May Face the Rising Sun* (London: Faber and Faber, 2002).

McRedmond, L., 'Many a Long Night: The Box with the Lighted Dial', *Written in the Wind, Personal Memories of Irish Radio 1926/1976* (Dublin: Gill and Macmillan, 1976).

Mac Gabhann, S., 'Continuity and Tradition in the Poetry of James Tevlin [1798–1873]', *Riocht na Midhe*, XVI (2005).

MacNeice, L., *Autumn Journal* (London: Faber and Faber, 1938).

— *Collected Poems* (London: Faber and Faber, 1966).

Meehan, P., *Mysteries of the Home* (Newcastle upon Tyne: Bloodaxe Books, 1996).

Montague, J., *Collected Poems* (Loughcrew, Oldcastle, Co. Meath: The Gallery Press, 1999).

— *Smashing the Piano* (Loughcrew, Oldcastle, Co. Meath: The Gallery Press, 1999).

— *Drunken Sailor* (Loughcrew, Oldcastle, Co. Meath: The Gallery Press, 2004).

Muldoon, P., *Madoc: A Mystery* (London: Faber and Faber, 1990).

Murphy, R., *The Battle of Aughrim and The God Who Eats Corn* (London: Faber and Faber, 1968).

— *The Price of Stone* (London: Faber and Faber, 1985).

— *Collected Poems* (Loughcrew, Oldcastle, Co. Meath, Ireland: The Gallery Press, 2000).

Ní Uallacháin, P., *A Hidden Ulster: People, Songs and Traditions of Oriel* (Dublin: Four Courts Press. 2003).

O'Connor, F., *A Short History of Irish Literature* (New York: Capricorn Books, 1968).

Ó Dúill, G., 'Sir Samuel Ferguson, Administrator and Archivist', *Irish University Review*, 16 (Autumn 1986).

— *Samuel Ferguson: beatha agus saothar* (Baile Átha Cliath: An Clóchomhar, 1993).

O'Faoláin, S., *'Midsummer Night Madness' and Other Stories*, Intro. Edward Garnett (London: Jonathan Cape, 1932).

— *A Purse of Coppers* (London: Jonathan Cape, 1937).

— *A Nest of Simple Folk* (London: Jonathan Cape; New York: Viking Press, 1934.

— *Bird Alone* (London: Jonathan Cape, 1936).

— *King of the Beggars: A Life of Daniel O'Connell* (London: Thomas Nelson & Sons, 1938).

— *The Great O'Neill: A Biography of Hugh O'Neill, Earl of Tyrone, 1550–1616* (London: Longmans, Green & Company, 1942).

— 'Yeats and the Younger Generation', *Horizon*, 5, 2 (1942).

— *The Collected Stories of Seán O'Faoláin*, Vol. 1 (London: Constable, 1980).

— *The Collected Stories of Seán O'Faoláin*, Vol. 2 (London: Constable, 1981).

— *The Collected Stories of Seán O'Faoláin*, Vol. 3 (London: Constable, 1982).

Ó hÓgáin, D., 'The Visionary Voice: A Survey of Popular Attitudes to Poetry in Irish Tradition', M. Harmon (ed.), *Images and Illusion: Anglo-Irish Literature and its Contexts. A Festschrift for Roger McHugh* (Dublin: Wolfhound Press, 1979).

Quinn, A., *Patrick Kavanagh: A Biography* (Dublin: Gill and Macmillan, 2001).

— (ed.), *Patrick Kavanagh Collected Poems* (London: Allen Lane, 2004).

Stuart, F., *We Have Kept the Faith* (Dublin: Oak Press, 1923).

— *Women and God* (London: Jonathan Cape, 1931).

— *Pigeon Irish* (London: Gollancz, 1932).

— *The Coloured Dome* (London: Gollancz, 1932).

— *The Pillar of Cloud* (London: Gollancz, 1948).

— *Redemption* (London: Gollancz, 1949).

— *Black List, Section H* (Carbondale: Southern Illinois University Press, 1971; London: Martin Brian & O'Keefe, 1974).

— *Memorial* (London: Martin Brian & O'Keefe, 1973).

— *A Hole in the Head* (London: Martin Brian & O'Keefe, 1977).

— *The High Consistory* (London: Martin Brian & O'Keefe, 1981).

— *We Have Kept the Faith: New and Selected Poems* (Dublin: Raven Arts Press, 1982).

— *Faillandia* (Dublin: Raven Arts Press, 1985).

— *The Abandoned Snail Shell* (Dublin: Raven Arts Press, 1987).

— *A Compendium of Lovers* (Dublin: Raven Arts Press, 1990).

— *King David Dances* (Dublin: New Island Books, 1996).

Wigzell, F., 'Dostoevskii and Russian Folk Heritage', W. J. Leatherbarrow (ed.), *The Cambridge Companion to Dostoevskii* (Cambridge: Cambridge University Press, 2000).

Willeford, W., *A Study in Clowns and Jesters and Their Audience* (London: Edward Arnold, 1969).

Yeats, W. B. (Intro. and notes), *A Book of Irish Verse, Selected from Modern Writers* (London: 1891).

— 'The Poetry of Sir Samuel Ferguson', *Uncollected Prose by W. B. Yeats, Vol. 1. First Reviews and Articles 1886-1896*, John P. Frayne (ed.) (London: Macmillan, 1970).

— *The Poems: A New Edition*, Richard J. Finneran (ed.) (Dublin: Gill and Macmillan, 1983).

INDEX

51; *The Great O'Neill* (1942) 65;
'Ireland after Yeats' (article, 1950) 46;
King of the Beggars (biography, 1938)
44, 64–5; *Midsummer Night Madness*
(1932) 63; *A Nest of Simple Folk*
(1934) 63–4; 'One World' series 69; *A
Purse of Coppers* (1937) 64; *Vive Moi!*
(1963) 42–3; 'Yeats and the Younger
Generation' (article, 1942) 46
O'Flaherty, Liam x, 4, 51, 99, 179
O'Hagan, Sheila 202, 203
Ormsby, Eric 206
O'Sullivan, Seamus 108
Outside History (Boland, 1990) xv

Parnell, Charles 64
'The Pattern' (Meehan) 190
PEN 43
Petrie, George 4, 33
Phoenix Park murders (1882) 34
The Playboy of the Western World (Synge,
1907) 16, 151
Poems 1963-1983 (Longley, 1985) 187
Poetry Ireland Review (ed. Harmon, 2001-
02) ix, 193, 195, 200–6
The Poetry of Thomas Kinsella (Harmon,
1974) xiii, 159
A Portrait of the Artist as a Young Man
(Joyce) 3
The Price of Stone (Murphy, 1985) 186
Protestant Repeal Association 31

Radio Telefís Éireann (RTE 1)
'Book Talk' 52
Cork radio station 54–5
drama 48–50, 51, 55, 57, 58
importance of 51–2, 55, 58
interviews with writers 57
Mobile Recording Unit 50–1
Modern Irish Poets series 48
payment for work 52–3
poetry 48, 52, 57, 109
short stories 50, 52, 53–4, 57
talks 48, 50, 52, 53, 54, 57
Thomas Davis lectures 55
Reeves, William 33
'Reply to a Poet' (Harmon) xv, 195, 196–9,
201
Riders to the Sea (Synge, 1904) 19-20

Robinson, Lennox 18, 53
Rodgers, W.R. 52
Rogha Dánta (Ó Dúill) 206
Rooney, Philip 53–4
Royal Irish Academy xi, 22, 35
Russell, George *see* 'AE'

'Santa Claus Says, No!' (McCann) 50
'The Seals at High Island' (Murphy) 186
Seán O'Faoláin: A Critical Introduction
(Harmon, 1967) xii, 61
Seán O'Faoláin, A Life (Harmon, 1994) 61
Seán O'Faoláin - A Centenary Celebration
(conference, Turin, 2000) 61
*Select Bibliography for the Study of Anglo-
Irish Literature and its Backgrounds*
(Harmon, 1977) xii, xiii
Shakespeare's Language (Kermode) 122
Sinn Féin 62
*Sir Samuel Ferguson in the Ireland of his
Day* (Lady Mary Ferguson, 1896) 24
Somerville and Ross 3
Stephens, James 52
Stokes, Whitley 33
'Stone Games' (Harmon) xvi
Stuart, Francis
attacks on Irish society 85, 87, 94
background 82
characterisation 84, 85, 86, 88, 89, 91–2
on Emily Brontë 92, 93
language and style 84, 87–8, 91–2, 93–4
radio contributions 48
social realism 83
themes
new ways of seeing 83–4, 85, 86, 87,
90
redemption through suffering 83,
84–5, 86, 87
religion and belief 83, 85–6, 87, 90,
91, 94
search for truth and reality 89, 90,
91–2, 93, 94
triumph out of adversity 83, 86, 87
works: *The Abandoned Snail Shell*
(1987) 87; *Black List, Section H*
(1971) 88–91; *The Coloured Dome*
(1932) 83; *A Compendium of Lovers*
(1990) 91; *Faillandia* (1985) 91; *The
High Consistory* (1981) 91; *A Hole in*